Programming Microcomputers for Psychology Experiments

Richard Deni
Rider College

Wadsworth Publishing Company
Belmont, California
A Division of Wadsworth, Inc.

To my wife Kristine, and children Leah and Michael

Psychology Editor: Kenneth King
Production Management: Miller/Scheier Associates
Designer: R. Kharibian & Associates
Copy Editor: Susan Weisberg

Printed in the United States of America

1 2 3 4 5 6 7 8 9 10—90 89 88 87 86

ISBN 0-534-05442-0

Library of Congress Cataloging in Publication Data

Deni, Richard.
  Programming microcomputers for psychology
experiments.

  Includes index.
    1. Psychology—Experiments—Data processing.
2. Microcomputers—Programming.   3. Basic (Computer
program language)   4. Real-time data processing. I. Title.
BF39.5.D46 1985   150'.72   85-7181
ISBN 0-534-05442-0

CONTENTS

PREFACE

This book is about one special area of computer applications in psychology: real-time laboratory computing. You can control a psychology experiment with a computer, directing every feature of a procedure as it is administered to the subject. You can program a computer to present stimuli, regulate processes, record behavior, and manage data, all during the actual experimental session (hence, the phrase *in real time*). You can interface—that is, link—a computer with other apparatus in the laboratory to further extend its control capabilities. And you can reprogram a computer an infinite number of times in a multitude of different ways. These are just some of the reasons computers are fast becoming an integral part of laboratory courses in psychology.

This book assumes no special preparation in computers. Even if you have never seen a computer before, this book won't leave you behind. It has most of the qualities of a primer, but will still challenge the active computer user because its focus is on applications beyond the common uses and perceived limitations of computers. It's a text for learning to *apply* the methods of laboratory research in experimental psychology, learning, cognition, perception, and biopsychology. It will gradually integrate real-time computer applications into the way you do research.

What are the programming techniques of real-time laboratory computing? To put it simply, they allow you to use a computer system and its resources to conduct an experiment, administer a research procedure, and measure behavior by counting or timing. It may sound complicated if you are uninitiated, but this book is designed to initiate you. With its emphasis on what are called stand-alone projects, the book will have you writing BASIC programs to run computer-controlled experiments using little more than the microcomputer itself as the test apparatus. If you have access to additional equipment, the book also teaches how to use a laboratory interface device to allow the computer to control external apparatus, such as an operant chamber for animal learning research. Extra lab equipment is optional, however, and you may pass over the interface projects in favor of concentrating on stand-alone applications.

I hope you don't think it extreme to direct the focus of psychology laboratory courses toward computer-based procedures. And I hope you don't think of this approach as a gimmick, or as a diversion from substance. Your psychology lab course should provide you with the opportunity to express creativity. Given that, you'll need the most flexible set of tools available. The microcomputer—the personal computer—is able to replicate most of the functions of the commonly used apparatus in the psychology teaching lab. In fact, with the help of this book, you'll transform a personal computer into your personal psychology laboratory, with a nearly unlimited range for applications. No other equipment is needed; with this flexible tool, you'll be better able to apply the principles of research design to the problems of translating an experimental idea into a laboratory reality. You'll be more creative.

This book will unlock the doors to increased productivity and the ability to do higher-level scholarship. And it will do it relatively quickly. The turn-around time, from reading textbook and journal descriptions of research procedures, to translating them into computer programs able to conduct experiments will be surprisingly short. Of course, you'll have to invest time in learning this approach very carefully. However, the rewards will be visible and tangible. You will be more productive, efficient, and able to pursue a broader range of problems in the laboratory. The tangibles will include an actual "tool kit" based on the software programs you'll write for the computer.

You're a rare student if you are already familiar with the techniques of real-time computing covered in this book, even though the field itself is not new. If you want to learn more about the field in general, read its research journal, *Behavior Research Methods, Instruments and Computers* and get acquainted with its professional society, The Society for Computers in Psychology. Even if you know computers well, this book will open new doors.

Finally, this is not a general text on programming, although it does teach you how to write programs. It is special in the *kind* of programming it teaches—namely real-time programming. The focus of the programming lessons is not computer literacy, but computer specialty in the area of laboratory control and experimentation in psychology.

Acknowledgments

Substantial support for my own real-time computer laboratory at Rider College was provided by the New Jersey Department of Higher Education through the *Computers in Curricula* program. Substantial support for my writing efforts was provided by a small group of my dedicated students at Rider College—Richard Coffee, Kathleen Cameron, Joyce Dixon, Christina Fantauzzo, Jennifer Makin, and Janusz Przeorek, who contributed ideas and helped to evaluate my work. I wish to acknowledge the helpful comments of the following reviewers of the manuscript, who made valuable suggestions for its improvement: Bruce Brown, Brigham Young University; Terry F. Pettijohn, Ohio State University at Marion; Paul Forand, East Texas State University; Debra Poole, Beloit College; Paul Wellman, Texas A & M University; Robert Seibel, Pennsylvania State University. I also wish to thank Dr. James Hogge of Peabody College, Vanderbilt University, for turning my attention toward computer applications in psychology. Finally, I would like to thank my family for their continuous support and inspiration in this project.

PART ONE

GETTING STARTED

Chapter 1 is a broad introduction to the text. First, I present a brief survey of the most common uses for computers in psychology and introduce the concept of real-time programming to control experiments. Next, I indicate which microcomputer systems and programming languages are covered in the text. Finally, I introduce you to the concept of a disk operating system (DOS). This chapter prepares you for one of two follow-up actions. If you are a novice, you should proceed slowly through the next two chapters. As you work your way through them, and indeed through the remainder of the book, go frequently to the computer and apply the lessons on commands and programming. Make the examples work on the computer as you are learning about their derivation and purpose. If you are a skilled computer user and know your system well, move ahead quickly to Part 2, where the coverage of real-time programming techniques begins in Chapter 4.

Chapter 2 is a concise handbook on how to operate your computer system. It has no lessons on programming, but covers the commands and procedures you'll use to manipulate the computer system as you create program files and store them for later use. Here I begin teaching you the various DOS commands and cover the procedures for starting the computer system.

Chapter 3 introduces the concept of a BASIC program and covers a special group of DOS commands that I refer to as BASIC commands. They are part of the programming process, but not part of the program itself.

CHAPTER 1

Microcomputers in the Experimental Psychology Laboratory

How Psychology Students Use Computers

Even though computers have become increasingly commonplace in our lives, no one knows all the uses to which they can be put. If you have had some prior experience programming computers, your first academic encounter probably involved computational tasks. On the computer's keyboard, you typed a list of instructions, called a **program,** to do arithmetic of one sort or another. The computer was good for the job because it could do many numeric computations very quickly. But the computer can manipulate text as well as numbers. By **text** I mean letters, words, paragraphs, and even whole manuscripts. Taken together, these two types of usage—number and text processing—account for a large measure of what people do with computers. But there are also more specialized applications, many of which are useful for psychology students.

Data Analysis and Statistics. Psychology students use computers to analyze research data and perform statistical tests. Psychological research usually produces lots of numbers. Researchers rely upon computers to store the information and then manipulate it. They use computers to summarize data and repeatedly solve formulas required as part of statistical testing of data. In addition, it is quite reasonable for students to learn to write simple statistics programs, like those required for central tendency and variability measures, chi-square, and the like. However, a large array of commercially produced programs are available to do data analysis and statistics, and advanced students

3

learn to use these for more difficult problems and very large sets of data. Commercial programs are also widely used for converting sets of numbers into charts and graphs.

Text Processing. Psychology students use commercial text processing (also called **word processing**) programs to write term papers, research reports, and other manuscripts. They store these written documents on the computer and manipulate the text in a number of ways to delete, add, change, format, and print the material as it is developed.

Database Access. One of the newest uses for computers is to store, manipulate, and retrieve specific information at the request of the user. A program that does such work is known as a **database** manager. Psychology students capitalize on this application when they do their literature searches for writing term papers and developing topics for research. Commercial information services provide access (for a fee) to databases stored on computer. For example, *Psychological Abstracts*, the foremost indexing and abstracting publication on literature in psychology, is available as a computer database. Through the use of these database services, students are able to obtain lists of pertinent journal articles on any subject in a matter of seconds. Though these services are costly, they are powerful time-saving tools, and their use is increasing rapidly.

Micro to Mainframe Connections. Most colleges and universities have at least one large, central **mainframe** computer on campus. Big computers are needed to store large amounts of data and to run complex programs. Many users are able to share the resources of a single mainframe because it can execute dozens of separate programs so quickly that it appears they are all working at once.

The other side of the coin is the small personal computer designed primarily for one person and one program at a time. This is the **microcomputer,** with a small, compact electronic processor. Microcomputers now fit nicely into work environments where mainframes used to dominate, thanks to commercial software that allows the small computer to "talk" to its big sibling on campus. The connection itself may be a direct cable from the mainframe to an electronic interface in the microcomputer, or over a special device called a **modem,** which allows users to transmit information over telephone lines. Any text or numeric data can be exchanged using this capability. Once on the mainframe, the text or data may be used with the sophisticated programs available on the large machine. The proliferation of these interconnections among computers of different size and function is called **networking.**

Undoubtedly, every psychology student will use at least one of these applications for computers. However, one course in particular brings several of these uses together and combines them with a fifth and very advanced application. The fifth application is referred to by a variety of names, including **real-time, on-line,** and **laboratory** computing. The essence of real-time computing is use of the machine to carry out actual laboratory experiments under the control of a program developed by the experimenter.

The Personal Psychology Laboratory

Where We Came From.   Apparatus for psychological research, and the capability to control it, evolved at a modest pace before the widespread introduction of computers. In the experimental psychology course, psychology majors became familiar with devices with strange-sounding names like memory drum, operant chamber, relay rack, and snap lead. The method for controlling much of this apparatus with so-called electromechanical devices was itself a major technical challenge to students (and their professors!). Very few students learned how to set up laboratory apparatus from scratch to conform to the experimental idea they wanted to test.

If they did attain this specialized knowledge and skill, students often found themselves further hindered by the lack of available control devices, either in number or in type. Equipment catalogs frequently list dozens of separate types of electromechanical modules. Furthermore, once the modules were set up using a series of so-called snap leads, experimenters developed an abiding tendency not to dismantle them. Few arrangements of these devices allowed several different experiments to be controlled using the same modules. There was no easy way to make the technology flexible. On the other hand, making the technology unusable was easy! Just take off one of the snap leads, and you have rendered the equipment useless.

Where We're Going.   The introduction of microcomputers has marked the beginning of a new way of controlling experiments in the psychology laboratory. In fact, a new kind of laboratory is evolving as a result. It is not limited by the inventory of equipment, availability of modular components, or willingness of other students to give up their treasured electromechanical setups. This new development is the "personal psychology laboratory" that this textbook shows you how to create.

This new laboratory is personal because each student can use the computer to design as many different experimental procedures as creativity allows. It is further personal in that the essence of the experiment is preserved in the computer program written to control it, not in the temporary configuration of devices. Finally, it is personal in a very concrete sense. The author of the program forever owns the procedure and the ability to use it. The student need only have access to a computer, and not necessarily even the same type of computer on which the program was developed. You will soon be writing programs that are transportable in that, with only minor modifications, they can be made to work on a variety of different computer systems. For these and other reasons, the personal psychology laboratory promises to give students new independence, open up new creative opportunity, and increase productivity in laboratory research.

I am classifying the research made possible by computer control into two broad categories: stand-alone projects and those requiring the use of an interface (an additional electronic component).

Stand-alone Projects. The **stand-alone** projects in this book require only the computer system itself as apparatus. The computer hardware, and the program operating it, will produce all the necessary functions, including stimulus display, event counting, and timing. Your subjects will sit at the computer console during testing and make responses at the keyboard. Most of the projects covered in the book will be of this type.

Interface Projects. A computer **interface** is an electronic device that allows two-way communication between the computer and external laboratory apparatus. For example, specialized test apparatus, such as operant chambers, can be controlled by the computer. This book will describe a limited number of interface projects.

The Computer Systems

The topics I'll be covering in this text will be generic in that the point of any given lesson will not depend upon a specific make and model of computer. However, when specific hardware and software attributes are mentioned, I will provide examples for use with one or more of the following computer systems: The IBM Personal Computer (and IBM PC–compatible work-alike systems), the Apple IIe (and earlier II series systems), and the TRS-80 Model 4 (and earlier Model III). These systems must have disk storage capability, a printer, and the appropriate disk operating system and BASIC language (I'll be defining disks and operating systems in Chapter 2 for the uninitiated). The text will provide you with all the material needed for you to work on one or more of these systems, and reference to owner's manuals and other technical sources will be necessary infrequently.

If you're using the IBM PC, I assume that your system has graphics capability (though it is not required). If you don't have the graphics adapter, you can skip the advanced lessons that require it. If your computer is called IBM compatible, you will have an implementation of the MS-DOS operating system and Microsoft BASICA/GW BASIC. Most compatibles also have the graphics adapter as standard equipment. Simply work your way through the text as if you had an IBM PC. If you're in the Apple camp, you may have an older model of the II series, or the newer IIc. The Apple IIe lessons will work without problems. Be advised, however, that the interface unit covered in this text cannot, as yet, be connected to the Apple IIc. And what about the Macintosh? Again, no problem. You must have the Microsoft BASIC master disk, and you should work with the IBM PC examples (but there's no interface capability on the Mac, as yet).

Most campuses have a central computer facility, within which resides the mainframe. This large central computer could, in most respects, accommodate the kind of lessons taught in this text. However, there will be certain qualifications. First, the mainframe is a **time-sharing** machine, meaning that many jobs (from many users) are running at the same time. Consequently, real-time computer control is never accurately attainable. Timing functions can be distorted by the number of users—it is like a clock that slows down depending upon how many people use it. However, the bottom line is that the mainframe *can* be used for both the principles and techniques of real-time laboratory computing, using stand-alone projects only. Appendix H gives you the necessary information to modify the IBM PC lessons for use with Digital Equipment Corporation mainframes, including the 2060 (using BASIC-PLUS-2), the PDP-11 series (using BASIC-PLUS), and the VAX series (using VAX-11 BASIC).

Although an expanding variety of interfacing equipment is available for microcomputers, I have geared the interface projects in this text to a specific system: the LVB Interface by Med Associates, Inc. I'm teaching you how to use the LVB Interface because it supports the IBM PC (and compatibles), the Apple II series, and the TRS-80 Models III and 4 (only TRS-80 Model 4 systems with catalog number 26-1069A support the LVB Precision Timer). No other interface supports so many different microcomputers. In addition, I think its operation through BASIC is very straightforward. Appendix A includes a set of instructions on how to set up the LVB interface.

The Computer Language: BASIC

Why learn to write computer programs anyway? Hundreds of programs are commercially available for microcomputers, leading many people to believe that no matter what computer application they have in mind, a program has been written for it. And programming seems to be the kind of skill you might have to learn for a course (in this case, a psychology lab) that is not likely to serve you beyond the immediate need. Does this sound convincing? I hope not!

Imagine if parents of young children believed that their child's time could be better spent watching stories on television rather than learning to read and write them. What if teachers suddenly said that there were already too many books, essays, and articles in print, so students would no longer have to learn to write technical or creative prose. There is a real danger that programming computers will become less and less a part of using them. However, for students of behavioral science, real-time programming skills are valuable assets. The ability will let you go beyond those problems that a limited amount of apparatus will *allow* you to study, to pursue the problems you *want* to study.

Fortunately, computers arouse strong interest. I feel confident in predicting that you'll actually enjoy learning how to use the computer in the laboratory.

But you still might ask why learn the BASIC programming language? Your friends majoring in electrical engineering or computer science might try to make you feel inadequate because you're not working with their favorite programming language. Pay no attention. Don't forget that you are learning about psychology, not computer science. This text will teach you the working technology of laboratory computing. BASIC is more than adequate for the job at hand, and its capabilities are well suited to the specific real-time applications involving interface control. No one is going to change the technology on you. When it comes to controlling psychology experiments with microcomputers, what you get from these pages will remain current for a long time.

Two Levels of Learning: DOS and BASIC

There are two distinct levels of functioning on microcomputers. The "outer" level on most computer systems is **DOS** (an acronym pronounced like *sauce*), which stands for *disk operating system*. For our purposes, the "inner" level will be the BASIC programming language. The **disk** itself is the physical device where all the programs and data reside. DOS makes the disk-based system work.

At DOS level you have access to a variety of capabilities, all having something to do with the disk storage device or the manipulation of disk files. A **file** is a specific unit of information. It may contain a program or sets of text or data. Disk files are much like paper files in that information in them can be labeled, stored, retrieved, and modified. DOS commands, for example, are single words and acronyms that direct the computer to perform manipulations of program and data files.

DOS is itself a set of programmed instructions to the computer that you, as user, do not see. These instructions reside on the **system master disk** provided by the computer manufacturer. When a master disk is inserted in the disk drive unit, DOS will be started automatically whenever the computer is turned on. You probably won't be surprised to learn that each manufacturer has a different name for its DOS (in fact, the names are trademarks).

PC-DOS (*pee see dauce*), a trademark of International Business Machines, Inc., and MS-DOS (*em ess dauce*), a trademark of Microsoft, Inc., are similar. They are found on the IBM PC and work-alike IBM PC–compatible systems, respectively. Several versions of this DOS exist. Each new, improved version of DOS gets a higher number. The IBM PC examples in this text are specifically geared for DOS 1.25 or higher. Newer IBM PC and compatible systems have DOS 2.0 or higher. This advanced version of DOS has capabilities not found in earlier versions; however the BASIC language is essentially the same. The IBM PC examples in this text will also work with the newest versions of PC-DOS and MS-DOS.

The Apple IIe (and IIc) uses either DOS 3.3 or ProDOS (*pro-dauce*), trademarks of Apple Computer, Inc. Only DOS 3.3 is covered in this text. If you have an older II series computer (II or II+), be sure to upgrade to DOS 3.3.

TRSDOS (*triss-dauce*), a trademark of Tandy Corp., is found on Tandy's TRS-80 Model III and 4 computers. The series 6 TRSDOS is the version currently being included on Tandy Model 4 and 4P (the portable Model 4) systems.

Each time a DOS command is presented in the text, examples for each of these three systems (IBM PC, Apple IIe, and TRS-80) will be given.

BASIC is also actually a program. It allows instructions (called **statements** and **functions**) to be interpreted by the processing hardware of the machine. BASIC can be thought of as a list of statements and functions, built around English-language terms and acronyms that perform numeric, text, and computer system manipulations. BASIC also resides on the master disk, and, depending upon the machine, you may need to start it with a specific DOS command. Again, different computers have different versions of BASIC. The PC-DOS and MS-DOS version is called BASICA or GW BASIC. The Apple IIe BASIC is called Applesoft, and the Tandy systems have TRSDOS BASIC. Throughout the text, specific programming techniques are exemplified in listings labeled for each of the three computer systems. When a listing is not specifically labeled, it can apply to any of the three systems.

A Note on Setting Up and Connecting the LVB Interface

Appendix A presents a list of hardware components and step-by-step instructions for connecting the LVB Interface to the three computer systems covered in the text. It also describes how to connect an operant chamber to the LVB Interface. With the proper equipment, each of the three computer systems covered can operate the interface. However, not all TRS-80 Model 4 systems will be able to operate the Precision Timer circuit of the interface. See Appendix A for the details.

Closure

If you are a novice at computer applications, you may have had to reread certain sections of this chapter in order to better comprehend them. Like any new subject, laboratory computer programming will present you with a new vocabulary and concepts. My advice is to work slowly and carefully. Refer as often as necessary to the glossary at the back of the book, and don't be afraid to ask questions if you get stuck.

If you are already initiated into the world of microcomputers, you can move quickly through the first part of this book. Chapter 4 begins the presentation of the real-time programming techniques that are the substance of the text.

CHAPTER 2

Fundamentals of Disk Operating Systems

Forethoughts and Preparations

If you are a confident computer user, know your operating system commands, and already have a working copy of your system master disk, move quickly through this chapter. If not, continue at a deliberate pace and try out these new commands and capabilities as you go along.

Disk Drives and Master Disks. I must caution you concerning the care and handling of flexible disks. Careless handling of disks will result in the loss of programs and data, and may lead to hardware problems in the disk drives. The disk itself, in its flat square covering, should ALWAYS be stored in its protective envelope. Never let the black square rest anywhere other than in the envelope or inside the drive. When you remove the disk from its envelope, handle it only on the edge with the label sticker. Never touch the exposed magnetic-sensitive surfaces. Always insert disks label side up into drives. Open and close drive doors gently but firmly. Use gentle pressure and never bend or buckle the disk during insertion or removal. Just pretend it costs a lot more than three or four dollars, because depending upon what programs and data are stored on it, your disk could be *worth* a lot more.

The **disk drives** are the system components that store and retrieve files from flexible disks. With this text you need a minimum of one disk drive. In two-drive systems, one drive has the role of default drive. In computer terminology the **default** is the choice *the computer* *makes for you* when you fail to specify an option. The default drive is the drive in which the computer expects to find the master disk when the power is initially turned on or the system is manually reset. Following power-on or reset, the computer works on its own, not giving you a chance to specify a drive.

As you have come to expect, each maker has labeled (and located) the default drive differently. It is called *Drive A*: on the IBM PC (and located on the left), *Drive 1* on the Apple IIe, and Drive :0 on the TRS-80 (and located on the bottom). Each disk drive has a red indicator light to show when the motor (and disk) are spinning. If this light is not conspicuous enough, you should have little trouble hearing the motor. DO NOT INSERT OR REMOVE A DISK WHEN THE DRIVE IS RUNNING.

Included with each computer should be a master disk supplied by the manufacturer. THIS DISK SHOULD NOT BE USED FOR DAILY OPERATION OF THE SYSTEM *because it might become worn or damaged*. Instead, you should create a working master disk by copying (or backing up) the manufacturer's master onto a new blank disk. Format the blank disk before (TRS-80) or during (Apple IIe and IBM PC) the copy process so that the disk can store information. Formatting will be explained a little later in this chapter.

How to Start Each System. Next, I will cover how to start up each system and prepare a working master disk. Before turning on the computer, first switch on any peripheral equipment. **Peripheral** is a computer term that refers to any device or component added to a computer system. Printers and detached video displays are examples of peripherals. So is the LVB interface. All these peripherals lead to a lot of AC cords winding their way around your work area. The solution is to obtain yet another peripheral. Power distribution strips (often containing a circuit that protects against power surges) are products that allow the entire system to be turned on by a single switch.

The IBM PC power switch is located on the right side of the system unit. The Apple IIe switch is on the back of the system unit, to the left. The switch on the TRS-80 is under the keyboard to the extreme right. Why don't the engineers put a big red power switch right up front where you can easily find it? Because they don't want you to bump it accidentally and lose your program.

Having found the appropriate power switch, you are ready to turn on the power to the computer itself. But wait! Two of the three systems, the IBM PC and the Apple IIe, require that the master disk be inserted into the default drive *before* the power is turned on. The TRS-80 can also start this way, but the technical manuals do not recommend it. Rather, you are supposed to (a) turn the power on, (b) wait for the default drive (which has no disk in it) to run for several seconds and then stop, and (c) then insert the master disk and start up the system. The three procedures are outlined below.

STARTING-UP EACH SYSTEM

IBM PC	Apple IIe	TRS-80

turn on peripherals
insert master disk
   in Drive A:
turn on computer
enter date/time
	turn on peripherals
	insert master disk
	   in Drive 1
	turn on computer
		turn on peripherals
		turn on computer
		wait for Drive :0
		   to stop
		insert master disk
		   in Drive :0
		press orange reset
		   button
		enter date

Only the Apple IIe places you firmly in DOS with the flick of the computer's on switch. The other two systems need additional steps, in the form of date and time entries. The TRS-80 *requires* that a date be entered and won't go any further without it. Enter dates in the form mm/dd/yy—for example, 06/18/85. Don't forget the zero before one-digit months and days. The IBM PC lets you ignore its attempts to get date and time by simply pressing ⟨return⟩ in reply to its prompts. If you do enter a date be sure to use a dash between numerals.

Next, you should see the DOS **prompt.** This is the signal from DOS that it is ready to receive a command. Purists will recognize that on the Apple IIe what I'm calling the DOS prompt will also be called the BASIC prompt (BASIC and DOS are at the same level on the Apple IIe).

DOS PROMPTS

IBM PC	Apple IIe	TRS-80
A>	]	TRSDOS Ready
...or...		
A:		

Formatting a Blank Disk. All systems require that a blank disk be **formatted,** or prepared to receive information, before files can be stored on it. In fact, FORMAT is a DOS command on the IBM PC and TRS-80. The formatting process is also an automatic part of the Apple

IIe and IBM PC disk duplication programs. On the IBM PC and TRS-80 the formatting procedure varies slightly depending upon whether your system has one or two disk drives. Most IBM PC systems have double-sided drives (they store information on both sides of the disk), although single-sided drives do exist (refer to the command variations below).

In this text all the examples I'll be showing are set off in "windows." The prompts and messages displayed by the computer during any given operation are enclosed in parentheses. What you are supposed to type is not. Always end each line of typing by pressing the ⟨return⟩ key, unless otherwise instructed. This key is labeled *enter* on the TRS-80 and with a down-to-left arrow symbol on the IBM PC. Any key that you are supposed to press will be printed within the ⟨ and ⟩ symbols (e.g., ⟨return⟩).

FORMATTING BLANK DISKS (ONE-DRIVE SYSTEMS)

IBM PC	notes
	Working master disks need not be formatted separately but will be formatted as part of the disk duplication process.
(A>) FORMAT A:/S	Use with double-side drives.
or	
FORMAT A:/1	Use with single-side drives.
(...insert blank disk...)	Remove master disk from Drive A: and replace with blank disk
(...etc...)	Follow remaining prompts

TRS-80	
(TRSDOS Ready)	
FORMAT :0 (Q=N)	
(Load Destination Disk...)	Remove master disk from Drive :0 and replace with blank disk. Press <enter> to continue.
(...are you sure...)	If the disk is not blank, you will be asked to type "yes" to continue.
(...etc...)	Follow remaining prompts.

```
FORMATTING BLANK DISKS (TWO-DRIVE SYSTEMS)
```

IBM PC	notes
	Working master disks need not be formatted separately but will be formatted as part of the disk duplication process.
(A>) FORMAT B:/S	Use with double-side drives.
or	
FORMAT B:/1	Use with single-side drives.
(...insert blank disk...)	Place blank disk in Drive B: (second drive)
(...etc...)	Follow remaining prompts

TRS-80	
(TRSDOS Ready)	
FORMAT :1 (Q=N)	
(Load Destination Disk...)	Place blank disk in Drive :1 (top drive) Press <enter> to continue.
(...are you sure...)	If the disk is not blank, you will be asked to type "yes" to continue.
(...etc...)	Follow remaining prompts.

Making a Working System Master.   Next, you need to duplicate the system master disk, provided by the manufacturer, onto a new disk. Again, a DOS command (or DOS program) does the job, and there are slight variations depending upon whether you have a one- or two-drive system. The Apple IIe and IBM PC disk duplication programs automatically format during the copying process. For the jargon buffs, the specialized terms of disk duplication are source disk, target disk, and destination disk. The *source disk* is your original, which you usually insert in the default drive on a two-drive system. The *target* or *destination disk* is the disk you are copying to, which you usually insert in the second drive on a two-drive system. On one-drive systems both the source and target disks must occupy the same drive, but at different times, necessitating a certain amount of disk swapping during the duplication process. Both processes are described on the following page.

DUPLICATING A DISK (ONE-DRIVE SYSTEMS)

IBM PC	notes
	Start with master disk in Drive A.
(A>) DISKCOPY A: A:	You are saying that both the source and target disks will be in Drive A.
(...insert source disk...)	You will have to alternate between the two disks until the job is complete.
(...etc...)	Follow remaining prompts.

Apple IIe	
(]) RUN COPYA	Start with master disk in Drive 1.
(ORIGINAL SLOT:) 6	Drive 1 should be controlled by Slot 6 inside the computer.
(DRIVE:) 1	You are saying that the original disk is in Drive 1.
(DUPLICATE SLOT:) 6	
(DRIVE:) 1	Both the original and duplicate will use Drive 1.
(...etc...)	You will have to alternate disks. Follow remaining prompts.

TRS-80	
(TRSDOS Ready)	Start with master disk in Drive :0.
BACKUP :0 :0 (X)	Both the source and destination disks will be in Drive :0.
(...insert...)	You are asked to change back and forth from the master to the destination disk.
(...are you sure...)	If the destination disk is not blank you will be asked to to type "yes" to continue.

DUPLICATING A DISK (TWO-DRIVE SYSTEMS)

IBM PC	notes
(A>) DISKCOPY A: B:	You are saying that the source disk will be in Drive A and target in B.
(...insert target disk...)	
(...etc...)	Follow remaining prompts.

```
Apple IIe

(]) RUN COPYA                          Disk duplication program.

   (ORIGINAL SLOT:) 6                  Drive 1 should be controlled by
                                         Slot 6 inside the computer.
             (DRIVE:) 1                You are saying that the original
                                         disk is in Drive 1
(DUPLICATE SLOT:) 6

             (DRIVE:) 2                You are saying that the duplicate
                                         disk is in Drive 2.
(...etc...)                            Follow remaining prompts.
```

```
TRS-80

(TRSDOS Ready)

BACKUP :0 :1                           Source disk will be in Drive :0
                                         and destination disk in :1.

(...insert...)                         Follow remaining prompts.

(...are you sure...)                   If the destination disk is not
                                         blank you will be asked again.
```

You are ready to put away the manufacturer's master disk and use only your working copy from now on. Furthermore, now that you know how to make duplicates of your master disk, you can get into the habit of regularly backing it up. That is to say, you should periodically duplicate your working master disk onto another disk that you keep safe just in case your working disk fails. Believe me, it can happen. If it does, at least your programs and data are on the backup disk.

Two-drive Systems.   If you have a two-drive system, you'll need to learn the difference between selecting and designating a different disk drive. Remember that the default drive was originally set when you started the system. This is A: on the IBM PC, Drive 1 on the Apple IIe, and Drive :0 on the TRS-80. **Selecting** a different disk drive essentially means that you change the default drive. When you **designate** a disk drive, you simply tell a DOS command to limit its function to the specified drive. The default drive remains unchanged. The IBM PC and Apple IIe allow selection of different drives. The TRS-80 does not; Drive :0 is always the default drive. When you want to select a different drive on the Apple IIe, you type the drive label *after* a DOS command. In other words, the DOS command function will be performed on the indicated drive, which will then become the new default. In the examples below the two drives are labeled A: and B: on the IBM PC, D1 and D2 on the Apple IIe, and :0 and :1 on the TRS-80.

SELECTING DIFFERENT DISK DRIVES

IBM PC	Apple IIe	TRS-80
(A>)B:	(])CATALOG, D2	
(B>)A:	(])CATALOG, D1	
(A>)		

The IBM PC and TRS-80 allow designation of another drive. The default drive is not changed, and the DOS command will function on the indicated disk.

DESIGNATING ANOTHER DISK DRIVE

IBM PC	Apple IIe	TRS-80
(A>)DIR B:		(TRSDOS Ready)
		DIR :1 (A)

Fundamentals of DOS and the Most Common Commands

As you learn these DOS commands, keep in mind that they are actually "invisible" programs that perform a variety of information management tasks on program and data files stored on the disk.

Entry into DOS. You know you are at DOS level when you have the DOS prompt. Of the three systems covered in this book, only the Apple IIe has no special DOS prompt. The Apple IIe uses a single prompt for both BASIC and DOS level.

DOS PROMPTS

IBM PC	Apple IIe	TRS-80
A>	]	TRSDOS Ready

After invoking DOS, you may want to invoke BASIC. Be sure to have the ⟨caps lock⟩ key engaged. All your typing in BASIC should be done with uppercase letters.

```
TO INVOKE BASIC FROM DOS
```

IBM PC	Apple IIe	TRS-80
(A>)BASICA	not relevant	(TRSDOS Ready)
(...headings...) (Ok)		BASIC
		(...headings...) (Ready)

Notice that the IBM PC and TRS-80 have different prompts for their BASICs. When you are finished with BASIC level and want to return to DOS level on these systems, you do so with the same command—SYSTEM. Remember, going back and forth from DOS to BASIC is not relevant on the Apple IIe. However, on the IBM PC and TRS-80, GOING FROM BASIC TO DOS CAUSES ANY BASIC PROGRAM THAT WAS IN MAIN MEMORY TO BE ERASED. So know where you're going before you go anywhere.

```
TO INVOKE DOS FROM BASIC
```

IBM PC	Apple IIe	TRS-80
(Ok) SYSTEM	not relevant	(Ready) SYSTEM
(A>)		(TRSDOS Ready)

DIR and CATALOG to Find Out What Files are on a Disk.
Obviously this is a very important operation. The IBM PC and TRS-80 recognize that the contents of the disk are kept in a **directory,** while the Apple IIe prefers the term **catalog.** In addition, each system's DOS reports different information about the files it displays.

```
DOS COMMANDS FOR LISTING THE CONTENTS OF A DISK
```

IBM PC	notes
(A>)DIR	Orders the directory for Drive A.
(A>)DIR B:	Orders the directory for Drive B.

```
(PROJECT   BAS     3440...)     Directory information includes:
(...ETC...)                         filename, extension, size-bytes,
                                    date; DOS 2.0 or higher will show
                                    free space also.
```

Apple IIe	notes
(])CATALOG	Orders the catalog for current Drive.
(])CATALOG, D2	Toggles to Drive 2 and orders catalog.
(...HEADING...)	Catalog information includes:
(* A 008 PROJECT)	lock status, * means locked;
(...ETC...)	file type, A means Applesoft
	BASIC program;
	file size in disk sectors;
	filename.

TRS-80	notes
(TRSDOS Ready)	
DIR (A)	Orders directories of both Drives.
(Filespec ...etc...)	No less than 10 types of file
(------------------)	information are provided, the most
(PROJECT ...etc...)	useful of which are:
(...etc...)	filename (filespec here);
	file size in bytes;
	the date the file was created
	or last modified.

There are also different procedures for having the list of files printed on the printer. Before using any printer commands, be sure that the printer is connected properly and that all necessary switches and settings are correct. If you are entering or editing a program, be sure to save it on disk before printing. If an attempt to use the printer fails, DOS may "hang up," temporarily jamming the computer (see the section below on restarting DOS). The IBM PC requires the use of certain control key sequences in order to print a directory. These are explained below.

```
LISTING THE CONTENTS OF A DISK ON THE LINE PRINTER
```

IBM PC	Apple IIe	TRS-80
(A>)<CTRL-P>DIR	(])PR# 1	(TRSDOS Ready)
(...printing...)	(])CATALOG	DIR (A,P)
<CTRL-N>	(...printing...)	
(A>)	(])PR# 0	

Did you catch the use of those **control key sequences** on the IBM PC? The trick to control sequences is to *press and hold* the ⟨Ctrl⟩ key, then *press and release* the other key. If your IBM PC has DOS 2.0 or higher, you can turn the printer on and off by pressing ⟨Ctrl-PrtSc⟩ or use the sequence above; but press ⟨Ctrl-P⟩ again, instead of ⟨Ctrl-N⟩, to turn the printer off.

The Apple IIe requires the PR# command for its printer. The PR# 1, above, activates the #1 expansion slot inside the computer cabinet, and you have your printer interface in that slot. The PR# 0 command will deactivate the printer. Finally, on the TRS-80 the printer is activated by a P in parentheses after a printable command.

REN and RENAME to Change the Name of a Disk File.   The most important thing here is not to use a file name that already exists. If you do, you will erase the file that was already on disk under that name. You may want to do that intentionally sometime, but be sure you're aware of the result. I'll explain file names in detail in Chapter 3.

```
DOS COMMANDS TO RENAME FILES
```

IBM PC	Apple IIe	TRS-80
(A>)REN PX1.BAS PX2.BAS	(])RENAME PX1, PX2	(TRSDOS Ready)
		RENAME PX1 PX2

DEL, DELETE, and REMOVE to Erase a File from Disk.   You must exercise caution whenever you erase files from disk. Check file names carefully before using these erase commands, so that you don't accidentally erase the wrong file.

```
DOS COMMANDS TO ERASE FILES
```

IBM PC	Apple IIe	TRS-80
(A>)DEL PROJECT.BAS	(])DELETE PROJECT	(TRSDOS Ready)
		REMOVE PROJECT

LOCK, UNLOCK, and ATTRIB to Protect Files from Being Changed.   Can you think of why you might not want a file to be changed? One reason is to protect it from accidental erasure. The Apple IIe and TRS-80 both allow some form of protection on files. When a file is **locked,** or protected, it can be used but not changed or deleted. In order to change or delete the file, you must first unlock it.

```
DOS COMMANDS TO LOCK AND UNLOCK FILES
```

TRS-80	notes
(TRSDOS Ready)	
ATTRIB PROJECT (OWNER="PASSWORD",PROT=READ)	Locks PROJECT.
ATTRIB PROJECT.PASSWORD (PROT=FULL)	Unlocks PROJECT.

Apple IIe	notes
(])LOCK PROJECT	Locks the file PROJECT.
(])UNLOCK PROJECT	Unlocks the file PROJECT.

How and When to Restart DOS

Restarting DOS is a touchy subject, because it usually is required after some error from which you cannot get back to DOS or BASIC level. For some unknown (to you) reason, the computer is **frozen,** or **locked-up.**

You wouldn't want to restart DOS accidentally because any program in memory at the time you restart DOS is *erased from memory*. Note that I didn't say erased *from disk*. If you have the program or file on disk, you're safe.

Any system can be restarted by turning the power switch off and on, with a master disk in the default drive. This is not recommended, however. It is better to use the reset button or restart keystroke sequence specific to the system. The reset button on the TRS-80 is a recessed orange button to the right of the keyboard. If you press this button, DOS instantly restarts whenever a master disk is in the default drive. The IBM PC and Apple IIe have keystroke sequences to restart DOS.

```
KEY-PRESS SEQUENCES TO RESTART DOS
```

IBM PC	notes
<Ctrl><Alt> <Del>	Press and hold down the <Ctrl> and <Alt> keys, then press <Del>; release all keys; respond N to the Test Memory? prompt.

```
Apple IIe                     notes
<CONTROL><OPEN-APPLE>  <RESET>  Press and hold down the <CONTROL>
                               and <OPEN-APPLE> keys, then
                               press <RESET>; release all keys.
```

DOS Commands from BASIC Level

Based on what you've read so far, you might now believe that the IBM PC and TRS-80 do not allow you to execute DOS commands from BASIC level (the Apple IIe does because it makes no distinction in the first place). However, you're in luck! The IBM PC and TRS-80 have special commands that work from BASIC level when you have the BASIC prompt showing. They will be covered later under BASIC commands.

Closure

Each computer system has a full technical manual to describe the intricacies and permutations of its DOS. I have covered only a tiny fraction of the available set of DOS commands. The above commands are actually all that you need to manage the disk storage of the programs you will write. You may want to keep the technical manuals handy, however, especially if you have a new IBM PC or work-alike system using DOS 2.0 or higher. Whenever I mention a feature that is different in higher versions of PC-DOS, I will be sure to alert you to Appendix F, where the differences are outlined.

CHAPTER 3

Fundamentals of Programming in BASIC— BASIC Commands

What is a BASIC Program?

A BASIC program is a series of numbered lines, each containing at least one BASIC statement. If you're going to put more than one statement on a given line, you must separate them with a colon. The line numbers you select for each line in your program should not be consecutive, or you won't have any free lines to add new statements in between existing ones. Instead, jump your numbers by tens or twenties (20, 40, 60, etc.). However, don't worry too much about line numbering, since you can renumber a program whenever you need extra spacing between lines. Finally, it's important to know that you don't need to type the lines in any particular order. Every time you finish a line and press the ⟨return⟩ key, BASIC will put that line exactly where it belongs according to its line number.

BASIC programs can exist in different places. Their permanent residence will be the flexible disk you just made into your working master. But *permanent* is not completely foolproof, so you should take precautions to safeguard your programs and data. There are two ways: keep a **backup** disk, and keep up-to-date printed listings of your programs and data. *Always* get a printed listing of the current version of a program after any editing. Learn the compulsive behavior patterns of a computer-savvy student—you'll be glad you did.

To create, edit, or run a program, it must first be present in the computer's main memory. If you're getting confused about where your program actually *is* in the computer at any point, let me summarize the situation. Each list on the following page assumes that you have correctly invoked BASIC and are at BASIC level.

MAJOR STEPS IN PROGRAM DEVELOPMENT AND USE

Creating	Editing	Running
1. Type statements from hand-written notes	1. Load program from disk	1. Run program from disk
2. List program on screen as needed	2. Add, change, delete lines	If errors, go to Editing -- Step 2
3. Run program to test it	3. List program on screen as needed	
4. List program on line printer	4. Run program to test it	
5. Save program on disk	5. List program on line printer	
6. Verify program on disk	6. Save program on disk	
	7. Verify program on disk	

BASIC Commands

I'm sure you remember the three BASIC prompts from Chapter 2. Whenever you see one on the screen near your **cursor** (the flashing line or little square), you are at BASIC level and can type a BASIC command or statement. You'll have to learn BASIC commands before you get into BASIC statements because the commands are aids to programming, and you should be familiar with them from the start. Experienced Apple users will want me to refer to certain of the commands below as DOS commands, because Apple manuals do. However, let me repeat that the Apple does not distinguish between DOS and BASIC levels.

The NEW Command. Use NEW to erase the program (if any) currently in main memory. It allows you to start entering program statements with a blank slate.

NEW COMMAND

IBM PC	Apple IIe	TRS-80
(Ok)	(])NEW	(Ready)
NEW		NEW

The LOAD Command and File Names. If a certain program is stored on disk, use LOAD to bring it from disk to main memory. After a program has been loaded, it may be listed, edited, or executed (put into action). LOAD commands must be used with a specific file name. **File names** are the unique labels you give each BASIC program.

The IBM PC uses a two-part file name. The first part may be up to eight characters long and should include *only* numbers and letters. The second part, called an **extension,** allows another three characters. BASIC programs on the IBM PC will automatically be given the extension BAS. A period separates the two parts of the file name (e.g., PROJECT.BAS).

The TRS-80 also uses a two-part file name, although an extension is not required for BASIC programs. The first part must not exceed eight characters, must start with a letter, and can contain only letters and numbers. Extensions are limited to three characters and are separated from the first part of the file name by a slash.

The Apple IIe allows file names up to 30 characters long, including letters, numbers, spaces, hyphens, and periods, but never a number as the first character.

Finally, there are certain "illegal" file names. These are usually the words (known as **reserved** words) that are also used as BASIC commands or statements. In general, you should avoid overly complex file names to keep from making typographical errors while trying to enter them. Please note the use of quotation marks around file names on the IBM PC and TRS-80.

```
LOAD COMMAND
```

IBM PC	Apple IIe	TRS-80
(Ok)	(])LOAD PROJECT	(Ready)
LOAD "PROJECT.BAS"		LOAD "PROJECT"
or		
LOAD "PROJECT"		

The LIST Command. Use the LIST command to display one or more program lines on the screen. If you ask for a range of lines to be listed, the display will move so quickly that you will be unable to read it. You can stop this **scrolling** effect of the display. On the IBM PC press ⟨Ctrl-NumLock⟩ to stop the display, and any other key to start it again. But if you want to stop the display and return the BASIC prompt, use ⟨Ctrl-Break⟩. On the Apple IIe press ⟨CONTROL-S⟩ to stop, and the same keys again to resume the display. Also on the Apple IIe, press ⟨CONTROL-C⟩ to stop a listing and return the BASIC prompt. On the TRS-80 press ⟨Shift-@⟩ to stop, and any other key to resume.

There are many variations of the LIST command: you can list the entire program, a range of lines, a single line, and the current line. The **current** line can be either the line where the program stopped due to an error, or the line you have just typed or edited.

```
LIST COMMAND
```

IBM PC	Apple IIe	TRS-80	notes
(Ok)		(Ready)	
LIST	(])LIST	LIST	Entire program
LIST 30-300	LIST 30,300	LIST 30-300	Inclusive range
LIST 30-	LIST 30,	LIST 30-	Line downward
LIST -300	LIST ,300	LIST -300	Start to line
LIST 285	LIST 285	LIST 285	Single line
LIST .		LIST .	Current line
LIST .-		LIST .-	Current to end
LIST -.		LIST -.	Start to current

When you give the LLIST command in place of LIST, both the IBM PC and TRS-80 will direct listings to the line printer rather than the screen. The Apple IIe has a different procedure. You must first select printer output with the PR#1 command. Then use LIST commands as shown above. Finally, reselect screen output with the PR#0 command.

The DELETE and DEL Commands.   It's only natural that you will need to erase specific lines as you are developing or editing your program. Please be cautious and double-check your commands before pressing that ⟨return⟩ key. Once lines are erased, they may not be recoverable. I say *may not* because there is actually one marginally useful recovery method for those times when you accidentally erase the wrong part or too much of your program. This recovery method is quite simple. Just reload the original disk version of the program, thereby wiping out what editing and erasing you just did. The trade-off with this recovery method is obvious: you may have to repeat some of your editing changes. To erase lines on the IBM PC and TRS-80, you have nearly all the options available with the LIST command shown above. Not so with the Apple IIe.

DELETE AND DEL COMMANDS

IBM PC	Apple IIe	TRS-80	notes
(Ok)		(Ready)	
DELETE 30-300	DEL 30,300	DELETE 30-300	Inclusive range
DELETE -300		DELETE -300	Start to line
DELETE 285		DELETE 285	Single line
DELETE .		DELETE .	Current line
DELETE .-		DELETE .-	Current to end
DELETE -.		DELETE -.	Start to current

Each system allows you to erase any single line by typing its line number only. This is actually the most common method used.

The RUN Command. RUN is probably the most important BASIC command: it gets your program working. Everything else is subordinate to it. RUN has only three variations: alone, with a file name, and with a line number. Before actual program execution starts, RUN sets all variables equal to zero (variables are covered in detail in Chapter 4).

RUN COMMAND

IBM PC	Apple IIe	TRS-80	notes
(Ok)		(Ready)	
RUN	(])RUN	RUN	Start program execution
RUN 300	RUN 300	RUN 300	Start program at line
RUN "PROJECT.BAS"	RUN PROJECT	RUN "PROJECT"	Erase main memory,
or			Load program, and start
RUN "PROJECT"			

How do you stop a program that is already running? It's simple. Just type the **break** sequence. You will be returned to BASIC level, and the program and variables will be unaffected.

BREAK SEQUENCES TO INTERRUPT A BASIC PROGRAM

IBM PC	Apple IIe	TRS-80
<Ctrl-Break>	<CONTROL-RESET>	<BREAK>
	or	
	<CONTROL-C>	

Only the TRS-80 allows you to stop a running program by pressing a single key, the ⟨BREAK⟩ key (located in the upper right part of the keyboard). The other two systems require a control sequence: first press and hold the ⟨CONTROL⟩ key, then press the other key, then release all keys. Don't ever try break sequences while loading or saving programs on disk.

The SAVE Command.   Use SAVE to store the program currently in main memory on disk. Make sure you have the master disk in the default drive before using this command (even though I can't think of any good reason why you should take the master out of the drive in the first place). SAVE must always be accompanied by a "legal" file name. Since you specify the file name, it is possible to store the current program under a different name from any previous version of the program on the disk. If you specify the same file name as a previous version, the current program is stored *in its place*, effectively erasing the old version. There is ample opportunity for accidentally erasing a program on the disk, so be careful to double-check file names before using them.

A useful option with the SAVE command for the IBM PC and TRS-80 is called **ASCII** (pronounced *as-key*) format. ASCII format stores the program as literal text, not in a compressed unreadable code, which is the mode for the straight SAVE command. With ASCII format you take up more disk space, but it is needed for certain other techniques, such as program merging (to be introduced in Chapter 10).

SAVE COMMAND

IBM PC	Apple IIe	TRS-80	notes
(Ok)		(Ready)	
SAVE "PROJECT.BAS"	(])SAVE PROJECT	SAVE "PROJECT"	Compressed format
SAVE "PROJECT.BAS",A		SAVE "PROJECT",A	ASCII format
or			
SAVE "PROJECT"			

The VERIFY Command. By now you may be feeling quite paranoid about all the different "glitches" that can strike your programs. For whatever reason, rare disk errors occur on any disk drive. These errors may be detected by the computer and you may get an error message, but more often than not, they go undetected until you attempt to load or run the program and it doesn't work or look right. Happily, there is a command called VERIFY that deliberately rechecks the disk version of a program against the version in main memory. The IBM PC verifies automatically with each SAVE command. The Apple IIe requires a separate VERIFY command after each SAVE. The TRS-80 allows you to select a VERIFY mode from TRSDOS level, which then automatically verifies after each SAVE used from BASIC level.

```
VERIFY COMMANDS
_____
Apple IIe                         TRS-80

(])VERIFY PROJECTOR               (TRSDOS Ready)

                                  VERIFY (YES)
_____
```

The example above for the TRS-80 uses the VERIFY command from TRSDOS level. BE VERY CAREFUL WITH THIS. If you are at BASIC level with a program in main memory, and you type SYSTEM to return to TRSDOS level to use VERIFY, the program in memory will be lost if you don't save it first. Also, remember that you need only use the TRS-80 VERIFY command once. The best time to use it is just after you start up the system and before you invoke BASIC. The Apple IIe VERIFY should be used after *each* SAVE command.

The FILES Command on the IBM PC. The IBM PC allows you to get a listing of the files stored on disk from BASIC level. In other words, you do not have to leave BASIC and use the DOS DIR command.

```
FILES COMMAND
_____
IBM PC                            notes

(Ok)

FILES                             File names only will be displayed
                                  on the screen
_____
```

The SYSTEM Command on the TRS-80. The TRS-80 allows nearly all DOS commands to be executed from BASIC level, provided they are part of a SYSTEM command. You have to be extra careful with SYSTEM because if it is used alone, you will jump out of BASIC, and the program in main memory will be lost. Below is an example of the SYSTEM command used to execute a DOS command from within BASIC.

```
SYSTEM "DIR" COMMAND
```

TRS-80	notes
(Ready)	
SYSTEM "DIR (A)"	File names only will be displayed on the screen
SYSTEM "DIR (A,P)"	Same as above, but listed on the line printer

The KILL Command on the IBM PC and TRS-80. Again, there is a way to erase a file from the disk without leaving BASIC and invoking DOS. On the IBM PC and TRS-80, use the KILL command. KILL must be accompanied by a file name enclosed in quotation marks.

```
KILL COMMAND
```

IBM PC	TRS-80
(Ok)	(Ready)
KILL "PROJECT.BAS"	KILL "PROJECT"

Closure

The BASIC commands from this chapter (and the DOS commands you've already studied) should be your constant companions during programming. There will be more of them, however. The advanced commands and utilities won't come until later chapters. Even so, you have enough knowledge of DOS to get started on simple projects. What you need next is BASIC statements.

PART TWO

APPLICATIONS

If you are already an experienced programmer, you've been quickly skimming the material in the last two chapters. The four chapters of Part 2 are the backbone of this text. In this part you'll learn what real-time computer programming is all about by doing it.

Chapter 4 is a review of BASIC statements, along with your first real-time programming assignment to make the computer act like a simple slide projector to display verbal stimuli.

Chapter 5 is new business. Here you will get an early introduction to the computer interface that allows real-time control over laboratory apparatus. You must study Appendix A before you attempt to work with the interface examples in Chapter 5. Also in this chapter is full coverage of how to use real-time clocks within your experimental control programs. The abilities to measure time and to control events based on time parameters are essential features of real-time programming. Be advised that the types of clocks that are available to you vary considerably, so go through this material very carefully and methodically. Additional programming techniques and BASIC statements will be introduced gradually as new material is presented.

Chapter 6 continues the coverage of real-time programming principles by presenting techniques for the measurement of a subject's behavior, the dependent variable of an experiment. Your first interface project on operant learning comes in this chapter. Also, an important programming project on the semantic differential procedure is introduced.

Chapter 7 closes this part of the book with coverage of techniques for creating and displaying stimuli. The examples on presentation of stimuli include operant reinforcement, verbal learning materials, and sound cues. Three new programming projects are introduced: how to control schedules of operant reinforcement, conduct the study phase of a paired-associate memory experiment, and conduct a time-perception test.

CHAPTER 4

Fundamentals of Programming in BASIC— Statements

Experimenter and Subject

With this chapter you'll begin to create real-time computer programs. Keep in mind that these programs are going to be used to carry out psychological experiments or procedures. You are the programmer and experimenter, but someone else will be the subject of your research. The computer (and its program) will be the test apparatus used by the subject in your experiments. Your subjects probably will not know how the program that is testing them was written, as they won't see the program listing. They will only be exposed to the stimuli, prompts, and instructions that you (the programmer-experimenter) designate. While you are developing programs, you will also take the role of subject, as you work out any bugs in the procedure. It helps if you try to think and function like a true subject, someone who has little or no idea what the plan or objective of the experiment (or program) is.

Constants, Parameters, Stimuli, and the DATA Statement

Numeric Constants. BASIC recognizes many different kinds of numbers in a program, including zero, positive or negative integers (whole numbers), or real numbers (those having a decimal fraction). Numbers in a program are called **numeric constants.** You'll often use numeric constants as **parameters,** values that control or limit a process within the program. For example, let's say you wanted to display a series of 10 words on the video screen. The process involved is the display of a given word, and you want to repeat the process 10 times. In this case the number of repetitions of the process is a parameter.

String Constants. BASIC also recognizes text in the form of characters, words, and the like. These are called **strings** in computer lingo. String constants are enclosed in quotation marks so the computer can distinguish them from numeric constants or other data. It should be easy to see that each of the 10 words you want to display is actually a string constant serving as a stimulus. **Stimuli** are simply the information or events that subjects are going to react to. This brings me to the first BASIC statement.

The DATA Statement. You use DATA statements to hold numeric and string constants used as either parameters or stimuli. Consider the example of the 10 words displayed in a series on the screen. You've got one parameter—the number of words (10)—and a set of stimuli—the 10 actual strings.

By now you should be familiar with BASIC prompts, so I will stop showing them in my window examples.

```
DATA STATEMENT
```

program segment	notes
100 DATA 10	
110 DATA "HOUSE","HARP","HORSE","HOT"	With more than one item per
120 DATA "HIM","HER","HOWL","HAPPY"	statement, separate items
130 DATA "HUNT","HAWK"	with commas, but don't
	end the line with a comma.

DATA statements are flexible enough to accommodate both numeric and string constants at the same time. Each DATA statement can hold several items or just one; it's up to you. If you're starting to wonder how the program will use these data items, I'll get to that in a minute.

Variables and the READ and RESTORE Statements

Numeric and String Variables. A number or string may be represented in a computer program as a **variable.** The first thing you should learn about variables is that they each must have a different name. This name is a code for a specific location in the computer's memory. A single number or string can be stored in each such memory location (in each variable, in other words).

Let's compare variables with constants for a moment. The value (either numeric or string) of a constant is obvious, because you have the number or string before you. The value of a variable is not obvious, because you see only the code name. For example, if you make the letter *V* a variable, you activate a numeric storage site in the computer's memory. You may store any number in that site. If you wrote a statement that said, "Put 12.6 into *V*," for example, *V* would have the value of 12.6. You could also write a statement to multiply *V* by 2. The new value of *V* would be 25.2. The *V* never changes; only its value changes. Just try to keep in mind that the variables you use in a BASIC statement represent locations in computer memory that can accept a range of values.

Rules for Naming Variables. There are certain universal rules. The name must begin with a letter, A–Z. String variable names must end with a dollar sign. Before a value is assigned, numeric variables equal 0 and string variables equal " " (the two quote marks side-by-side represent nothing, or a **null** string).

Other rules vary by computer system. Both IBM PC and TRS-80 allow up to 40 characters (letters and digits) in a variable name. This effectively allows you to use meaningful words and phrases as variables names. BUT DON'T USE ANY SPACES. The Apple IIe allows a whopping 239 characters (letters and digits) in a variable name! But only the first two characters count; all the rest are ignored by the computer and are only for your reference.

My advice for all systems is to use short variable names (1–6 characters) for simplicity and to save typing time. Finally, a variable name should not contain a BASIC statement, function, or other reserved word. You may think LETTER$ makes a good variable name, but it will cause a program error because LET is contained within it (LET is a BASIC statement reserved word). On the Apple IIe these errors are indicated when you list the line. The variable name is broken up with the reserved word portion separated from the rest to tip you off that it needs correcting (LETTER$ would be shown as LET TER$). Other systems will simply report "Syntax Error," leaving you to find it (the technical manual for each system will list reserved words). You have to learn to watch out for these little pitfalls!

VARIABLE NAMES

IBM PC and TRS-80	Apple IIe	notes
AA	TRIAL	Numeric variable
ITEM$	SLIDE$	String variable

The READ Statement. Use READ to assign a constant, in a DATA statement list, to a variable. READ works in an unusual way. It does not know in advance how many items are in the DATA statements. The program must control the READ statement so that it does not go beyond the last data item. READ can, however, keep track of the last data item assigned. READ has its own **pointer,** which clicks down (and across) the list of data items as each one is assigned. It always proceeds from top to bottom, and left to right, among a series of DATA statements. READ also can't tell the difference between a numeric and a string data item. The program must ensure that READ assigns strings to string variables and numbers to numeric variables. Let me give you an example, based upon the 10 stimulus words listed on page 36.

READ STATEMENT

program segment	notes
100 DATA 10 110 DATA "HOUSE","HARP","HORSE","HOT" 120 DATA "HIM","HER","HOWL","HAPPY" 130 DATA "HUNT","HAWK"	From the previous example
500 READ NUM 510 READ S1$ 520 READ S2$	Assigns 10 to variable NUM Assigns HOUSE to variable S1$ Assigns HARP to variable S2$

The pointer that READ uses is now set at "HORSE" in the data list. The next time a READ statement occurs, this is the item that will be assigned. If you should ever want to send the pointer back to the top of the list, to the first data item, use the RESTORE statement.

RESTORE STATEMENT

program segment	notes
...continuing from above	
600 RESTORE 610 READ FULL	Sends pointer back to top. Assigns 10 to variable FULL

Arithmetic and the LET Statement

BASIC uses five symbols to carry out simple arithmetic. Add to these the left and right parentheses, and you have a powerful way of solving long formulas and computations. The LET statement gives you the capacity to solve a formula and assign the result to a variable *at the same time*. LET always uses an equal sign to split the statement into left and right portions. The right portion is solved and then assigned to the variable in the left portion. Only single variables can appear in the left portion of the statement. Equations, constants, or variables can appear in the right portion. Finally, LET is convenient because the reserved word (LET) need not be typed in the statement itself. Here are some examples.

```
LET STATEMENT
```

program segment	notes
100 B1=45	Assignment of a constant
110 XY=YY	Assignment of a variable
120 F=A+B	Addition
130 G=A-B	Subtraction
140 H=A*B	Multiplication
150 I=A/B	Division
160 J=A^2	Exponentiation; also note that on the TRS-80 the ^ symbol is <Shift ;>
170 K=(F+G)/((H-I)*J)	Using parentheses

Using parentheses can be tricky. The computer will do the *innermost* set first when it encounters nested sets. It always solves parenthetical formulas before performing operations on nonparenthetical material. As a quick, but far from flawless, check on the correct use of parentheses, you can count the left and right parentheses separately. The two counts should match; otherwise there will be a problem.

The INPUT and PRINT Statements

The INPUT Statement. DATA and READ statements are fine for assigning parameters and stimuli to variables, but how about getting numeric and textual information directly from the keyboard? Keyboard input will be a fundamental requirement for using the computer to conduct an experiment. INPUT statements assign keystrokes to a variable. Again, it's up to the program to differentiate between numeric and string entries by making assignments, through the INPUT statement, to either numeric or string variables.

You know now that INPUT assigns keystrokes to a variable. How does the subject (at the keyboard) know when to type the information? It's simple. INPUT can also print a prompt on the screen. This prompt is a string constant. The IBM PC and TRS-80 will automatically add a question mark after the prompt string; the Apple IIe will not. And how does the computer know the subject has finished typing the series of keystrokes that INPUT will assign to a variable? That's simple too. There is a **line terminator** keystroke, the ⟨return⟩ key (⟨Enter⟩ on the TRS-80). Pressing that key terminates the entry sequence. However, if ⟨return⟩ is the first key pressed, then the INPUT statement will attempt to assign "nothing" to the variable. If INPUT has a string variable, zero characters are assigned to it; the string variable becomes blank. This can be a handy feature, as you'll soon see. Below are some examples of INPUT in use.

At this point, I'm going to start using screen diagrams to show you what effect your statements have when the computer executes them.

INPUT STATEMENT

program segment	notes

300 INPUT "NUMBER OF TRIALS";NT
310 INPUT "NUMBER OF WORDS";NW
	Notice that the prompt string
	    is separated from the
	    variable by a ;

400 INPUT "SUBJECT'S NAME";SN$	String input.
410 INPUT "SUBJECT'S GROUP";SG	Numeric input.
	On the Apple IIe the ? is not automatic.

(when you RUN the above, you must respond to each prompt in sequence...)

```
                              screen
    NUMBER OF TRIALS? 6
    NUMBER OF WORDS? 3
    SUBJECT'S NAME? J.SMITH
    SUBJECT'S GROUP? 1
```

The PRINT Statement.   PRINT is a very useful statement. With it you control what appears on the display screen and the line printer. The different types of information that can be printed are: numeric constants and variables, string constants and variables, and arithmetic solutions. Yes, you can solve equations with PRINT statements. Here is an example.

PRINT STATEMENT

program segment	notes
300 INPUT "NUMBER OF TRIALS";NT	
310 INPUT "TRIAL DURATION IN MINS";TD	
315 PRINT	Skip one line.
320 PRINT D*NT;"MINS REQUIRED"	Multiply and print.

```
                        screen

    NUMBER OF TRIALS? 5
    TRIAL DURATION IN MINS? 2

     10 MINS REQUIRED
```

Punctuation is a critical factor within PRINT statements. You use two kinds of punctuation symbols to format, or structure, the way information is displayed on a line. The semicolon will print items next to each other on the line. There still may be spaces separating the items, however. On the IBM PC and TRS-80 all numbers are printed with a trailing blank, positive numbers are printed with a leading blank, and negative numbers are printed with a leading minus sign. On the Apple IIe the semicolon will give no blank spaces between numeric print items. The comma will cause a jump to the next **print zone** on the line. There are 5 print zones per line on the IBM PC and TRS-80, and they are located every 16 and 14 spaces, respectively. The Apple IIe has only 3 print zones, 17 spaces apart. If you leave a trailing semicolon or comma at the end of a PRINT statement, the cursor will wait where it left off, and the next item printed will be displayed at that location.

If you want to direct your print statements to the line printer instead of the screen, it's simple on the IBM PC and TRS-80. Just use LPRINT instead of PRINT. On the Apple IIe you must activate the printer with the PR#1 statement. Any PRINT statements to follow will be directed to the line printer. To activate the screen again, use the PR#0 statement (both PR#1 and PR#0 are line-numbered statements just like all the others).

Programming Repetitions with FOR-NEXT Statements

The FOR-NEXT Statements.   This is a special functional combination of two statements working together to perform what are called loops in computer lingo. A **loop** is a series of statements, enclosed within a FOR-NEXT combination, that will be repeated a number of times. A number of parameters control the action of each loop. Each parameter is present in the FOR statement. The critical parameter is the number of times the loop will repeat. The FOR statement determines this parameter by indicating that a numeric variable increments through a specified range. This variable is like any other, but I'm giving it the special name of **loop variable.** The FOR statement gives the value for the loop variable at the start and finish of the repetition process, in effect determining the number of times the loop repeats.

```
FOR-NEXT LOOPS
```

program segment	notes

800 FOR I = 1 TO 10
     .
     .
	I is the loop variable; I is 1 to start, increments by 1 each time loop repeats until I equals 10.

900 NEXT I	This loop repeats 10 times.

950 FOR J = 1 TO FULL
     .
     .
	This time the loop repeats until J equals variable FULL.

990 NEXT J	

The NEXT statement shouldn't give you any problems. I recommend referencing the same loop variable used in the matching FOR statement. The loop variable J is used in both line 950 and line 990.

So far I haven't considered what statements should go inside a loop, other than to say that they will be repeated a number of times. I'll pull together the previous examples on READ-DATA, INPUT, PRINT, and FOR-NEXT to give you an idea of how all these statements work. Remember that I originally wanted to display a list of 10 words.

PROGRAMMING EXAMPLE: FOR-NEXT LOOP IN A PROJECTOR PROGRAM

program segment	notes
100 DATA 10	The number of stimuli
110 DATA "HOUSE","HARP","HORSE","HOT"	The data list of 10 stimuli.
120 DATA "HIM","HER","HOWL","HAPPY"	
130 DATA "HUNT","HAWK"	
300 READ FULL	FULL now equals 10 (from DATA statement at line 100).
400 FOR I = 1 TO FULL	
410 READ W$	W$ now equals HOUSE.
420 PRINT ,W$	Skip 1st zone, print HOUSE.
425 INPUT "RETURN FOR NEXT WORD";E$	Program waits for key press.
430 NEXT I	W$ changes with each pass through the loop, and the next data item is printed.
500 END	END statement is always last

```
                              screen
              HOUSE
RETURN FOR NEXT WORD?
              HARP
                .
                .

              HAWK
RETURN FOR NEXT WORD?
```

Controlling Where Text Is Displayed on the Screen

The CLS and HOME Statements.   With a little imagination you may be able to make your program simulate a slide projector, advancing from one word to the next as you press the ⟨return⟩ key. However, what if you want only one word on the screen at a time? You'll have to **clear** the screen before each repetition of the loop.

CLS AND HOME STATEMENTS

IBM PC and TRS-80	Apple IIe
402 CLS	402 HOME

If you run your slide projector program with a clearing statement added, you'll get only the prompt and stimulus on each of ten screens. Maybe you would like to print the stimulus in the center of the screen and the prompt at the bottom. It can be done.

The LOCATE Statement on the IBM PC. LOCATE is very useful and easy to use. The standard size screen on the IBM PC contains a grid of 24 lines down and 80 columns across, so there are many different positions at which you can start to print something. The trick is to get your cursor to just the right position. Use LOCATE to position the cursor *before* printing. The row and column values in the LOCATE statement may be constants, variables, or equations.

```
LOCATE STATEMENT
```

IBM PC	notes
420 LOCATE 12,40	Puts the cursor at line 12, column 40; the center point of screen.
422 PRINT W$	Printing starts at new cursor position.

The VTAB and HTAB Statements on the Apple IIe. Apple IIe does it a little differently. You have 24 lines by 40 columns in the standard system (an 80-column option is available). VTAB moves the cursor to a given line, while HTAB moves the cursor to a given column.

```
VTAB AND HTAB STATEMENTS
```

Apple IIe	notes
420 VTAB 12 : HTAB 20	A multiple-statement line; cursor first goes to line 12, then column 20; screen center point.
422 PRINT W$	

The PRINT @ Statement on the TRS-80. Here you find a similar approach. The standard TRS-80 Model 4 screen is also 24 lines by 80 columns, and the PRINT @ statement refers first to the line, then to the column. This statement is roughly the same as LOCATE on the IBM PC and may have variables or equations as the row and column values. It differs from LOCATE in that the items to be printed may be listed in the PRINT @ statement. However, it is possible to use PRINT @ just to position the cursor. In that case you must have a semicolon at the end. And by the way, there must be a space between the PRINT and @.

```
PRINT @ STATEMENT
```

TRS-80	notes
420 PRINT @ (12,40), W$	Don't forget the comma between the cursor coordinates and the print list.

Let's see what one of the 10 screens in the PROJECTOR program will look like after you insert the appropriate cursor movement statements.

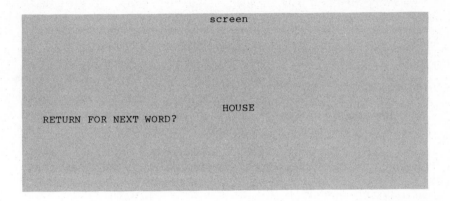

Documenting The Program Listing

The REM Statement.   REM is one of the most important BASIC statements since it will allow you to place notes and remarks directly in the program listing without affecting the program itself. These notes to yourself will keep you informed about what parts of the program are doing long after you have forgotten. Use REM statements as often as you want.

```
REM STATEMENT
```

program segment	notes
500 REM TRIAL LOOP STARTS HERE	
900 REM SUBJECT MUST ALSO PRESS <RETURN>	

Closure

You covered a lot of ground in this chapter, but you are now on your way toward an understanding of how the computer program uses parameters and stimuli to carry out an experimental procedure. Now that you're writing programs, double-check the use of those DOS and BASIC commands covered in earlier chapters.

The SLIDE PROJECTOR program I built up in the previous examples is a very simple prototype, but by studying it, you should be able to see how word or sentence stimuli can be presented to subjects via the video display. The projects suggested below are designed to get you to elaborate upon the skills you've learned.

Tips on Developing New Programs from Old Programs. Throughout the text, you will be asked to develop new programs and modify or expand old programs. Please realize that YOU DO NOT HAVE TO RETYPE STATEMENTS ALREADY SAVED IN A PROGRAM. For example, if your assignment is to modify or expand program X, which you already have stored on disk, simply load program X, delete and/or add lines to make the modifications, and then save the program under a new name. The old version will remain intact on disk. Take the time to develop the "cut-and-paste" skills needed to avoid retyping statements already entered as part of another similar program.

Projects

Stand-alone Project: SLIDE PROJECTOR II.   Using the sample program above, make the necessary changes so that pairs of words are printed at the center of the screen, side-by-side. The word list is as follows: HOUSE, SHACK, CAR, SEDAN, HORSE, PONY, BUNDLE, SATCHEL, PAIL, BUCKET.

Stand-alone Project: SLIDE PROJECTOR III.   Redesign the program in the first project to display the first word of the pair in the center of the screen, followed by a prompt for the second word. When the subject responds, print the second word of the pair directly below the first, followed by a prompt for the next pair.

CHAPTER 5

Fundamentals of Real-Time Computing

ADVANCING BASIC: New Statements and Functions

So far you have practiced the fundamentals of BASIC programming and written a few short programs. Now you're ready to learn some of the more advanced features of BASIC. These will be presented in special sections entitled ADVANCING BASIC:. . . . I have a special purpose in mind for these advanced features: I want you to design programs to conduct experiments. You're going to use these new features to manipulate parameters and stimuli and to collect and organize the responses of your subjects.

You're still a novice in one area—real-time computing techniques. That's what this chapter is about. You'll begin learning about computer interfacing hardware and the software used to control it. You'll also practice some sophisticated programming techniques to control real-time clocks and timers.

The Hardware of Real-Time Computing

The interfacing projects in this text rely on one particular product because it can be connected to each of the three computer systems I cover (IBM PC, Apple IIe, and TRS-80). This product, called the LVB Interface, is available from Med Associates, Inc., Box 47, East Fairfield, Vermont 05448, phone (802) 827-3825.

The LVB Interface. Simply put, the LVB Interface is a "black box" containing some specially designed circuitry that enables the computer to communicate with other devices and apparatus. With the interface the computer can receive signals from an apparatus (the computer receives input) and send signals to an apparatus (the computer produces output). Let's say you have an operant learning apparatus (for people or animals) that you want to control with a computer system. The LVB Interface gives you two essential capabilities. First, it allows the computer to detect the occurrence of any switch closure representing an operant response (e.g., when a rat presses the response lever, or a person presses a button). Second, it allows the computer to turn on various electrical devices that provide stimuli and reinforcement used as part of an operant test apparatus (e.g., when a pellet dispenser provides a food pellet to a rat, or when a slide projector advances to a new slide in order for a person to receive a new visual stimulus).

The input and output (I/O) capabilities of the interface are very flexible. Virtually any switching device can generate an input signal to the interface, and virtually any electrical apparatus can be activated by the output circuits. There is a third circuit inside the interface that you'll learn about, the Precision Timer. This is not an ordinary clock, but a programmable clock with flexible features. It's also able to measure very small intervals. Think of it as the computer's stopwatch. These functions are provided by four LVB Interface I/O circuit cards: Switch Input, DC Driver (output), Relay (output), and Precision Timer. If you have not studied Appendix A, which describes the LVB Interface in detail, go to it now and then return to this chapter.

There are two other kinds of timers available for stand-alone projects (those that don't require the interface). I'm calling these **DOS clocks.** They are activated by commands within the disk operating system of the computer. DOS clocks keep track of the time of day just like a digital watch, giving you hours, minutes, and seconds. Some DOS clocks will give you fraction-of-a-second resolution as well. DOS clocks are built in to the operating systems of the IBM PC and TRS-80. A special optional clock circuit card must be added to the Apple IIe. Appendix C provides additional information on these clock cards for the Apple IIe. Now, I want you to turn your attention back to the LVB Interface.

LVB Precision Timer—1080-54A. Appendix A contains a short course in how to assemble and install the components of the LVB Interface. As I've said, make sure you are familiar with the material in Appendix A before you proceed to the interface lessons in this chapter. I am first going to cover how the LVB Precision Timer card operates and the techniques for programming it.

Each computer system uses a slightly different method of communicating with the LVB Precision Timer. For example, as you have learned from Appendix A, the IBM PC and the TRS-80 use the **port** system. Correct installation of the timer card for the TRS-80, for example, requires that the I/O card dip switches be set to port 10. Port 10 is the **control line** for the LVB Precision Timer. Instructions for setting the various timer functions are sent to the interface from Port 10. Port 11 automatically becomes the **data line** carrying timer readings back to the computer. For the IBM PC and TRS-80 there are statements and functions that allow the program to have direct access to ports, using the port number as a parameter. The Apple IIe, however, has a different kind of system, which involves the use of its **memory map.** Without confusing you any further, let's just say that the two systems are functionally equivalent, but the parameters are different. You'll see this more clearly in the programming examples below.

ADVANCING BASIC: OUT and POKE Statements, INP and PEEK Functions

Microcomputer I/O Systems.   An I/O (input/output) **system** allows the computer to connect to outside equipment. The I/O system is not the same on all computers, so the parameters used by specific I/O functions or statements will vary. The derivation of the parameters used by I/O commands is not particularly interesting, but for those that need to know, the information is in the LVB technical manuals. Here you'll learn only what you need in order to use the interface for experiments. If you intend to do interface projects, you must have completed all steps outlined in Appendix A for the connection of the LVB Interface to your computer and the operant learning apparatus you will be using in your lab. In general, the IBM PC and TRS-80 use the INP function for interface inputs, and the OUT statement for interface outputs. The Apple IIe uses the PEEK function for interface inputs and the POKE statement for interface outputs.

Controlling the LVB Precision Timer from BASIC.   To begin, I want to point out that the LVB Precision Timer has several modes of operation. You will learn just one mode that allows you both to record response latencies and to program time intervals. The other modes of operation are outlined in the LVB technical manuals.

First, I'll review the port numbers (IBM PC and TRS-80) and memory map parameters (Apple IIe) that you'll use with the Precision Timer. Real-time control programs will require a series of LVB parameter statements. These are LET statements that assign specific values to variables for use in your programs. The LVB parameter statements should always appear at the beginning of each program. They differ by system, so be sure to keep them straight. Throughout the book, as I add capabilities, I will present expanded listings of LVB parameter statements.

LVB PARAMETER STATEMENTS: Precision Timer -- Port and Memory Map
                         Values

IBM PC program segment	notes
10 TCLVB = 240	Timer Control on port 240.
12 TDLVB = 241	Timer Data on port 241.

TRS-80 program segment	notes
10 TCLVB = 10	
12 TDLVB = 11	
18 OUT 236,16	Required to turn on the LVB (TRS-80 only).

Apple IIe program segment	notes
...assumes adapter card in Slot #2...	As described in Appendix A.
10 TCLVB = -16222	Memory map values instead
11 TDLVB = -16221	of port numbers.

IMPORTANT: The memory map parameters given above for the Apple IIe require that the LVB computer connection card be located in slot 2 inside the Apple IIe system unit.

You'll be using one of two output statements, OUT or POKE, to communicate with the Precision Timer control line. Each will require a pair of additional parameters in order to work. The pair includes the port number (or memory map value), and a binary number representing a Precision Timer function. As an example, I'll begin with a fairly obvious function: reset and start timing.

LVB PRECISION TIMER: RESET-AND-START-TIMING

IBM PC and TRS-80	notes
20 OUT TCLVB, 64+2	The parameter 64 resets Timer.
	The next parameter is the time base; if:
	0, the Timer has .001-second increments; ranging from 0-9.999;

```
                                    1, the Timer has .01-second
                                    increments; ranging from 0-99.99;

                                    2, the Timer has .1-second
                                    increments; ranging from 0-999.9.
```

Apple IIe	notes
20 POKE TCLVB, 64+2	Same as above (Just using POKE instead of OUT)

Of course, the system-specific LVB parameter statements are present before these reset statements. The reset statements above will give you 999.9 seconds of time before the Precision Timer rolls over back to 000.0 again.

The next LVB Precision Timer function I'll cover is reading the clock. Reading the Timer first requires an output to the interface to enable the Timer (that is, get it ready to report data). Then input commands will retrieve the Timer's data. This is done in two steps with the INP or PEEK function. Raw time data is in binary form and needs to be converted to decimal before it can be used in the program. Be advised that there are two different models of the LVB Precision Timer, and so two different routines for reading the clock. The routine for the current model, 1080-54A, is given below. The routine for the earlier model, 1080-54, is given in Appendix B.

```
LVB PRECISION TIMER: READING THE CLOCK (1080-54A ONLY)
```

IBM PC and TRS-80	notes
50 OUT TCLVB, 128+2	The 2 preserves .1 sec interval; (it varies with the time base).
52 T1 = INP(TDLVB) * 256	Part 1 of Timer raw data.
54 OUT TCLVB, 4+2	The 2 preserves .1 sec interval. (it varies with the time base).
56 T2 = INP(TDLVB)	Part 2 of Timer raw data.
58 TIME = (T1 + T2)/10	Add parts 1 and 2 and divide by 10 (because the time base was set to .1 secs; this denominator also varies with the time base)

Apple IIe	notes
50 POKE TCLVB, 128+2	
52 T1 = PEEK(TDLVB) * 256	Part 1 of Timer raw data.
54 POKE TCLVB, 4+2	
56 T2 = PEEK(TDLVB)	Part 2 of Timer raw data.
58 TIME = (T1 + T2)/10	Add parts 1 and 2 and divide by 10.

The variable TIME now holds the clock reading. This reading is a digital **running time,** and quite different from a time-of-day reading in hours, minutes, and seconds. The running time is reported only in seconds. So if you're thinking in minutes, stop! The LVB Precision Timer works in seconds (and fractions of seconds) only. Again, remember that the above example applies only to the model 1080-54A Precision Timer. Each of the three systems can make use of the Precision Timer card, provided they are connected to the LVB Interface. The second type of real-time clock is what I'm referring to as a DOS Clock, to be covered next.

DOS Clocks

How the DOS Clock Works. Unlike the LVB Precision Timer, the DOS clock is a time-of-day clock that runs all the time. You can do only two operations with it: reset it to some desired value, or read it. As you read this clock, you will convert the time of day to running time. Also note that the IBM PC and TRS-80 have their DOS clocks built in to the operating system. The Apple IIe requires an optional clock card in order to have DOS clock capability (see Appendix C). The approach will be simple. As the program starts, it will reset the DOS clock to 00:00:00 (no hours, no minutes, no seconds).

```
DOS CLOCK: RESET

IBM PC                          TRS-80

20 TIME$ = "00:00:00"           20 SYSTEM "TIME 00:00:00"
```

Resetting the DOS clock on the IBM PC and TRS-80 may take a few seconds of actual time, so don't do it when time is critical. The reset statement should occur only once at the beginning of the program, well before any critical timing operations begin. If you have a clock card installed in your Apple IIe system, refer to the owner's manual for the reset procedure. These clock cards do not normally need to be reset in each program, since they run continuously with either a wall charger or internal battery.

ADVANCING BASIC: String Functions and Reading the DOS Clock

The DOS Time String.   When the DOS clock is read, it returns a time string in the form of hours:minutes:seconds. That's an eight-character string of six numbers and two colons. You need to convert that time string into digital running time in seconds. To do this you separate the time string into three substrings, one for each data item. This is done with a string function.

The MID$ String Function.   Before you can use the MID$ function to extract a substring from the time string, you need to know the exact locations of each character. Starting with the extreme left character in the time string, the characters are numbered from 1 upward. For example, the two-character substring for hours begins at character number 1 and contains two characters. These are the two essential parameters for the MID$ function. Let's look at MID$ in action, extracting three substrings from the time string. Watch what happens to the colons.

```
DOS CLOCKS: MID$ FUNCTION TO OBTAIN HOURS, MINUTES, AND SECONDS

IBM PC and TRS-80                    notes

80 T$=TIME$                          LET statement reads DOS clock and
                                       assigns time string.
82 H$=MID$(T$,1,2)                   Extracts substring H$ from T$.
84 M$=MID$(T$,4,2)                   Extracts substring M$ (mins).
86 S$=MID$(T$,7,2)                   Extracts substring S$ (secs).
```

Now you have three separate substrings, H$ for hours, M$ for minutes, and S$ for seconds. Notice the two parameters used with the MID$ function: beginning character position, and number of characters. Also note the string parameter used with the MID$ function: T$ was the string from which the substrings were obtained. So when you want to obtain part of a string, MID$ is the function to use.

Functions are certainly different from statements in BASIC. Think of a function as part of a statement (LET, PRINT, etc.) that the computer recognizes as a special instruction. Now you're ready to convert the three substrings into actual numbers, so you can compute the digital running time. For that you need a second type of string function called VAL, which will convert the string form of a number to its numeric value.

The VAL String Function. If you subject a string to the VAL function, the computer will convert it to a number. The string must be numerals in the first place, or a program error will result. You don't have that problem with time string conversions, however, since the colons were removed when you extracted substrings with the MID$ function. Remember, VAL makes numbers out of strings, so you can use VAL within formulas and equations. That's what you're going to do here. Remember that your objective is to produce digital running time in seconds from separate values of hours, minutes, and seconds. First, ask yourself how many seconds are in an hour, and then how many seconds are in a minute. If you wanted to transform these hour and minute values into seconds, what would you do, arithmetically? You need to multiply the time units by certain constant values, as you'll see below.

DOS CLOCKS: VAL STRING FUNCTION TO CONVERT TIME SUBSTRINGS

IBM PC and TRS-80	notes
...continuing from above...	
88 HS = VAL(H$) * 3600	HS is the number of hrs expressed as secs.
90 MS = VAL(M$) * 60	MS is the number of mins expressed as secs.
92 SS = VAL(S$)	Direct VAL conversion to get secs.
94 TIME = HS + MS + SS	Add up components to get running time in secs.

Now you have harnessed the DOS clock capabilities to add a timer to your computer programs. You can easily substitute the LVB Precision Timer routines for DOS clock routines. The Apple IIe DOS clock is also a very useful high-speed timer like the LVB Precision Timer card, since the DOS clock on the Apple IIe is based on a clock card that can resolve time to the nearest .001 second. Apple IIe clock cards also use the above string functions to convert the time string into a digital running time (see Appendix C for substitute statements). Also, new versions of the IBM PC or work-alikes may have fractions of a second in their version of the DOS clock if they have PC-DOS (and GW BASIC) version 2.1 or higher (see Appendix D for substitute DOS clock statements on these systems and Apple's Macintosh). Next, I'll cover the programming technique for reading the clocks in the most efficient manner.

ADVANCING BASIC: Subroutines and Reading the Clock

Subroutines in BASIC.   Think of a **subroutine** as simply a part of a program. Subroutines are designed to conduct certain limited procedures that otherwise would have to be repeated throughout the program. Now you can see why a subroutine to read the clock is a good idea. Consider the example above, using the DOS clock statements. If your program reads the clock in several situations, you'd have to retype these statements several times. It's much more efficient to use a clock subroutine.

Subroutines are controlled by two statements: GOSUB and RETURN. GOSUB requires a parameter in the form of the line number where the subroutine begins. The GOSUB statement is not part of the subroutine itself. The RETURN statement is part of the subroutine, and is always placed as its final statement. RETURN causes the computer to go back to where it left off before it was called to the subroutine (the very next statement after the last GOSUB). So, whenever you use GOSUB you can jump around from the main program to any number of parts, or subroutines. Before looking at specific examples, let's list all the possible variations in clock subroutines. You're going to see a new statement here—GOTO; I'll explain it shortly.

```
SUBROUTINES TO READ REAL-TIME CLOCKS: IBM PC and TRS-80

LVB Precision Timer (1080-54A)        notes

...LVB parameter statements...        Varies by system.

30 GOTO 100                           Branch past the subroutine.

50 OUT TCLVB, 128+2                   First statement of subroutine.
52 T1 = INP(TDLVB) * 256
54 OUT TCLVB, 4+2
56 T2 = INP(TDLVB)
58 TIME = (T1 + T2)/10
60 RETURN                             Last statement of subroutine

DOS Clock

30 GOTO 100

50 T$=TIME$
52 H$=MID$(T$,1,2)
54 M$=MID$(T$,4,2)
56 S$=MID$(T$,7,2)
58 HS = VAL(H$) * 3600
60 MS = VAL(M$) * 60
62 SS = VAL(S$)
64 TIME = HS + MS + SS
66 RETURN
```

SUBROUTINE TO READ REAL-TIME CLOCK: APPLE IIe

LVB Precision Timer (1080-54A)	notes
...LVB parameter statements...	Varies by system.
30 GOTO 100	Branch past subroutine.
50 POKE TCLVB, 128+2	First statement of subroutine.
52 T1 = PEEK(TDLVB) * 256	
54 POKE TCLVB, 4+2	
56 T2 = PEEK(TDLVB)	
58 TIME = (T1 + T2)/10	
60 RETURN	Last statement of subroutine.

DOS clock based on optional clock card (from Appendix C)

IMPORTANT: Card shown is installed in slot #5.

20 D$ = CHR$(4)	Allows program control of DOS commands
30 GOTO 100	
50 PRINT D$	Clock subroutine begins.
51 PRINT D$; "PR#5"	Sets output to clock card.
52 PRINT D$; "IN#5"	Sets input from clock card.
54 INPUT " ";T$	
56 HS = VAL(MID$(T$,7,2))	Time string conversions.
58 MS = VAL(MID$(T$,10,2))	
60 SS = VAL(MID$(T$,13,2))	
62 FS = VAL(RIGHT$(T$,4))	
64 HS = HS * 3600	Conversions to seconds.
66 MS = MS * 60	
68 TIME = FS + SS + MS + HS	
70 PRINT D$; "IN#0"	Returns input to keyboard.
72 PRINT D$; "PR#0"	Returns output to screen.
74 RETURN	Last line of subroutine.

The new statement at line 30, GOTO, is absolutely necessary. You never want to enter a subroutine unless it's through the GOSUB calling statement. So I used GOTO as a way of branching around the subroutine and continuing with normal program execution.

Also notice that I started each subroutine (regardless of type of clock) at line 50. This is important because, from this point onward, you will be developing programs without reference to specific types of clocks. The specific type of clock subroutine you use will depend upon the type of project (stand-alone vs. interface) and the types of clock you have available. Though designed for use with DOS clocks, stand-alone projects can use the LVB Timer.

To make sure you understand this, I'll take the trouble to list each possible clock subroutine variation within an actual program you've already developed: the first PROJECTOR program from Chapter 4. The program is not developed yet to the point where it is able to use the clock. I'm only interested in your seeing where the clock subroutine fits within the program.

PROGRAMMING EXAMPLE: PROJECTOR PROGRAM WITH LVB TIMER

IBM PC and TRS-80 program segment	notes
...LVB parameter statements...	Varies by system.
...clock reset...	

```
30 GOTO 100

50 OUT TCLVB, 128+2                    First statement of subroutine.
52 T1 = INP(TDLVB) * 256
54 OUT TCLVB, 4+2
56 T2 = INP(TDLVB)
58 TIME = (T1 + T2)/10
60 RETURN                             Last statement of subroutine

100 DATA 10                           The number of stimuli
110 DATA "HOUSE","HARP","HORSE","HOT" The data list of 10 stimuli.
120 DATA "HIM","HER","HOWL","HAPPY"
130 DATA "HUNT","HAWK"
300 READ FULL
400 FOR I = 1 TO FULL
402 CLS
410 READ W$
420 PRINT ,W$
425 INPUT "RETURN FOR NEXT WORD";E$
430 NEXT I
500 END
```

Apple IIe program segment	notes
...LVB parameter statements...	Varies by system.
...clock reset...	

```
30 GOTO 100

50 POKE TCLVB, 128+2                   First statement of subroutine.
52 T1 = PEEK(TDLVB) * 256
54 POKE TCLVB, 4+2
56 T2 = PEEK(TDLVB)
58 TIME = (T1 + T2)/10
60 RETURN                             Last statement of subroutine.

100 DATA 10                           The number of stimuli
110 DATA "HOUSE","HARP","HORSE","HOT" The data list of 10 stimuli.
120 DATA "HIM","HER","HOWL","HAPPY"
130 DATA "HUNT","HAWK"
300 READ FULL
400 FOR I = 1 TO FULL
402 HOME
410 READ W$
420 PRINT ,W$
425 INPUT "RETURN FOR NEXT WORD";E$
430 NEXT I
500 END
```

PROGRAMMING EXAMPLE: PROJECTOR PROGRAM WITH DOS CLOCK

IBM PC program segment	notes

```
20 TIME$ = "00:00:00"
```
Resets DOS clock.

```
30 GOTO 100
```

```
50 T$=TIME$
```
First statement of subroutine.
```
52 H$=MID$(T$,1,2)
54 M$=MID$(T$,4,2)
56 S$=MID$(T$,7,2)
58 HS = VAL(H$) * 3600
60 MS = VAL(M$) * 60
62 SS = VAL(S$)
64 TIME = HS + MS + SS
66 RETURN
```
Last statement of subroutine

```
100 DATA 10
```
The number of stimuli
```
110 DATA "HOUSE","HARP","HORSE","HOT"
```
The data list of 10 stimuli.
```
120 DATA "HIM","HER","HOWL","HAPPY"
130 DATA "HUNT","HAWK"
300 READ FULL
400 FOR I = 1 TO FULL
402 CLS
410 READ W$
420 PRINT ,W$
425 INPUT "RETURN FOR NEXT WORD";E$
430 NEXT I
500 END
```

TRS-80 program segment	notes

...same as above except...

```
20 SYSTEM "TIME 00:00:00"
```
Different DOS clock reset statement.

Apple IIe program segment	notes

DOS clock based on optional clock card (from Appendix C)

IMPORTANT: Clock card is installed in slot #5.

```
20 D$ = CHR$(4)
```
Allows program control of DOS commands

```
30 GOTO 100
```

```
50 PRINT D$
```
Clock subroutine begins.
```
51 PRINT D$; "PR#5"
```
Sets output to clock card.
```
52 PRINT D$; "IN#5"
```
Sets input from clock card.
```
54 INPUT " ";T$
56 HS = VAL(MID$(T$,7,2))
```
Time string conversions.
```
58 MS = VAL(MID$(T$,10,2))
60 SS = VAL(MID$(T$,13,2))
62 FS = VAL(RIGHT$(T$,4))
64 HS = HS * 3600
```
Conversions to seconds.
```
66 MS = MS * 60
68 TIME = FS + SS + MS + HS
70 PRINT D$; "IN#0"
```
Returns input to keyboard.
```
72 PRINT D$; "PR#0"
```
Returns output to screen.
```
74 RETURN
```
Last line of subroutine.

```
100 DATA 10
```
The number of stimuli

```
110 DATA "HOUSE","HARP","HORSE","HOT"    The data list of 10 stimuli.
120 DATA "HIM","HER","HOWL","HAPPY"
130 DATA "HUNT","HAWK"
300 READ FULL
400 FOR I = 1 TO FULL
402 HOME
410 READ W$
420 PRINT ,W$
425 INPUT "RETURN FOR NEXT WORD";E$
430 NEXT I
500 END
```

With that out of the way, you can get on with learning how to actually use the clock (LVB Timer or DOS clock) to regulate the passage of time. For this you'll need a new BASIC statement.

ADVANCING BASIC: The IF-THEN Statement

Operating the real-time clock requires a certain amount of common sense. Remember, it's nothing more than a glorified digital stopwatch. Remember also that it times everything in seconds. Suppose you wanted to modify the PROJECTOR program so that the subject does not need to activate the slide advance by pressing the ⟨return⟩ key. Instead, you want the slides to advance automatically every 5 seconds. Here's what your program needs to do, in common-sense terms, before each slide. If your goal is to wait 5 seconds between each slide change, then your first act must be, in effect, to look at your watch and note the current time. Then you'll probably want to recheck the watch continuously until it reads 5 seconds more than that first reading. If the reading is less than 5 seconds more, then you'll continue rechecking it. If it is 5 seconds more, then you'll know time is up, and the next slide should be shown. That description was full of "if's," and that's the type of statement you're going to use to operate the clock.

The IF-THEN Statement. This statement compares two entities and determines the relationship between them. The IF part of IF-THEN uses what are called **relational operators** to make such comparisons. These operators include the equal sign, less-than symbol, and greater-than symbol, among others. The relational operator you choose is an important parameter of the statement. The two entities you are comparing provide additional parameters. They can be constants, variables, or equations. The THEN part of IF-THEN is concerned with the *consequence* of the particular comparison involved, which is expressed in the form of another statement (most often a GOTO). If the comparison staged by the IF-THEN statement is true, then the consequence is executed. If the comparison proves false, the computer executes the next numbered line. Once you see examples, it should all become clear. In the next program segment, I'll translate the common-sense actions described into BASIC statements.

IF-THEN STATEMENT: OPERATING A CLOCK

program segment	notes
415 GOSUB 50	Call clock subroutine; TIME now holds current value.
416 START = TIME	LET statement assigns TIME to a variable.
417 GOSUB 50	Call clock again; update TIME.
418 IF TIME < START + 5 THEN 417	IF statement with GOTO consequence (GOTO can be omitted).
420 ...program continues...	

In this example I sent the computer into an "endless" loop between lines 417–418 *until* the IF-THEN statement proved false. At that point, the program executes the next line below. Now I'm going to add real-time control to the PROJECTOR program. Remember, I'm not showing the actual clock reset statements and subroutine (use the LVB Timer or DOS clock, whichever is available to your system).

PROGRAMMING EXAMPLE: PROJECTOR PROGRAM WITH REAL-TIME CONTROL

IBM PC program segment	notes
...clock reset, etc...	
...clock subroutine...	
100 DATA 10	The number of stimuli
110 DATA "HOUSE","HARP","HORSE","HOT"	The data list of 10 stimuli.
120 DATA "HIM","HER","HOWL","HAPPY"	
130 DATA "HUNT","HAWK"	
300 READ FULL	
400 FOR I = 1 TO FULL	
410 READ W$	Get next slide.
415 GOSUB 50	Take first reading on clock.
416 START = TIME	
417 GOSUB 50	
418 IF TIME < START + 5 THEN 417	Keep reading clock.
419 CLS	After 5 secs. clear screen.
420 LOCATE 12,40	
422 PRINT W$	Display next slide.
430 NEXT I	
440 CLS	Clear screen after last slide.
500 END	

```
Apple IIe program segment              notes

...same as above except...

419 HOME
420 VTAB 12 : HTAB 20
440 HOME
```

```
TRS-80 program segment                 notes

...same as above except...

420 PRINT @ (12,40), W$
422                                    Delete this line.
```

This marks a milestone in your laboratory computing career. When you get this modified PROJECTOR program to work, be sure to congratulate yourself! You've learned how to use a simple **interval timer** to control a process within your program.

As you have gone through the various program examples, you have no doubt noticed how, as I develop new examples, I frequently add line numbers between two previous statements. I am certainly in danger of running out of room for these ever-expanding programs. Now's a good time to learn how to use the line-renumbering functions available on the IBM PC and TRS-80, and the RENUMBER program in the Apple IIe DOS.

ADVANCING BASIC: How to Renumber the Lines of a Program

The RENUM Function. Both the IBM PC and TRS-80 use a BASIC function called RENUM to renumber lines within a program. At this point you'll learn how to do the simplest renumbering steps. I'll cover more complex options in Chapter 10; in the meantime, you can consult your system's technical manual. Suppose you simply want more room between each statement in the program currently residing in main memory (it's already been loaded successfully, or typed in from scratch). However, you have the clock subroutine at line 50, and you want to keep it there, so you need to start renumbering at line 100.

```
RENUM FUNCTION (Starts Renumbering at Line 100)
```

IBM PC	TRS-80
RENUM 100,100,20	RENUM 100,100,20

The first parameter on page 61 (100) specifies where the new line numbers will begin. The second parameter (100) specifies the original line number where renumbering is to start. The third parameter (20) specifies the renumbering increment. Type this command from BASIC level, with or without the BASIC prompt showing. The new numbering will begin with line 100 and increase by 20 throughout. Don't forget to save the renumbered version now in main memory!

The procedure on the Apple IIe requires that you use a DOS program.

RENUMBER PROGRAM ON THE APPLE IIe

Apple IIe	notes
...first save the original program on disk as a backup...	
(])RUN RENUMBER	Refers to DOS RENUMBER program.
...the RENUMBER title screen appears...	
press <RETURN>	
(])LOAD ...program...	Re-load the program you want to renumber.
(])& FIRST 100, START 100, INC 20	Calls for renumbering with first new line at 100, starting at old line 100, incrementing by 20.
...continue programming...	BE CAREFUL: don't forget to save the new version.

Closure

This chapter was your introduction to real-time computing, with a heavy dose of real-time clocks. Let's take a moment to recap some of the new principles laid down in this discussion. First, you now know the difference between the LVB Timer and a DOS clock. You also should know whether your computer has access to either or both; develop your future programs accordingly. From this point on I'll be using programming examples that do not specify the type of clock in use. I'll only be concerned with universal procedures to control the clock functions. Only one such timing procedure has been covered thus far, the interval timer. The clock lesson in the next chapter concerns programming a process or latency timer. Real-time clocks will be with you from this point onward.

Also reflect back on what you learned about the LVB Interface. The statements and functions that allow I/O communications will continue to be of use, but the type of application will broaden in coming chapters. I have yet to cover the switch input, DC driver, and relay output functions provided for by the LVB Interface.

Projects

Stand-alone Project: SLIDE PROJECTOR IV.   Redesign the SLIDE PROJECTOR III program (from Chapter 4) to the following specifications. Use interval timing techniques to present five pairs of words, one above the other in the center of the screen, at regular intervals. Make the time interval a variable holding a parameter value read from a DATA statement.

CHAPTER 6

Measurement of Subject Behavior

The Computer as a Measurement Device

Your computer system can be used to detect and record the behavior of subjects. However, that behavior must be a motor response suited to the hardware and software capabilities of the machine. In this chapter I will discuss two major categories of computer-based measurement: keystroke/keyboard input and switch input via the LVB Interface.

Keystroke input should have obvious appeal to you at this point in your programming experience. After all, you have so far developed a series of programs that use the video screen as a slide projector and the ⟨return⟩ key as the slide advance button. In this chapter you'll learn additional ways of measuring subject keystrokes, and using those responses as events that determine the operation of a computer-controlled experimental procedure.

The LVB Switch Input card will come as a new topic. However, you should recognize it as one of the three interfacing I/O circuits. Here the subject operates a switch (you do this all the time around the house, in your car, and so on). I will show how switch input capabilities can be used with operant test apparatus for learning experiments. I will focus on the typical operant test chamber and its response lever as the switch device to be monitored by the computer.

ADVANCING BASIC: Reading Single Keystrokes

The INKEY$ Function. Both the IBM PC and TRS-80 have a specific capability that allows the computer to detect a single keystroke without the subject's needing to press the ⟨return⟩ key. This is done using the INKEY$ string function. Because it is a function, INKEY$ is used within a LET statement to assign a keystroke to a string variable. The Apple IIe requires a special routine for keystroke entry, and I'll cover that shortly.

```
INKEY$ FUNCTION
```

IBM PC and TRS-80	notes
500 I$ = INKEY$	

Unlike the INPUT statement, INKEY$ does not interrupt the execution of the program or prompt you with a question mark. This is a vital feature for programs that must continuously monitor the keyboard for a subject response that could come at any time. For example, imagine a sample program to measure a person's processing time on an information analysis task. In other words, you want to measure how long it takes the individual to complete a given task.

My example is a spin-off of the classic semantic differential, where the subject is given a word as the stimulus, and then required to assign a value to the word. Value assignments are based on where the word fits along a dimension of meaning; for example, good vs. bad. I am assigning the ⟨1⟩ key to *good* and the ⟨9⟩ key to *bad*. The intermediate keys fall within the range. Now if I were to present the word DOLLAR, which key would you press? I'm not concerned with your semantic judgment at this stage. The point is that the subject must select from a variety of response options. In addition to recording the choice itself, you also want to record how much time it takes to make each choice. The time measure should be based on one keystroke, not two, as would be the case if you used INPUT, since that would require an accompanying press on the ⟨return⟩ key.

How does INKEY$ do all this? Each time INKEY$ is assigned, the status of the keyboard is determined. If a key has been pressed, the character represented is assigned by INKEY$. If no key has been pressed, INKEY$ assigns the null string (""). And there's one more point. There may be a need to clear the keyboard if the subject is likely to press keys during times when you are not scanning for keystrokes (e.g., during an intertrial interval). In that case, use INKEY$ in a LET statement just prior to the start of the keystroke entry routine. This will serve to clear away any unwanted premature keystrokes. See if you can identify these features in the following sample program.

PROGRAMMING EXAMPLE: MEASURING THE SEMANTIC DIFFERENTIAL

IBM PC program segment	notes
...clock reset, etc...	
...clock subroutine...	
100 DATA 2	
110 DATA "HAWK","HAPPY"	
200 READ N	2 Trials to be run.
210 FOR I = 1 TO N	
215 X$ = INKEY$: X$ = INKEY$	Clears the keyboard.
220 CLS : LOCATE 12,1	Clear and position cursor.
230 PRINT "GOOD BAD"	Display semantic choices.
240 PRINT "1 2 3 4 5 6 7 8 9"	
250 PRINT	
260 READ W$: PRINT " ";W$	Read and display stimulus.
300 GOSUB 50 : START=TIME	Start process timer.
310 I$ = INKEY$	Assign keystroke.
320 IF I$ = "" THEN 310	Endless loop until keypress.
330 GOSUB 50	Read process timer.
340 PRINT	
350 PRINT TIME-START,"= PROCESS TIME"	Display data.
355 PRINT I$,"= CHOICE"	
360 GOSUB 50 : START=TIME	
365 GOSUB 50	
370 IF TIME < START + 5 THEN 365	5-sec pause timer.
380 NEXT I	Continue with next trial.

TRS-80 program segment	notes
...same as above except...	
220 CLS : PRINT @ (12,1),;	Clear and position cursor.

You should recognize some familiar routines in the above program. Each trial in the procedure is controlled by a FOR-NEXT loop (just like the PROJECTOR program). Also, the number of trials, and each stimulus, are read from DATA statements. Finally, cursor positioning statements are used to move the display toward the center of the screen. What's new is that the INKEY$ function is used within an endless loop to wait until a keystroke is made. Remember, if no key is pressed, INKEY$ assigns the null string (""). Also, I used the clock twice. First, I used a *latency* timer or *process* timer to record elapsed time between two events: stimulus display and keystroke response. I used the clock a second time as an *interval* timer to maintain a specific intertrial interval. The results should look like this when you run the program:

```
                              screen




GOOD          BAD
1  2  3  4  5  6  7  8  9

      HAWK

   4                   =PROCESS TIME
   8                   =CHOICE
```

Don't be alarmed when this screen disappears after the 5-second intertrial interval. I programmed it that way. If you have a printer connected to your IBM PC or TRS-80, you can get on-line printing (as the program executes) by substituting LPRINT for PRINT in lines 340–355.

ON-LINE PRINTING OF RESULTS

IBM PC or TRS-80 program segment	notes
...same as above except...	
340 LPRINT	
345 LPRINT "TRIAL",I	Print trial number as heading.
347 LPRINT W$,"=STIMULUS"	Print stimulus word.
350 LPRINT TIME-START,"= PROCESS TIME"	Print data.
355 LPRINT I$,"= CHOICE"	
...continued as above...	

Since this is a paper printout, you will want it to show all the details of the procedure. In this case each section on the printout will be clustered by trial and will show all the information used or measured by the program. Make sure the power and on-line switches on your printer are set correctly before you run the program.

Reading the Apple IIe Keyboard. You can perform the same keystroke input operations on the Apple IIe. A preliminary lesson is required on ASCII character codes.

Every key on the computer keyboard has a corresponding numeric ASCII code. Each alphabetic, numeric, and symbol key can be expressed two ways: as a character and as an ASCII code. Even other keys, which have no obvious character equivalency, can be expressed as an ASCII code. For example, the ⟨return⟩ key has the ASCII code of 13. The full listing of ASCII codes for any computer is given as an appendix in the owner's manual or BASIC language manual.

You will have occasion to use ASCII code values to read individual keystrokes on the Apple IIe. The method I'm about to introduce is functionally the same as the capabilities provided by the INKEY$ function on the IBM PC and TRS-80. However, you must make two important modifications in your thinking in order to use the Apple IIe keystroke routine. First, recall that INKEY$ assigns the actual string. Unlike INKEY$, the Apple IIe keystroke routine assigns *only* an ASCII code (but I'll show you how to convert it back into a character). Second, in an endless loop, INKEY$ automatically assigns the null string ("") if no key has been pressed, effectively clearing the keyboard before each keystroke. The corresponding Apple IIe routine requires that the subject clear the keyboard by pressing a key (other than a response key) that the program can recognize. In my examples this clearing key will be the ⟨return⟩ key.

Let me review what I've said concerning the Apple IIe keystroke routine: (a) It's the functional equivalent of INKEY$ on the IBM PC and TRS-80; (b) it assigns an ASCII code rather than a string, which must be converted back to a string; and (c) it requires a separate keystroke to clear the keyboard.

Before you can proceed with an example, you first must have the capacity to convert ASCII codes to character strings. This is done using the string function CHR$(X), where X is an ASCII code. CHR$(X) is treated by the computer *as the string it represents*. In other words, the computer sees no functional difference between CHR$(13) and the ⟨return⟩ key.

APPLE IIe KEYSTROKE ENTRY ROUTINE

program segment	notes
500 INPUT "PRESS <RETURN> TO START";R$	Subject clears keyboard with <return>.
	Keystroke entry routine.
510 KEY = PEEK (-16384)	Reads the keyboard as KEY.
520 POKE -16368,0	Resets the keyboard.
530 IF KEY > 127 THEN 550	If new key has been pressed.
540 GOTO 510	If not, read keyboard again.
550 KEY$ = CHR$(KEY-128)	Convert keystroke to string.

Below line 550, KEY$ will equal the string representing the last key pressed by the subject. Don't be alarmed by the PEEK function and the POKE statement in this routine. The status of the keyboard is represented within the main memory of the computer, and these features are needed in order to evaluate those memory locations and return their status to the program.

At this point you need to see all this in action, so I'll transform the SEMANTIC DIFFERENTIAL program example into its Apple IIe version. Remember, you are obtaining semantic differential judgments from the subject following the display of a single stimulus word.

PROGRAMMING EXAMPLE: MEASURING THE SEMANTIC DIFFERENTIAL

Apple IIe program segment	notes
...clock reset, etc... ...clock subroutine...	
100 DATA 2 110 DATA "HAWK","HAPPY"	
200 READ N 210 FOR I = 1 TO N	2 Trials to be run.
215 HOME 217 INPUT "PRESS <RETURN> TO START";R$	Clear screen. Subject clears keyboard with <return> key (ASCII 13).
220 HOME : VTAB 12 230 PRINT "GOOD BAD" 240 PRINT "1 2 3 4 5 6 7 8 9" 250 PRINT 260 READ W$: PRINT " ";W$	Clear and position cursor. Display semantic choices. Read and display stimulus.
300 GOSUB 50 : START = TIME	Start process timer.
302 KEY = PEEK (-16384) 304 POKE -16368,0 306 IF KEY > 127 THEN 310 308 GOTO 302 310 KEY$ = CHR$(KEY-128)	Keystroke entry routine (chapter 6). If new key has been pressed. Convert keystroke to string.
330 GOSUB 50 340 PRINT 350 PRINT TIME-START,"= PROCESS TIME" 355 PRINT KEY$,"= CHOICE"	Read process timer. Display data.
360 GOSUB 50 : START=TIME 365 GOSUB 50 370 IF TIME < START + 5 THEN 365 380 NEXT I	 5-sec pause timer. Continue with next trial.

The PEEK and POKE combination in the Apple IIe keystroke routine actually make possible the transfer of information from the keyboard to variables in the program, much the same as the INKEY$ function does on the other systems. Also, it's not necessary to worry about unwanted keystrokes because the subject clears the keyboard before each trial can continue.

At this point, you may want to print subject data on-line using the Apple IIe. Unlike the other systems, the Apple IIe does not have a special PRINT statement for the line printer. Instead, you have to activate the printer with the PR# 1 statement. Usually the printed data are also displayed on the screen as well, so the subject will see them. Until I cover disk output files, you should clear the screen (using the HOME statement) immediately after subject data are printed. Here are the changes to make in order to get smooth on-line printing.

```
ON-LINE PRINTING OF RESULTS
```

Apple IIe program segment	notes
...all the above except...	
335 PR# 1	Activates line printer.
340 PRINT	
350 PRINT TIME-START,"= PROCESS TIME"	Display data.
355 PRINT KEY$,"= CHOICE"	
357 PR# 0	Deactivate line printer. IMPORTANT: You cannot use these printer commands with disk output files (to be covered in chapter 9).
...continued as above...	

Switch Inputs Using the LVB Interface

Review of the LVB Interface.   Appendix A covered the steps to set up and connect the LVB Interface, and also gave some background on its method of operation. Next, you covered the use of the Precision Timer I/O circuit card in Chapter 4. It would be wise to take a break here and reread the relevant sections you have already covered.

Next, I'm going to go over the binary labeling system used by the LVB for its various input and output channels. (You should remember this system from setting dip switches according to the instructions in Appendix A.) The LVB Switch Input card has eight input channels. These are labeled using numeric values derived from a binary number consisting of eight-bit units. The numeric labels are decimal, but each of the eight binary units can be only 0 (off) or 1 (on).

NUMERIC CHANNEL LABELS AND CORRESPONDING BINARY BIT NUMBERS

BIT NUMBER	7	6	5	4	3	2	1	0
CHANNEL LABEL	128	64	32	16	8	4	2	1
CHANNEL NUMBER	8	7	6	5	4	3	2	1

The channel numbers (1–8) are available for connection to different input devices. In the examples I will be using just one input device, an operant lever, so I need only one channel, *labeled* 1. If you had additional input devices—for example, a second lever and a photo cell—you would assign these (by actually wiring their NO circuit to the Switch Input card edge connector) to channel number 2 and channel number 3. Your BASIC program, however, will only use **channel labels** because they are the binary equivalents. So if you meant to read an input from the photo cell, you would read the channel *labeled* 4 (this is channel *number* 3, however). Mercifully, when your input device is wired to channel number 1, it is also labeled 1.

If you did have several switches connected to the Switch Input card, and more than one switch was on, the card would send the sum of all those channel labels. For example, if channels *numbered* 1, 2, 3, and 4 were on at the same time, the card would report the value 15, the sum of the four *label* values (1 + 2 + 4 + 8). The value reported by the card is the sum of all the binary equivalents for the channels that are on at the time of the reading. (See Appendix I.)

Naturally, before you can do any programming you must be sure that the correct external voltage is supplied to the input device, the operant lever. Wiring instructions are presented in Appendix A. If that's all in order, you can proceed to measure operant behavior using the computer. Switch Inputs are read on the IBM PC and TRS-80 using the INP function, and on the Apple IIe using the PEEK function. Each time these functions are used, they must refer to a specific port number or memory map value (just like the Precision Timer card routines). Here are the port number and memory map value for the Switch Input card.

LVB SWITCH INPUT -- PORT NUMBERS AND MEMORY MAP PARAMETER

I/O Card Line	IBM PC	TRS-80	Apple IIe
Switch Input	208	1	-16224

Get in the habit of placing the relevant LVB parameter statements related to the use of the Precision Timer at the top of all your interface programs. I've already listed these Timer parameters, but now is a good time to expand the list to include the above Switch Input values.

```
LVB PARAMETER STATEMENTS: Precision Timer and Switch Input
```

IBM PC program segment	notes
10 TCLVB = 240	
12 TDLVB = 241	
14 SLVB = 208	Switch Input on port 208.

TRS-80 program segment	notes
10 TCLVB = 10	
12 TDLVB = 11	
14 SLVB = 1	Switch Input on port 1.
18 OUT 236,16	Turn on ports (TRS-80 only).

Apple IIe program segment	notes
10 TCLVB = -16222	
12 TDLVB = -16221	
14 SLVB = -16224	Switch Input memory map value.

Since INP and PEEK are functions, they must be used within LET statements to assign a value to a variable. The value returned by INP or PEEK indicates the input channel(s) activated.

```
LVB SWITCH INPUT -- IBM PC AND TRS-80
```

program segment	notes
...LVB parameter statements...	Varies by system.
300 LEVER = INP(SLVB)	Reads all input channels; Assigns channel label to variable.

In my example, with just one input channel in use, this system is not very sophisticated. But what if more than one channel were in use at the same time? Then things get interesting. Remember, INP will assign a value that is the *sum* of all channel labels activated. For example, if channels number 1 and 3 are both active (switches closed, voltage present), INP returns 5 because channel number 1 has a label of 1 and channel number 3 has a label of 4, and 1 plus 4 equals 5.

Before going any further, I'll show you how switch inputs are done on the Apple IIe. The PEEK function is used instead of INP, and a different parameter is required: the memory map value.

```
LVB SWITCH INPUT -- APPLE IIe
```

program segment	notes
...LVB parameter statements...	Varies by system.
300 LEVER = PEEK(SLVB)	Reads all input channels; Assigns value to variable.

Clearing Unwanted Inputs. Because the Switch Input card has its own internal memory, it may frustrate you in one particular situation. Let's say that the power switches are all on, your subject is in the operant chamber and ready to go, but you have not yet run the computer program that will control the test session. The subject can still press the lever and have the response, which occurred before the official start of the program, detected automatically when the program starts. The circuitry allows this type of false first response to be detected under certain circumstances. To avoid a problem, you should clear the Switch Input card simply by reading it, but not doing anything with the result. Thus, if any false readings are stored there, they will be cleared away just before the procedure actually starts. You'll see an example of this below.

Determining Which Switch Has Been Activated. Reading a switch is not unlike reading the keyboard. When no switch is active, INP(SLVB) and PEEK(SLVB) will return a value of 0 (when you have a bad connection, INP will return 255). If you want to scan continuously until the switch is pressed, then you need an endless loop constructed from an IF-THEN statement. Let's say you wanted to count the number of presses on the response lever (wired to channel 1 on the LVB Switch Input card, of course).

```
PROGRAMMING EXAMPLE -- COUNTING OPERANT LEVER PRESSES
```

IBM PC and TRS-80 program segment	notes
...LVB parameter statements...	Varies by system.
300 LEVER = INP(SLVB)	Assigns active channels.
310 IF LEVER = 0 THEN 300	Determines if a channel is active (not zero).
320 COUNT = COUNT + 1 330 GOTO 300	If active, increase variable.

Apple IIe program segment	notes
...same as above except...	
300 LEVER = PEEK(SLVB)	

It should be fairly obvious, at this point, how to apply the LVB Switch Input routines to a practical problem. As your programming example, you'll record an operant baseline on the subject in the operant test chamber. You may recall that reinforcement is not given during baseline sessions. This is a simple exercise and requires that the program run for a certain amount of time (session length) and record the total number of lever presses.

PROGRAMMING EXAMPLE: OPERANT BASELINE

IBM PC and TRS-80 program segment	notes
...LVB parameter statements... ...clock reset, etc... ...clock subroutine...	
100 REM	Start of main program.
105 GOSUB 50 : START = TIME 110 EMPTY = INP(SLVB)	Begin session timer. Clears Switch Input card.
290 GOSUB 50 295 IF TIME > START + 180 THEN 400 300 LEVER = INP(SLVB) 310 IF LEVER = 0 THEN 290	Is the 3-min session over? Assigns active channels. Determines if a channel is active (not zero).
320 COUNT = COUNT + 1 330 GOTO 290	If active, increase variable.
400 PRINT COUNT,"=TOTAL LEVER PRESSES" 500 END	

Apple IIe program segment	notes
...same as above except...	
110 EMPTY = PEEK(SLVB)	
300 LEVER = PEEK(SLVB)	

You'll get more programming experience with the Projects section below, but before going to that, let's complete the discussion of behavioral measurement using the computer.

The Range of Dependent Variables Available

The examples used in this chapter have touched upon both types of dependent variables available under computer control. They are, broadly speaking, measures of a target behavior that are related to either time or frequency of occurrence.

Measures Related to Time. The computer programs you write will operationally define time-related measures as either response latencies or durations. I have already discussed latency or process time measurement within the context of the SEMANTIC DIFFERENTIAL program. Let's take a moment to expand on that. A **latency** is simply how much time it takes to make a response. The purest form of this measure would be a simple reaction time. You start a timer following the presentation of a stimulus, and stop the timer at the instant of the subject's response to the stimulus (hence, *reaction time*). The latency is the time difference. When you require the subject to make some sort of judgment or decision about the stimulus, you might refer to *process time* as opposed to reaction time (as we did in the SEMANTIC DIFFERENTIAL program). Both measures are types of latencies.

Another time-related measure is a **duration** between two responses. A good example is the case of operant response chaining, where two or more distinct responses are performed in sequence to obtain reinforcement. To measure the time interval between two responses, you start a timer as the first response is detected, and stop the timer as the second response is detected. The time difference is the duration.

You can exercise a lot of creativity by applying the different time-related measures to the specific research problems you tackle using computer control. It sure beats a pocket full of stopwatches!

Measures Related to the Frequency of Behavior. Counting the occurrence of target behaviors is a simple task. The simple counter used in the OPERANT BASELINE program was a kind of LET statement. I'm going to explain it in more detail now, because it will be used throughout future work.

COUNTING STATEMENT

program segment	notes
200 K = K + 1	Each time it executes, K is is increased by 1.

As with any LET statement, the expression to the right of the equals sign is solved first. So, K is incremented by 1. This new value is then assigned to the variable to the left of the equals sign. The prior value for K is *replaced* with the new value ($K + 1$). The next time this statement is executed, K will increase by 1 again, and so on. It's a simple counter.

The same statement can be used to maintain a **cumulative sum** of measurement. A good example would be the case where your program recorded a separate response latency for each trial in a series, but you wanted to compute the average latency. In order to do that, you would first need the cumulative sum of all the individual latencies. The sum of the latencies would then be divided by the number of trials. You'll get a chance to try out this version of the counting statement when you try the projects below.

Closure

This chapter on using the computer to record the behavior of a subject puts you two-thirds of the way toward mastery of the three standard I/O functions in real-time computing. You now know how to use the real-time clock, and both input from the keyboard (INKEY$ and the Apple IIe keyboard routine) and LVB Interface (Switch Input card). Only the computer-generated outputs remain, and I'll cover that next.

In addition, I have attempted to bring certain general principles of behavioral research together with computer-based procedures, as evidenced in the discussion of how dependent measures are operationally defined in computer terms. The translation of measurement needs into their computer-based equivalents is a vital component of real-time computer control of experiments.

Projects

Stand-alone Projects. Take the SEMANTIC DIFFERENTIAL program example presented in the chapter and develop it further. Set up a second version of the program based on the semantic differential of STRONG–WEAK. Use the word list from the PROJECTOR program as the stimuli, or make up your own word list.

Interface Projects. Modify the OPERANT BASELINE program to print interim response totals every X minutes during a session Y minutes long. In other words, make the program subdivide the operant session into equal intervals. Record and print the number of responses during each interval and the overall total.

CHAPTER 7

Control of Stimulus Presentation

The Computer as a Stimulus-Generating Device

Most experimental procedures for the study of learning, cognitive processes, and perception require that the subject be stimulated in some way. Stimuli may be presented to the subject during learning, as with verbal items to be remembered, or after learned responses, as with reinforcement. In stand-alone applications the stimuli will be primarily visual—displays of character strings and graphic images on the computer's video screen. Certain audio stimuli are also available on most systems. Interface applications add the capability to operate external devices such as food pellet dispensers or slide projectors through the use of the LVB DC Driver and Relay I/O circuit cards.

Furthermore, the stimuli presented usually constitute levels of the independent variable and vary by groups in the research design. This last point is important to you as a real-time programmer, since programs must be written as templates that can accept *any* specific stimulus and present it correctly. This may be hard to visualize, so I'll begin my coverage with a simple example drawn from verbal learning research: the paired-associate word list. Your first task will be to display the items to be associated in the center of the screen.

ADVANCING BASIC: Centering Strings on the Display Screen

The Problem. To understand how to develop a routine to center a string, you must first visualize what information you need at your disposal. Let's work backward from the solution. The goal is to display a string at the midpoint of a line on the screen. Does this mean that the string is printed beginning at the halfway mark on the line? Not necessarily. It means that the midpoint of the string overlaps the midpoint of the line. The midpoint of the line is a constant: either 40 or 20. How can it be either 40 or 20?

Changing Screen Dimensions. Each system allows you to change the width of the screen to either 40 or 80 columns. The IBM PC and Apple IIe require special optional circuit cards for this capability. The IBM PC needs a graphics adaptor for a true 40-column mode (enlarged print), and the Apple IIe needs a special card for 80-column mode (small print). It is preferable, though not required, to be able to present enlarged text on the screen in 40-column mode. If you have an IBM PC without the graphics adaptor, simply keep all the following examples in 80-column mode by using a value of 40 as the midpoint of a line. Most of the examples to follow will benefit from this enlarged display capability.

The Apple IIe starts in 40-column mode, so you're all set on that system. The IBM PC can be switched to 40-column mode using the WIDTH statement, while the TRS-80 requires that you print a special ASCII code. You may remember that ASCII codes are printed using the CHR$ string function (I covered this in Chapter 6 in the context of keyboard input on the Apple IIe).

```
CHANGING SCREEN WIDTH
```

IBM PC	TRS-80	notes
	20 CLS	
30 WIDTH 40	30 PRINT CHR$(23);	Sets 40-column mode.
200 WIDTH 80	200 CLS	Sets 80-column mode.

Changing the screen width on the IBM PC automatically clears the screen. However, on the TRS-80, clearing the screen automatically sets the screen width to 80. In effect, to remain in 40-column mode on the TRS-80, you must reset 40 columns after each CLS statement. Now I'll continue developing a technique for centering strings.

The LEN String Function.   LEN is a most valuable string function. It is used within a LET or PRINT statement to return the **length,** or number of characters, of a string. You need that information in order to center a string on the screen because you must identify the correct column where printing is to begin. Specifically, you need to know the length of the string divided by two. Remember, your goal is to get the midpoint of the string on the midpoint of the line. Here's one way. Divide the length of the line by two (40/2 = 20). There's your line midpoint. Now, if you find the column that marks half the length of the string, you'll have the target column. To find it, use the LEN function.

```
LEN STRING FUNCTION
```

program segment	notes
100 DATA "HOUSE"	
300 READ W$	
310 L = LEN(W$)	L now equals 5.

Whoops! One-half of five will be 2.5, and there are no half columns on the screen. The centering routine requires this value to be an integer. To convert it, use the INT function.

The INT Function.   Subjecting a value or equation to the INT function results in the **truncation,** or dropping off, of any decimal fraction. Keep in mind that this is not rounding (I cover rounding in Chapter 8).

```
INT FUNCTION
```

program segment	notes
100 DATA "HOUSE"	
300 READ W$	
310 L = LEN(W$)	L now equals 5.
320 HL = INT(L/2)	HL now equals 2.

The Target Column.   Before you can put all this together to get a centering routine, you have to add the final link: a screen-positioning statement. You should remember that these statements move the cursor to a specific location on the screen before the display of an item. They require line and column numbers as parameters. In the PRO-

JECTOR program developed in Chapter 5, you used these statements to position words near the center of the screen. Now, you want to position the words exactly in the center of the screen. To do it, you need to focus on the column parameter. The target column referred to above is, in fact, this value. Because cursor positioning statements differ by system, I'll show the string-centering routine separately for each.

PROGRAMMING EXAMPLE: CENTERING STRINGS ON THE SCREEN

IBM PC program segment	notes
20 WIDTH 40	
100 DATA "HOUSE"	
300 READ W$	
310 L = LEN(W$)	
320 HL = INT(L/2)	
330 TARG = (40/2)-HL	The target column.
340 LOCATE 12,TARG	Move cursor.
350 PRINT W$	

On the TRS-80 you substitute the PRINT @ statement at line 340. There's an important catch, however. The PRINT @ statement works differently when the TRS-80 is in 40-column mode. In 40-column mode, the column value of PRINT @ must be multiplied by 2 in order to work correctly. This is because the PRINT @ regards the screen as half as wide as the 80-column mode. Remember, this qualification applies only to 40-column mode on the TRS-80.

TRS-80 program segment	notes
...same as above except...	
20 CLS : PRINT CHR$(23);	Sets 40-column mode.
340 PRINT @ (12,TARG*2),;	Moves cursor to line 12, target column.

APPLE IIe program segment	notes
...same as above except...	
340 VTAB 12 : HTAB TARG	

Even with all these system variations, the centering routine is a nice tool to have at your disposal for string stimulus presentation.

Next, let's return to developing the display for a paired-associate learning procedure. At this point you have a routine to center a string on the display screen. But you may recall that paired associates are, in fact, two strings: a *stimulus term* and a paired *response term*. You may also recall that paired-associate procedures often make use of either the *anticipation* or *study-test* method. In this case you'll be programming the study-test method, which requires that the experiment be carried out in two phases: study and test. Simply put, the study phase requires that a list of paired associates be displayed, one pair at a time, stimulus term on the left, response term on the right. You know how to center a string, but can you center two strings? Just treat the two strings (stimulus term, response term) as one; the technique is described below. Then you can use the same routine you've already learned.

ADVANCING BASIC: String Concatenation, Paired-Associate Displays

If you want to make one string out of two, you must add, or **concatenate,** them. It looks as if you were adding numeric variables, but the result is a new, longer string consisting of the original strings attached to one another in series. You'll also have to concatenate spaces (" ") so that the stimulus and response terms are displayed as a pair of items and not run together.

STRING CONCATENATION

program segment	notes
100 DATA "HOUSE","HARP"	
300 READ LW$,RW$	Reads two items at a time.
305 W$ = LW$ + " " + RW$	W$ is now "HOUSE HARP"

Your program's next step should be the centering routine covered above. You shouldn't have any trouble converting the PROJECTOR IV program to a PAIRED ASSOC STUDY program, one that presents paired associates together in the center of the screen, one at a time, with a certain duration of exposure, and interpair interval. I'm making this an option in the Projects section at the end of this chapter. However, I won't be covering the corresponding PAIRED ASSOC TEST program until Chapter 9 because it requires a more sophisticated technique.

Now let's explore some of the other ways the computer system can stimulate subjects. In the interface configuration the computer will be able to control any electronic or electromechanical device capable of providing stimulation. In its stand-alone configuration each system has ways of generating audio stimuli. Audio stimulus production will be my next topic.

ADVANCING BASIC: Producing Sound and Tone Stimuli

Sounds and tones can be used throughout computer-controlled experimental procedures. They are ideal as signaling stimuli since they require little interpretation. They can also be used as informational stimuli in procedures requiring that they be analyzed, associated, and so on. For my example in this section, I'll use a simple procedure drawn from the study of perception: time judgments. You probably can anticipate the procedure. Your program will present the subjects with an audio signal, then they will have to estimate when a certain amount of time has passed and respond by pressing a certain key on the keyboard. You can then compare the actual elapsed time with the subject's estimate, to determine the level of accuracy in time perception.

The ASCII Bell Code. The standard audio stimulus available on most systems is the ASCII bell code. You produce it by printing CHR$(7). The bell code may not work within a TRS-80 BASIC program, so the SOUND statement (covered in the next section) should be used instead.

ASCII "BELL" CODE

IBM PC and Apple IIe program segment	notes
400 PRINT CHR$(7);	The semicolon prevents altering the screen.

The ASCII bell code produces either a buzz or a beep, depending upon the hardware. The bell code is adequate for use as an event signal when information value is not particularly important. In the example I'll develop for this section on time perception, the bell code would do well as the signal for subjects to begin and end their time judgments. The duration of the bell code cannot be controlled. However, it is presented at the same duration, pitch, and loudness each time it occurs.

This programming example will consist of a brief time perception procedure based on five test trials. Maybe you have been wondering if subjects will cheat and simply count out the seconds between beeps. Certainly they could if they wanted to. But if the standard were simply 1 second in duration, counting (and cheating) is somewhat less useful, so that's the way you'll do it. The five trials will be based on two low, two equal, and two high durations: 0.6, 0.8, 1.0, 1.2, and 1.4.

Here are the steps that will make up each trial in the procedure: (a) a pretrial waiting period of 5 seconds; (b) bell code at start and stop of stimulus interval; (c) display three response options—less than, greater than, or equal to 1 second; and (d) print each response. The LVB Precision Timer can be used on each system for this program since it has been set for a time base of 0.1 second. A DOS clock on the Apple IIe, based on an internal clock card, can also be used. And while I'm at it, I'll use keystroke entry for the responses.

PROGRAMMING EXAMPLE: TIME PERCEPTION

IBM PC program segment	notes
...LVB parameter statements...	Varies by system.
...clock reset, etc...	Remember, always have
...clock subroutine...	clock subroutine at 50.
100 DATA 5	
102 DATA 0.6, 0.8, 1.0, 1.2, 1.4	I am not concerned about
	order in this example.
200 CLS	
300 READ FULL	
310 FOR I=1 TO FULL	
320 GOSUB 50 : START = TIME	Begin pretrial timer.
330 GOSUB 50	
340 IF TIME < START + 5 THEN 330	
350 READ OVER	Assign interval value.
400 GOSUB 50 : PRINT CHR$(7);	Sound bell; begin interval
410 START = TIME	timer.
420 GOSUB 50	
430 IF TIME < START + OVER THEN 420	
440 PRINT CHR$(7);	Sound bell
500 PRINT " CHOICES:"	
510 PRINT	
520 PRINT "1 IF LESS THAN A SECOND"	
530 PRINT "2 IF EQUAL TO A SECOND"	
540 PRINT "3 IF MORE THAN A SECOND"	
600 A$=INKEY$: IF A$="" THEN 600	Reading keyboard.
610 PRINT : PRINT "CHOICE","ACTUAL"	
620 PRINT : PRINT A$,OVER	Printing results.

```
700 GOSUB 50 : START = TIME          Posttrial pause timer.
710 GOSUB 50
720 IF TIME < START + 5 THEN 710
730 CLS

800 NEXT I
1000 END
```

APPLE IIe program segment	notes
...same as above except...	DOS clock may substitute for LVB Timer.
200 HOME	
315 INPUT "PRESS <RETURN> TO START";R$	Needed to "clear" keyboard.
600 KEY = PEEK (-16384)	Keystroke entry routine
602 POKE -16368,0	(chapter 6).
604 IF KEY > 127 THEN 608	If new key has been pressed.
606 GOTO 600	
608 A$ = CHR$(KEY-128)	Convert keystroke to string.
730 HOME	

The differences in these two versions are related primarily to how the Apple IIe accomplishes keystroke input. If you're not quite sure of these routines, reread the appropriate sections in Chapter 6. One question at this point is what about "true" control over audio stimuli. Wouldn't it be nice if you could control the pitch of the signal? Or its duration? Certain systems give you that control.

ADVANCING BASIC: The SOUND Statement

Like other procedures you've seen, all SOUND statements are not created equal. The IBM PC gives you precise control over the pitch and duration of sound stimuli. The TRS-80 gives you relative control. Let's cover the IBM PC version first.

SOUND STATEMENT ON THE IBM PC

IBM PC program segment	notes
500 SOUND 200, 18	

The SOUND statement has two parameters. The first parameter is the pitch or frequency. It can range from 37 to 32767 Hertz units. That's precise control. The second parameter is duration. Here's the rub. It's not clock time, but rather a kind of computer time called a **tick.** There are 18.2 ticks per second (so the above statement specifies a duration of slightly less than a second). If you alter the above procedure slightly, you'll have precise control of both pitch and duration in the TIME PERCEPTION program. Just take the stimulus durations (now in DATA statements) and multiply them by the 18.2 (the tick/second factor). Now you should present a sound for the duration of the stimulus interval that is being judged, not beep a start and stop signal as before. The revised program is streamlined compared to the original.

```
PROGRAMMING EXAMPLE: REVISED TIME PERCEPTION PROCEDURE -- PRECISE
                 DURATION AND FREQUENCY OF SOUNDS
```

IBM PC program segment	notes
...LVB parameter statements... ...reset clock, etc... ...clock subroutine...	
...Delete lines 400-430	Clock routines not needed.
440 SOUND 200,18.2*OVER	Turns on 200 Hz sound for specified duration.

The TRS-80 allows only relative control in the SOUND statement. The frequency parameter can vary from 0 to 7 and is not in Hertz units. The duration parameter can vary from 0 to 31 and is not in computer tick units, or even seconds for that matter.

```
SOUND STATEMENT ON THE TRS-80
```

TRS-80 program segment	notes
500 SOUND 7, 5	

The first parameter above is the frequency; the second parameter is the duration. A very short sound can serve as a beep in the original version of the TIME PERCEPTION program. The ASCII bell code is not available in a TRS-80 BASIC program.

PROGRAMMING EXAMPLE: TIME PERCEPTION

TRS-80 program segment	notes
...LVB parameter statements...	Varies by system.
...clock reset, etc...	Remember, always have
...clock subroutine...	clock subroutine at 50.

```
100 DATA 5
102 DATA 0.6, 0.8, 1.0, 1.2, 1.4          I am not concerned about
                                            order in this example.
200 CLS
300 READ FULL
310 FOR I=1 TO FULL

320 GOSUB 50 : START = TIME               Begin pretrial timer.
330 GOSUB 50
340 IF TIME < START + 5 THEN 330
350 READ OVER                             Assign interval value.

400 GOSUB 50 : SOUND 5,1                  Sound beep; begin interval
410 START = TIME                            timer.
420 GOSUB 50
430 IF TIME < START + OVER THEN 420
440 SOUND 5,1                             Sound beep.

500 PRINT "     CHOICES:"
510 PRINT
520 PRINT "1    IF LESS THAN A SECOND"
530 PRINT "2    IF EQUAL TO A SECOND"
540 PRINT "3    IF MORE THAN A SECOND"

600 A$=INKEY$ : IF A$="" THEN 600         Reading keyboard.
610 PRINT : PRINT "CHOICE","ACTUAL"
620 PRINT : PRINT A$,OVER                 Printing results.

700 GOSUB 50 : START = TIME               Posttrial pause timer.
710 GOSUB 50
720 IF TIME < START + 5 THEN 710
730 CLS

800 NEXT I
1000 END
```

Finally, note that the IBM PC has a music capability in BASIC as well as the pure sound capability I've just discussed. I won't be going into music, but you may want to look up the PLAY statement in your IBM PC BASIC manual. There is potential for this approach to sound stimuli in laboratory applications.

ADVANCING BASIC: Sound Production on the Apple IIe

Sound production on the Apple IIe is accomplished with the PEEK function referencing a specific memory map location for the built-in audio circuit and speaker.

PEEK FUNCTION FOR SOUND PRODUCTION: APPLE IIe

Apple IIe program segment	notes
500 S = PEEK(-16336)	The S variable is needed for a legal LET statement.

The sound produced is a click. However, you can also produce a full range of beeps varying in pitch by adding the PEEKs and by putting the PEEKs inside loops. It is beyond the scope of this text to go further into sound production using the Apple IIe. Accurate music and sound production requires machine language routines, which are documented in many popular press volumes on the Apple II series (check your local bookstore).

Review of the Stand-alone Stimulus Options.   Before moving on to interface applications, let's look back over the ground already covered. First, I discussed the methods for displaying strings (text) on the computer's video screen. This stimulus option is by far the most flexible and useful for psychological research on learning, memory, and perception. Next, I showed you audio stimulus production on the three systems. In both cases you were able to bring together some of the earlier routines, including the use of real-time clocks and keystroke input. Every new lesson will require that you reach into your tool kit of programming routines to assemble a new structure for a new application. Now, you're ready to move on to interface outputs.

DC Driver and Relay Cards in the LVB Interface

These are the two primary output circuit cards used in the interface. Remember, however, that the Relay card is considered as optional equipment for the purposes of this text. My primary emphasis will be on the DC Driver card because it was specially designed for applications in operant learning. In the next section you'll learn first about using the DC Driver card to control a feeder/dipper inside an operant test chamber. Appendix A is your source for information on wiring and assembly of this equipment. I'll finish the chapter with a lesson on using the Relay card to control the functions of a carousel slide projector.

ADVANCING BASIC: OUT and POKE Statements

You first saw the OUT and POKE statements in connection with the LVB Precision Timer card. With regard to the DC Driver and Relay cards, they allow you to send a signal outside the computer to the LVB Interface, where another circuit interprets the command and operates one of the available drivers or relays. A **driver** is a circuit in the interface that provides the electrical power to a device such as a food pellet dispenser. A **relay** is an interface component that acts as a switch to turn a device on and off.

OUT and POKE each require two parameters. The first parameter is the port number on the IBM PC and TRS-80. On the Apple IIe the corresponding memory map value is required.

LVB OUTPUT CARDS -- PORT NUMBERS AND MEMORY MAP PARAMETERS

I/O Card Line	IBM PC	TRS-80	Apple IIe
DC Driver (1080-18)	176	96	-16223
Relay (1080-40)	242	30	-16220

It pays to establish these values as variables at the top of any program that will use the LVB interface. In the examples throughout this text, I will continue to refer to *LVB parameter statements*. You were exposed to these statements twice before, when you were setting up routines to run the LVB Precision Timer, and to obtain switch inputs from the interface. The approach I'm now taking with the DC Driver and Relay cards will be quite similar. In fact, now is the time to show the final version of the LVB parameter statements in a single routine. Remember, Appendix A describes how to configure these LVB components so that the parameters shown below will work.

COMPLETE LVB PARAMETER STATEMENTS: Precision Timer, Switch Input,
                                   DC Driver and Relay Cards

IBM PC program segment	notes
10 TCLVB = 240	Timer Control on port 240.
12 TDLVB = 241	Timer Data on port 241.
14 SLVB = 208	Switch Inputs on port 208.
15 DLVB = 176	DC Drivers on port 176.
16 RLVB = 242	Relays on port 242.

TRS-80 program segment	notes
10 TCLVB = 10	
12 TDLVB = 11	
14 SLVB = 1	
15 DLVB = 96	
16 RLVB = 30	
18 OUT 236,16	Required to turn on LVB (TRS-80 only).

```
Apple IIe program segment              notes

...assumes adapter card in Slot #2...

10 TCLVB = -16222                 Apple IIe uses memory map
12 TDLVB = -16221                    values, not port numbers.
14 SLVB = -16224
15 DLVB = -16223
16 RLVB = -16220
```

The second parameter in the operation of the LVB DC drivers or relays is the channel label. This should be a familiar concept since it was introduced in Chapter 6. To quickly refresh your memory, consider this.

NUMERIC CHANNEL LABELS AND CORRESPONDING BINARY BIT NUMBERS

BIT NUMBER	7	6	5	4	3	2	1	0
CHANNEL LABEL	128	64	32	16	8	4	2	1
CHANNEL NUMBER	8	7	6	5	4	3	2	1

Channel number refers to the actual wiring post used on the LVB output card (the top edge connector on DC Driver or Relay). **Channel label** is the binary equivalent used as the second parameter in the OUT or POKE statement. As you can see, you have eight drivers and eight relays at your disposal. However, you need only two drivers and one relay in the following programming examples. According to the instructions in Appendix A, the feeder/dipper of the operant chamber should be wired to driver #1 on the DC Driver card. The white cue light should be wired to driver #2.

To reiterate, the Relay card is optional, but if you have it and want to learn to use it, there is an example at the end of this chapter. Now let's concentrate on the DC Driver functions.

LVB DC Driver Card—Modes of Operation. Each of the eight drivers on this card can be set to one of two modes of operation by making a selection on a small dip switch. If toggle #1 on the switch is ON, then **pulse mode** has been selected. If the switch is OFF, then **level mode** has been selected.

Pulse mode allows you to adjust the duration of the operation of the driver. For example, feeders and dippers require pulsed operation. The driver that controls your feeder/dipper (driver #1) must be in pulse mode. The relative duration of the pulse is determined by dialing the control knob (use a small screwdriver) labeled for driver #1. You can select short or long pulses by adjusting this dial control.

Level mode is more like the light switches around your house. When you turn them on, they stay on until you turn them off. You'll be controlling the operant chamber's cue light with a driver #2 in level mode. Double-check those mode dip switches to make sure you've got them right.

Programming the DC Driver Card.   Because of the way these circuits are designed, there is one programming behavior that you must acquire. The DC Driver card *must be reset as one of the very first program statements*. This is because the drivers may come on automatically whenever you run a program using the LVB interface and both the LVB unit and 28-volt supply are also switched on. You'll see this DRIVER RESET statement highlighted in the programming examples to follow. *If you forget to put it in your programs, you may damage equipment like feeders or dippers.* It's serious enough to pay special attention to. A reliable fail-safe procedure is to keep the 28-volt supply off until you are ready to begin the operant test session and after your program has reset the drivers. I'll also integrate this fail-safe procedure into the programming example.

Operating drivers is very straightforward. Simply specify the channel label you want to operate. If you want to operate more than one channel at a time, specify the sum of the binary equivalents for those channels. If several drivers are on at once, and you wish to turn off certain ones selectively, reduce the sum by the binary equivalent of the channels you want to turn off. For example, if you turn on the drivers by specifying 15 (a sum of label values), you will get #1, #2, #3 and #4 ON at once (1 + 2 + 4 + 8). If you then want to turn off only #4, specify a label value of 7 (1 + 2 + 4). If the driver is in pulse mode, it will operate momentarily. If the driver is in level mode, it will lock on and require a separate off statement to terminate its operation (also, see Appendix J).

Finally, you can update the OPERANT BASELINE programs by operating driver #1 to give your subject operant reinforcement. Your first programming example will be a simple routine to allow the experimenter (you) to provide reinforcements by pressing the ⟨return⟩ key on the computer. A loop will limit the number of reinforcements to five. That routine will be followed by another segment to operate the cue light.

```
LVB DC DRIVER OUTPUT: Feeder/Dipper and Cue Light
```

IBM PC and TRS-80 program segment	notes
...LVB parameter statements... ...reset clock, etc... ...clock subroutine...	Varies by system.
200 OUT DLVB, 0	DRIVER RESET statement.
210 INPUT "NOW TURN ON 28 V SUPPLY";Z$	Suspends program execution; turn on 28-volt supply and press <return> to resume program.
250 FOR R = 1 TO 5 300 INPUT "PRESS RETURN TO FEED";Z$	Press <return> to operate driver.
400 OUT DLVB, 1	Operate driver #1 (pulse mode must be set).
410 NEXT R	
500 FOR R = 1 TO 5 510 INPUT "PRESS RETURN TO LIGHT";Z$ 520 OUT DLVB, 2	Operate driver #2 (level mode must be set).
530 GOSUB 50 : START = TIME	Start interval timer.
540 GOSUB 50	
550 IF TIME < START + 5 THEN 540	5 s interval specified.
560 OUT DLVB, 0	Turns off all drivers.
570 NEXT R	

Apple IIe program segment	notes
...same as above except...	
200 POKE DLVB, 0	POKE is used instead of OUT.
400 POKE DLVB, 1	
520 POKE DLVB, 2	
560 POKE DLVB, 0	

That was easy enough. Of course, it all hinges on the correct pre-settings on the driver card. You can never be too careful about checking and double-checking all the necessary settings and controls. In that vein, did you notice the DRIVER RESET statement and the fail-safe power supply message? You should clearly see the difference between programming pulse mode and level mode operations. Level mode (the cue light) requires a separate OFF statement; pulse mode does not.

Using LVB DC Driver Outputs: Schedules of Reinforcement

Now that you know how to activate the feeder/dipper and cue light in the operant chamber, you're ready to write programs to control operant conditioning procedures. A good starting point would be to present specific schedules of reinforcement. These are usually covered in the learning chapter of your introductory psychology text. You might want to dust that book off and reread those sections.

For a quick sample program, let's control a fixed-ratio (FR) schedule. The rule in any FR schedule is simple. A number of separate operant responses (one or more) must be made before a single reinforcement is given. The actual number of responses required is referred to as the *ratio*. In FR schedules the same ratio requirement stays in effect for a series of reinforcements.

Parameters. A good general-purpose routine for FR reinforcement will assign the ratio to a variable, so that any given ratio can work without the need for reprogramming. This ratio value is your first parameter. In fact, many hungry subjects will train themselves to press the lever on FR 1 if left inside the operant chamber long enough. Your second parameter will be the total number of reinforcements available. This value will be used to determine the end of a given operant test session.

Measures of Behavior. You're going to count lever presses, just as you did in the OPERANT BASELINE program developed in Chapter 6. In addition, you'll need to know exactly how much time elapsed before the allotment of reinforcements was received. This duration measure will be used to compute operant response rates.

Since FR responding involves repetition, there's a good chance that you can put a FOR-NEXT loop to use in the program. Come to think of it, two loops would do the job because there are two repetitious cycles. The first cycle is the repetition of the procedure until the total number of reinforcements is attained. Within each of those cycles, however, is a second cycle of repetition until the ratio response requirement is performed. So there are two cycles (loops), one within the other. This arrangement is called **nesting** loops, and now is a good time to cover some of the rules that apply.

First, nested loops must not overlap their cycles. Rather, inner loops must be completely contained within outer loops. It may seem obvious, but you must complete the inner loop cycle (NEXT J, above) before you complete the outer loop cycle (NEXT I, above).

NESTED FOR-NEXT LOOPS

correct program segment	incorrect !
200 FOR I = 1 TO 10 210 PRINT I	200 FOR I = 1 TO 10 210 PRINT I
220 FOR J = 1 TO 5 230 PRINT J	220 FOR J = 1 TO 5 230 PRINT J
240 NEXT J : NEXT I	240 NEXT I : NEXT J

The second rule to keep in mind concerns the use of specific loop variables. In the above example I used *I* and *J*. Always make sure to use variables that are different from each other and any other variable used in the program. That's the safest way to avoid foul-ups.

Now you're ready to develop your first program to control operant schedules. The measurement of operant behavior and the correct scheduling of reinforcement are early steps in the creation of real-time computer programs to conduct instrumental learning experiments.

PROGRAMMING EXAMPLE: FIXED RATIO SCHEDULES OF REINFORCEMENT

IBM PC and TRS-80 program segment	notes
...LVB parameter statements... ...reset clock, etc... ...clock subroutine...	Varies by system.
100 DATA 20 110 DATA 2	Total reinforcements given. FR value.
150 OUT DLVB, 0	DRIVER RESET statement.
160 INPUT "NOW TURN ON 28 V SUPPLY";Z$	Suspends program execution; turn on 28-volt supply and press <return> to resume program.
200 READ NR,FR 205 GOSUB 50 : SESS = TIME	Assigns parameters. Starting point of session.
210 FOR I = 1 TO NR 215 LEVER = INP(SLVB)	Outer loop for reinforcements. Clears Switch Inputs.
220 FOR J = 1 TO FR	Inner loop for responses.
230 LEVER = INP(SLVB) 240 IF LEVER = 0 THEN 230 250 NEXT J	
400 OUT DLVB, 1	Operate feeder/dipper.
500 NEXT I 510 GOSUB 50 : ELAPSE = TIME - SESS	Determine duration of test.

```
600 MELAPSE = ELAPSE/60              Convert to minutes.
610 PRINT (NR*FR)/MELAPSE,"RATE/MIN" Print operant response rate.

1000 END
```

Apple IIe program segment	notes
...same as above except...	
150 POKE DLVB, 0	
215 LEVER = PEEK(SLVB)	
230 LEVER = PEEK(SLVB)	
400 POKE DLVB, 1	Operate feeder/dipper.

Next, let's incorporate the cue light into an operant control program.

You've surely heard about conditioned reinforcement. In my example it can occur when a specific change in the environment is correlated with the delivery of the food or water reward for operant lever pressing. Let's present the cue light immediately after each reinforcement. Then, you can test for the strength of the conditioned reinforcement (the cue light) by presenting the light alone as the only consequence of lever pressing. The degree to which the light maintains lever pressing is the measure of its strength as a conditioned reinforcer. So, this sample program will have two phases. You'll give 20 reinforcements (at a specific FR value) and then move to the conditioned reinforcement phase, where you'll see how long it takes the rat to produce 20 presentations of the light only.

PROGRAMMING EXAMPLE: CONDITIONED REINFORCEMENT

IBM PC and TRS-80 program segment	notes
...LVB parameter statements...	Varies by system.
...reset clock, etc...	
...clock subroutine...	
100 DATA 20	Total reinforcements given.
110 DATA 2	FR value.
150 OUT DLVB, 0	DRIVER RESET statement.
160 INPUT "NOW TURN ON 28 V SUPPLY";Z$	Suspends program execution; turn on 28-volt supply and press <return> to resume program.
200 READ NR,FR	Assigns parameters.
205 GOSUB 50 : SESS = TIME	Starting point of session.
210 FOR I = 1 TO NR	Outer loop for reinforcements.
215 LEVER = INP(SLVB)	Clears Switch Inputs.

```
220 FOR J = 1 TO FR                    Inner loop for responses.

230 LEVER = INP(SLVB)
240 IF LEVER = 0 THEN 230
250 NEXT J

400 OUT DLVB, 1                        Operate feeder/dipper.
410 OUT DLVB, 2                        Operate light (level mode).
420 GOSUB 50 : START = TIME            Start interval timer.
430 GOSUB 50
440 IF TIME < START + 2 THEN 430       2 s interval.
450 OUT DLVB, 0                        Turn off all drivers.

500 NEXT I
510 GOSUB 50 : ELAPSE = TIME - SESS    Determine duration of test.

600 MELAPSE = ELAPSE/60                Convert to minutes.
610 PRINT (NR*FR)/MELAPSE, "RATE/MIN"  Print operant response rate.

700 REM...BEGIN PHASE TWO

710 FOR I = 1 TO NR                    Outer loop for reinforcements.
715 LEVER = INP(SLVB)                  Clears Switch Inputs.

720 FOR J = 1 TO FR                    Inner loop for responses.
730 LEVER = INP(SLVB)
740 IF LEVER = 0 THEN 730
750 NEXT J

800 REM...FEEDER/DIPPER NOT USED

810 OUT DLVB, 2                        Operate light (level mode).
820 GOSUB 50 : START = TIME            Start interval timer.
830 GOSUB 50
840 IF TIME < START + 2 THEN 830       2 s interval.
850 OUT DLVB, 0                        Turn off all drivers.

900 NEXT I
910 GOSUB 50 : ELAPSE = TIME - SESS    Determine duration of test.

920 MELAPSE = ELAPSE/60                Convert to minutes.
930 PRINT MELAPSE, "COND REINF STRENGTH" Print time it took to complete
                                          20 reinforcements.
1000 END
```

```
Apple IIe program segment             notes

...same as above except...

150 POKE DLVB, 0

215 LEVER = PEEK(SLVB)

230 LEVER = PEEK(SLVB)

400 POKE DLVB, 1                       Operate feeder/dipper.

715 LEVER = PEEK(SLVB)

730 LEVER = PEEK(SLVB)

810 POKE DLVB, 2                       Turn on cue light.

850 POKE DLVB, 0                       Turn off all drivers.
```

If you understand these examples, you'll have little trouble expanding upon the techniques for more complex operant control programs. In the Projects section at the end of this chapter, you'll get your chance to expand on what you've already learned. At this point I'm nearing the end of my coverage. But before I close, let's develop one quick example of an application for the LVB Relay card. Again, this card is optional, but if you have it in your system, you should learn how to use it. You're going to develop another example that involves operant behavior, this time in people. To keep things very simple, the operant response I'm targeting is simply a verbal command issued by the subject. The operant reinforcement will be to advance a carousel slide projector to a new slide. This is the ideal time to dig out all those slides from your past summer vacations. Pack them into the carousel, complete the wiring steps (described below), and you're ready to go. But first, I'll review the Relay output card.

The Relay I/O Circuit Card. A relay is a remote-controlled switch. Switch configurations are presented in Appendix A, so it might be wise to reread the appropriate sections. Since a relay is a switch, it can control other electrical circuits. Electrical signals enter the relay through its Common wiring post. However, they go no further as long as the relay remains unoperated. When the relay is operated, the signal passes out via the normally open post. A typical example for this in the psychology lab is controlling a carousel slide projector. The slide advance function can be accomplished under remote control by connecting the two poles of the advance circuit to the Common and NO posts of a relay. Let's be more specific. When you look at the back of a carousel projector and inspect the small panel above the off/fan/on switch, you see five little holes.

OFF/FAN/ON SWITCH PANEL OF A CAROUSEL PROJECTOR

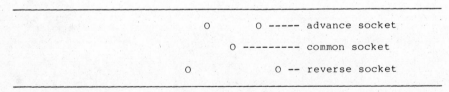

If you have the hand-held slide-advance control, you could insert its five-prong plug into this five-socket receptacle. Or you could obtain individual plugs and wire them for a custom remote-controlled projector. To get your computer to advance the projector, simply bring out the common and advance wires from the five-socket panel on the back of the carousel. Now back to the LVB Relay card (and the tables in Appendix A). With common connected to the Common pin of Relay #1 and advance connected to the NO pin of Relay #1, you're ready to roll.

My example will parallel the first operant program. You'll advance the carousel each time you press the ⟨return⟩ key.

LVB RELAY OUTPUT: Slide Advance on a Carousel Projector

IBM PC and TRS-80 program segment	notes
...LVB parameter statements... ...reset clock, etc... ...clock subroutine...	Varies by system.
200 OUT RLVB, 0	RELAY RESET statement.
210 INPUT "NOW TURN ON CAROUSEL";Z$	Suspends program execution; you then turn on carousel and press <return> to resume program.
250 FOR R = 1 TO 5 300 INPUT "PRESS RETURN TO ADVANCE";Z$	Press <return> to operate relay.
400 OUT RLVB, 1 402 GOSUB 50 : START = TIME 404 GOSUB 50 406 IF TIME < START + .75 THEN 404	Turn on relay #1. Start interval timer. .75 s duration.
408 OUT RLVB, 0	Turns off all relays.
410 NEXT R	

Apple IIe program segment	notes
...same as above except...	
200 POKE RLVB, 0	POKE is used instead of OUT.
400 POKE RLVB, 1	
408 POKE RLVB, 0	

What about that interval timer at line 402? What was it for? The device operated by the relay is the slide-advance mechanism. Unlike the cue light, this mechanism is designed to operate in brief episodes to ensure that its motor does not advance more than one position at each operation. If you were operating the hand-held button, you would press and release without holding.

You can do a fixed-ratio program requiring a certain number of verbal commands (operant responses) from your subject for each slide-advance operation (reinforcement). Tell your subjects to say "next slide" each time they want the carousel to advance. When you hear their command, press the ⟨return⟩ key.

PROGRAMMING EXAMPLE: FR SCHEDULES OF SLIDE-ADVANCE REINFORCEMENT

IBM PC and TRS-80 program segment	notes
...LVB parameter statements... ...reset clock, etc... ...clock subroutine...	Varies by system.
100 DATA 20 110 DATA 2	Total reinforcements given. FR value.
150 OUT RLVB, 0	RELAY RESET statement.
160 INPUT "NOW TURN ON CAROUSEL";Z$	Suspends program execution; you then turn on carousel and press <return> to resume program.
200 READ NR,FR 205 GOSUB 50 : SESS = TIME	Assigns parameters. Starting point of session.
210 FOR I = 1 TO NR	Outer loop for reinforcements.
220 FOR J = 1 TO FR	Inner loop for responses.
230 INPUT "PRESS RETURN TO ADVANCE";Z$	When you hear the command.
250 NEXT J	
400 OUT RLVB, 1 402 GOSUB 50 : START = TIME 404 GOSUB 50 406 IF TIME < START + .75 THEN 404	Turn on relay #1. Start interval timer. .75 s duration.
408 OUT RLVB, 0	Turns off all relays.
500 NEXT I 510 GOSUB 50 : ELAPSE = TIME - SESS	Determine duration of test.
600 MELAPSE = ELAPSE/60 610 PRINT (NR*FR)/MELAPSE,"RATE/MIN"	Convert to minutes. Print operant response rate.
1000 END	

Apple IIe program segment	notes
...same as above except...	
150 POKE RLVB, 0	POKE used instead of OUT.
400 POKE RLVB, 1	
408 POKE RLVB, 0	

Closure

This chapter marks the third of the three cornerstones in real-time computer control of experiments. You now have learned the principles of timing, input, and output. Your future programs will be full-fledged pieces of work, and you are certainly able to tackle more complicated translations of experimental procedures.

Again in this chapter you've seen a clear distinction between how stimuli are presented to subjects in stand-alone versus interface applications. The computer has a lot to offer in the way of flexible visual and audio stimulation in the stand-alone applications. I have yet to cover screen graphics as a stimulation medium, but that will come (Chapters 12 and 13).

In addition, the LVB Interface provides all the flexibility needed to operate devices outside the computer that are intended to stimulate subjects. When this system is viewed as a whole, computer plus interface, it represents the single most powerful and useful piece of laboratory apparatus at your disposal for psychological research.

Projects

Stand-alone Project. PAIRED ASSOC STUDY: This program will be an adaptation of the SLIDE PROJECTOR IV program completed earlier. Use the same data items. Read pairs of words as stimulus and response terms. Display each pair together in the center of the screen, following examples in this chapter. Select a display duration that will facilitate learning. (Note: the accompanying PAIRED ASSOC TEST program will be covered in Chapters 9 and 10.)

Stand-alone Project. TIME PERCEPTION II: Write a pair of programs that use the time perception routine. The first program should use sound stimuli in a manner similar to the chapter examples. The second program should use visual stimuli. Display a single * character in the center of the screen to represent the start signal in the time perception trial. Clear the screen as the stop signal.

Interface Project. ALTERNATING SCHEDULES II: You now know how to program an FR schedule of reinforcement. Write a program that will present two schedules during the same test session. Use a reinforcement criterion of 20. Alternate between any two FR schedules, changing schedules after every five reinforcements.

PART THREE

REFINEMENTS

Chapter 8 teaches you how to store, summarize, and print tables of raw data obtained from computer-controlled experiments. It introduces new principles for programming, including one- and two-dimension arrays and the operation of system line printers. The chapter also shows how to integrate the statistical computation of the mean and standard deviation for raw data into real-time programs. Finally, I cover special programming techniques for rounding off data values for neater printing and better organization of data tables. You will continue working with the SEMANTIC DIFFERENTIAL program and will apply what you learn in this chapter to the next level of revision.

Chapter 9 completes the coverage of storing data generated by real-time programs. It deals specifically with disk file storage. The chapter introduces printout format, or sequential-access disk files, and covers the special programming techniques for creating these files. A new programming example is developed: a PAIRED ASSOC TEST program. This is the second program of the two-part series for conducting a paired-associate verbal learning experiment (it is further refined into its finished version in Chapter 10). Finally, I discuss special methods for transferring disk files to the system line printer.

Chapter 10 is the final core chapter of the book. Its purpose is to teach how the requirements of experimental design are incorporated directly into real-time programs. I teach you techniques for controlling the order of presentation of conditions and stimuli within an experiment. The TIME PERCEPTION program exemplifies both counterbalancing and randomization techniques. In addition, you will develop the final version of the PAIRED ASSOC TEST program.

The remainder of the book will deal with advanced programming examples in specific topic areas.

CHAPTER 8

On-Line Storage and Display of Subject Data

Raw Data Versus Summary Data

Up to this point I have not introduced any sophisticated programming techniques for managing the data generated by an experimental procedure. In fact, the programs you've already written have simply printed subject data, as it was obtained, on the computer screen or line printer. Polished experimental control programs do not use these simple methods, so you must plunge ahead toward mastery of a full set of programming tools to store, organize, and display subject data. The first conceptual problem you face is the distinction between raw data and summary data.

Raw Data.   **Raw data** are generated each time the subject makes a response that is recorded by the computer. Most computer-controlled procedures will generate a large body of raw data. For example, think back to the SEMANTIC DIFFERENTIAL programs you have been working on. Each word listed in DATA statements at the top of the program represents a single trial of the procedure. Each trial generates a rating response and a process time value. That's two raw data values per trial. If you have 30 trials, 60 raw data values are generated. If you build an independent variable into the program, and test with two different types of words (two separate word lists), then the amount of raw data doubles, giving you 120 raw data values from just one subject. If you test 20 subjects, it's easy to see how raw data proliferate.

   Raw data must be managed carefully, so that you can return to them long after the experiment is over and still understand what they mean and how they were derived. Enter the **raw data table**. From now on you're going to build a raw data table for each run of the programs you use. This technique requires that you store the raw data as they are obtained, since these tables should not be printed while the program is testing the subject. I will cover data storage techniques shortly, but at this point I can say that data will be stored either inside the program (on-line storage) or outside the program (off-line storage). On-line storage is the major learning objective of this chapter. Off-line storage will be covered in Chapter 9.

Summary Data.   In this chapter **summary data** will take the form of measures of central tendency and variability. The mean and standard deviation will be used, whenever possible, to summarize raw data by category. Categories can represent a variety of entities, including different subjects, trials, levels of independent variable, type of dependent variable, and the like.

So if you're reading between the lines, yes, I am including a statistics lesson in this chapter on data management. First I will cover programming techniques for managing raw data, and I'll be introducing a major new concept called array storage.

ADVANCING BASIC: Data Tables and Array Storage

Data Tables "Inside" the Computer.   When you picture a table of numbers, certain basic features come to mind. Usually the numbers are organized or categorized in some way. A very common method would be to draw a series of rows on a piece of paper and place a different category on each row. For example, consider the raw data from the first SEMANTIC DIFFERENTIAL program. The program recorded a rating response representing a judgment (1 = good through 9 = bad). Tabled by rows, the data from five trials might look like this:

		Response
Row	1	3
	2	1
	3	8
	4	7
	5	5

That's simple enough. Now let me complicate it. First, the rating responses are not numbers; they are actually strings. (Skeptics will want to check the SEMANTIC DIFFERENTIAL program listings in Chapter 6.) There's nothing wrong with strings as data, as long as you don't want to do any arithmetic with them. But I want to calculate using this information, at least to get a mean and standard deviation, as promised above. So I must first convert the strings to numbers using a special string function called VAL.

```
VAL STRING FUNCTION
```

	notes
355 CH = VAL(I$)	Strings of words or letters will generate errors.

I'll be coming back to the VAL function, but now you're going to learn how the above table can be represented as a one-dimension array.

One-dimension Arrays. An **array** is quite similar to a variable, as far as the computer is concerned. For instance, arrays have names, just as variables have names. Values can be assigned to arrays using statements such as LET, READ, INPUT, and so on. The big difference is that an array can hold a *series* of values (either string or numeric), whereas a variable can hold only one. Each value, called an array **element**, is identified by a **subscript** indicating its location within the array. A subscript can be either a constant (a plain number) or a variable. Let's develop the example further, starting with a modification of the table above:

```
ONE-DIMENSION ARRAY
```

	NONCOMPUTER CONCEPT		ONE-DIMENSION ARRAY
	Response		
Row 1	3		RE(1) = 3
2	1		RE(2) = 1
3	8		RE(3) = 8
4	7		RE(4) = 7
5	5		RE(5) = 5

Do you see the subscripts (numbers in parentheses) in the RE array? Each response value from the original table is now assigned to a specific array element, indicated by the subscripts one through five. In this example the subscripts are shown as numeric constants. This is somewhat unrealistic, however, since most applications require that the subscript be a variable. Let's explore that idea further.

Take a close look at the subscripted variables in the RE array above. Each row of the array represents a different trial (stimulus word) in the original semantic differential procedure. To put it another way, there is a one-to-one correspondence between each trial number and each element (subscript) in the RE array. So, the variable that should represent the subscript in the RE array is the same variable that represents the trial number. To see this clearly, take another look at the SEMANTIC DIFFERENTIAL program listing (from Chapter 6).

PROGRAMMING EXAMPLE: ARRAY DATA STORAGE -- SEMANTIC DIFFERENTIAL
                     PROGRAM

IBM PC program segment	notes
...clock reset, etc... ...clock subroutine...	
100 DATA 2 110 DATA "HAWK","HAPPY"	
200 READ N	2 Trials to be run.
210 FOR I = 1 TO N	Start "trial" loop.
220 CLS : LOCATE 12,1	Clear and position cursor (IBM PC only).
230 PRINT "GOOD BAD" 240 PRINT "1 2 3 4 5 6 7 8 9" 250 PRINT	Display semantic choices.
260 READ W$: PRINT " ";W$ 300 GOSUB 50 : START=TIME	Read and display stimulus. Start process timer.
310 I$ = INKEY$ 320 IF I$ = "" THEN 310	Assign keystroke. Endless loop until keypress (IBM PC, TRS-80 only).
330 GOSUB 50 340 PRINT 350 PRINT TIME-START,"= PROCESS TIME" 355 PRINT I$,"= CHOICE"	Read process timer. Display data.
360 GOSUB 50 : START=TIME 365 GOSUB 50 370 IF TIME < START + 5 THEN 365 380 NEXT I	 5-sec pause timer. Continue with next trial.

The trial loop variable (in the above program represented by *I*) is the one to focus on. The variable *I* in this routine always equals the trial currently being presented. That means that should you add array storage of raw data to the above routine, RE(*I*) (spoken as "R E sub I") will always be the corresponding array element.

The actual rating response is represented by the variable *I$*, a string variable. It had to be that way to take advantage of keystroke input capabilities. This string must be changed into the number that it represents before it can be stored in a raw data array. You can use the VAL function to accomplish that.

Next, I want you to revise this section of the SEMANTIC DIF-FERENTIAL program beginning with line 340. Your goal is to store the subject's responses in a raw data array.

program segment	notes
	Delete line 340.
350 PRINT TIME-START,"= PROCESS TIME"	Display data.
355 RE(I) = VAL(I$)	Converts I$ string and assigns value to element in RE array.

While you're at it, why not assign the process time value to its own array? Use the name PT. It should look like this.

program segment	notes
	Delete line 340.
350 PT(I) = TIME-START	Assigns value to element in PT array.
355 RE(I) = VAL(I$)	Converts I$ string and assigns value to element in RE array.

The PT array is exactly like the RE array. Note that TIME-START is already numeric, unlike *I$*, which is a string and has to be converted before being assigned to an array element. You have replaced the PRINT statements in the program. But don't worry, I'll deal with that later as I cover methods for printing raw data tables.

That's the one-dimension array. You may be wondering if there are two-dimension arrays as well. Of course there are! And on some systems even three-dimension arrays, though you won't be using them here.

Two-dimension Arrays.   Imagine a data table organized by rows and columns. Continue with my working example from the SEMANTIC DIFFERENTIAL program. You still have rows of data representing each trial (word) in the procedure, but now add a column factor. How about running the experiment using two different sets of words, concrete and abstract? The first five trials (words) will present concrete words, the second five trials will present abstract words. The concept of the raw data table will be as follows (again, the actual ratings are made up for this example).

RESPONSES

		Column 1 concrete	2 abstract
Row	1	3	5
	2	1	2
	3	8	9
	4	7	3
	5	5	2

Now instead of having just row locations as subscripts, you also have column locations.

TWO-DIMENSION ARRAY

NONCOMPUTER CONCEPT			TWO-DIMENSION ARRAY	
	Column 1 concrete	2 abstract		
Row 1	3	5	XE(1,1) = 3	XE(1,2) = 5
2	1	2	XE(2,1) = 1	XE(2,2) = 2
3	8	9	XE(3,1) = 8	XE(3,2) = 9
4	7	3	XE(4,1) = 7	XE(4,2) = 3
5	5	2	XE(5,1) = 5	XE(5,2) = 2

Each array element now has two subscripts separated by a comma. The first subscript always references a row location, the second subscript a column location. Array elements now extend down (rows) and across (columns). Keep the following diagram as your mental image of what a two-dimension array looks like.

```
                          Columns

                          1     2    etc...
                         |—————|—————|—
              Rows   1   |  3  |  5  |
                         |—————|—————|—
                     2   |  1  |  2  |
                         |—————|—————|—
                 etc...
```

How large can such an array get? The amount of available memory in your system determines how large these dimensions can be. For two-dimension arrays the system automatically reserves 0–10 rows and 0–10 columns of space. You won't be programming with the 0th element; however, it is technically available. If your arrays are larger, you must reserve more space using a special statement.

The DIM Statement. DIM is used to reserve array space beyond the automatic value of 10 (all arrays have default dimensions of 10, which really means 11 if you add in the 0th element). Each array requested is listed in the DIM statement along with the corresponding number of rows and columns requested.

```
DIM STATEMENT
```

program segment	notes
5 DIM RE(20), RT(20)	20 rows in each.
15 DIM XE(20,2), XT(20,2)	20 rows x 2 columns in each.

Let's return to the expanded SEMANTIC DIFFERENTIAL program. Your first expansion covered assigning raw data, by trial, into two one-dimension arrays: RE for response ratings, and PT for process time. These factors were the two dependent variables in the experiment. The next expansion will be a little more complicated because I want you to incorporate two kinds of words, concrete and abstract.

Think about this. When I wanted the program to repeat the same procedure using five different words, I used a FOR-NEXT loop that cycled five times. Now, in addition to that, I want to repeat the five trials two times, once for concrete, once for abstract words. Should you use a second FOR-NEXT loop? Why not! In fact, it's your old friend nested loops, last seen in the OPERANT BASELINE programs of Chapter 6. Nested loops get values into and out of two-dimension arrays.

PROGRAMMING EXAMPLE: SEMANTIC DIFFERENTIAL WITH TWO TYPES OF WORDS
                     AND TWO-DIMENSIONAL ARRAY DATA STORAGE

IBM PC program segment	notes
...clock reset, etc... ...clock subroutine...	
100 DATA 5	Each word type has 5 words.
110 DATA "HAWK","HOUSE","HOLE" 112 DATA "HATCHET","HORSE"	Concrete word list.
120 DATA "HONOR","HELP","HOLY" 122 DATA "HOPEFUL","HORRID"	Abstract word list.
130 DIM XT(10,2),XE(10,2)	
150 READ N	5 trials per word type.
200 FOR J = 1 TO 2	"Outer" loop with 2 cycles, one for each word type.
210 FOR I = 1 TO N	Start "inner" trial loop.
220 CLS : LOCATE 12,1	Clear and position cursor (IBM PC only).
230 PRINT "GOOD BAD"	Display semantic choices.
240 PRINT "1 2 3 4 5 6 7 8 9" 250 PRINT	
260 READ W$: PRINT " ";W$ 300 GOSUB 50 : START=TIME	Read and display stimulus. Start process timer.
310 I$ = INKEY$ 320 IF I$ = "" THEN 310	Assign keystroke. Endless loop until keypress (IBM PC, TRS-80 only).
330 GOSUB 50	Read process timer.
350 XT(I,J) = TIME-START 355 XE(I,J) = VAL(I$)	Assign process time value. Convert string; assign rating value.
360 GOSUB 50 : START=TIME 365 GOSUB 50 370 IF TIME < START + 5 THEN 365 380 NEXT I	5-sec pause timer. Continue with next trial.
400 NEXT J	Continue with next word type.

In the sample program on page 110 look for three new features: (a) two sets of data statements, one for concrete, one for abstract words; (b) an outer loop that cycles two times (once for each type of word); and (c) statements that assign raw data values to elements of the two-dimension arrays.

Of course, if you're running this enhanced version of the SE-MANTIC DIFFERENTIAL program on the TRS-80 or Apple IIe, you must make certain modifications in screen positioning and/or keyboard input routines (just use the routines developed in Chapter 6 for the original version of this program). Once this sample program runs, you have evidence that you're progressing rapidly. It's the most full-featured piece of software you've developed so far. It includes a real-time clock, formatted screen display, keyboard input, one independent variable (more on this coming in Chapter 10), two dependent variables, and array storage of subject data.

The finishing touch remains to be added, however. Now that you've got your raw data neatly stored away in those two arrays, you need to get it out, preferably printed in a neat formatted table. Time for more nested loops.

Printing Data Tables from Arrays

The simple rule to remember when programming these printing routines is that the data are usually printed from arrays with the same steps used to place them into arrays. Take the expanded SEMANTIC DIFFERENTIAL program above and add a section that will produce a neat raw data printout. Keep in mind that since nested loops stored the data, nested loops will print them.

Printing Table Headings.   Since raw data tables are going to provide an archival record of your experiment, they should be properly labeled with text headings. Column headings are quite straightforward. Most of the time you can take advantage of the standard number of print zones available to you. If you remember, this requires that items in a PRINT statement list be separated with commas. The first step in the raw data table is to print the column headings. The next step is to start the repetition process controlled by the nested loops. The outer loop must control row data. The inner loop must control column data. That's because printing moves from left to right across each line. You'll find that if you reuse the row and column loop variables (I and J, in the program), it will help keep things clear.

PRINTING RAW DATA TABLES FROM ARRAYS

program segment	notes
500 REM PRINTOUT SECTION	
510 PRINT "RAW DATA: RATINGS"	Short table title.
515 PRINT	
520 PRINT "TRIAL","CONCRETE","ABSTRACT"	Column labels.
530 PRINT	
540 FOR I = 1 TO N	Outer (row) loop starts.
550 PRINT I,	Loop variable is trial number; trailing comma required
560 FOR J = 1 TO 2	Inner (column) loop starts.
570 PRINT XE(I,J),	Trailing comma required.
580 NEXT J : PRINT	Bare PRINT causes a return to left margin.
590 NEXT I	

In Chapter 4 I covered the technique for printing items in pre-assigned columns called print zones. You're using this method again in the above print routine. When you attempt to move across print zones using a loop while printing, however, don't forget to return to the left margin at the end of each row of printing. Line 580, above, shows the required technique. NEXT J indicates that a single row of printing is finished, but the trailing comma in Line 570 keeps the cursor (or print mechanism on a line printer) positioned out on the line. The bare PRINT statement in line 580 returns the cursor to the left margin. NEXT I at line 590 then causes the next row of the table to be printed.

Operating the Line Printer. Remember that the above print routine can work the line printer on the IBM PC and TRS-80 when you substitute LPRINT for PRINT. The above routine will also work on the Apple IIe after the line printer has been activated with the PR #1 statement (don't forget to deactivate with the PR #0 statement).

Well, I'm just about ready for your statistics lesson. As you look at the finished product (below) of your print routine, it still needs a couple of things to make it complete. Specifically, it needs summary data in the form of means and standard deviations.

PRINTING DATA TABLES FROM ARRAYS: SCREEN VIEW

	screen	
TRIAL	CONCRETE	ABSTRACT
1	3	5
2	1	2
3	8	9
4	7	3
5	5	2

Computing the Mean and Standard Deviation from Data in Arrays

The Formulas.   The formulas for the mean and standard deviation of a group of scores are not that difficult. What most students have trouble with is the conversion of the algebraic formula (out of a statistics textbook) to a computer formula (that could be used in a LET or PRINT statement). To remedy this, I'll show both versions.

The mean is simply the sum of scores divided by the number of scores.

FORMULA FOR THE MEAN

ALGEBRAIC: MEAN $= \dfrac{\Sigma X}{N}$

where . . . ΣX is the Sum of Scores
.N is the Number of Scores

COMPUTER: MN $=$ SS/N

where . . . MN is the Mean
SS is the Sum of Scores
N is the Number of Scores

Different formulas for the standard deviation can be found from textbook to textbook. I'll be using the following:

FORMULA FOR THE STANDARD DEVIATION

ALGEBRAIC   S.D. $= \sqrt{\dfrac{\Sigma X^2 - \dfrac{(\Sigma X)^2}{N}}{N-1}}$

where . . . ΣX^2 is the Sum Squared Scores
$(\Sigma X)^2$ is the Sum of Scores Squared
N is the Number of Scores

COMPUTER   SD $=$ SQR ((SQ $-$ (SS$\hat{\,}$2/N)) / (N $-$ 1))

where . . .   SD is the Standard Deviation
SQ is the Sum of Squared Scores
SS is the Sum of Scores
N is the Number of Scores

and . . .   SQR (?) is the square root function
in BASIC.

The computer versions of these equations may look mystifying, but in fact, there are only two variables within them that need to be computed in the SEMANTIC DIFFERENTIAL program: SS—sum of scores, and SQ—sum of squared scores. There is quite a difference between summing the scores and summing the squared scores, however. When you sum the scores you simply add them together. When you sum the squared scores you square the score *before* adding.

Summing the Scores and Squares. The concept of summing a series of values is obviously repetitive. You should be thinking in terms of loops. Summing is so simple it only requires a LET statement placed strategically within a loop. A LET statement that sums is very similar to a LET statement that counts. You've covered counting statements already, so these variations should give you no trouble.

For example, imagine a summing statement that computes the sum of scores of the rating responses in the early version of the SEMANTIC DIFFERENTIAL program.

SUMMING STATEMENT: SUM OF SCORES

program segment	notes
357 SS = SS + VAL(I$)	I$ was a string representing an individual rating.

You could use the same kind of statement to compute the sum of squares of the process times.

SUMMING STATEMENT: SUM OF SQUARES

program segment	notes
352 SQ = SQ + (TIME-START)^2	Square first, then add.

Next, you'll see how these summing statements would look within the newest version of the SEMANTIC DIFFERENTIAL program. But there's a problem. You will now need two sets of means and standard deviations since you'll have two sets of words, concrete and abstract. You'll be repeating the entire process, once for concrete and again for abstract words. Your mind should be picturing the outer loop that segregates the two types of words. You'll handle these summary data just as you handled the raw data—namely, by placing those values corresponding to concrete and abstract words into separate columns in an array.

The summary data array is identical to the raw data array on the column dimension. But do you see any need for a row dimension? There is none, since there is only one mean and one standard deviation for each column of raw scores. So column means and standard deviations will each be stored in one-dimension arrays.

If that explanation was a little fast for you, take another look at the raw data table. This time I'll add the summary data on the computer side.

SUMMARY DATA ARRAYS

		NONCOMPUTER CONCEPT		TWO-DIMENSION ARRAY for Raw Data	
		Column			
		1 concrete	2 abstract		
Row	1	3	5	XE(1,1) = 3	XE(1,2) = 5
	2	1	2	XE(2,1) = 1	XE(2,2) = 2
	3	8	9	XE(3,1) = 8	XE(3,2) = 9
	4	7	3	XE(4,1) = 7	XE(4,2) = 3
	5	5	2	XE(5,1) = 5	XE(5,2) = 2
				ONE-DIMENSION ARRAYS for Summary Data	
Mean		4.80	4.20	ME(1) = 4.80	ME(2) = 4.20
S.D.		2.86	2.94	SE(1) = 2.86	SE(2) = 2.94

As you move down each column in the two-dimension raw data array (XE), you are actually executing individual cycles in the inner row loop (the I loop in the sample program above). This means that you should place your summing statements inside the I loop. In the example below you will continue to expand the SEMANTIC DIFFERENTIAL program by adding another section using nested loops to compute means and standard deviations.

SUMMING STATEMENTS: SUM OF SCORES AND SQUARES

program segment	notes
600 FOR J = 1 TO 2	
605 SS = 0 : SQ = 0	Sum variables must begin as zero.
610 FOR I = 1 TO N	
620 SS = SS + XE(I,J)	Sum of scores (ratings)
630 SQ = SQ + XE(I,J)^2	Sum of squares (ratings)
640 NEXT I	
650 REM: BOTTOM OF COLUMN REACHED	
660 REM: COMPUTE MEAN AND S.D.	
670 ME(J) = SS/N	Formula for mean.
680 SE(J) = SQR((SQ-(SS^2/N))/(N-1))	Formula for S.D.
690 NEXT J	Cycle to next column.

Next, you can print the means and standard deviations.

program segment	notes
700 PRINT	
720 PRINT "MEAN",	Row label at left margin.
730 FOR J=1 TO 2	
740 PRINT ME(J),	Means printed across row.
750 NEXT J : PRINT	
800 PRINT "S.D.",	Row label at left margin.
810 FOR J=1 TO 2	
820 PRINT SE(J),	S.D.s printed across row.
830 NEXT J : PRINT	

This is getting to be quite an involved program with all these separate sections of nested loops! Here's what the screen output should look like now.

```
                              screen

     TRIAL            CONCRETE            ABSTRACT

     1                   3                   5
     2                   1                   2
     3                   8                   9
     4                   7                   3
     5                   5                   2

     MEAN              4.8                 4.2
     S.D.              2.863564            2.949576
```

When you get this jazzed-up SEMANTIC DIFFERENTIAL program to run, you've reached a new peak in computer expertise. Remember, however, that the examples dealt with only the rating response raw score array (the XE array). You'll have to plug in the proper statements for similar operations on the process time raw score array (the XT array). This will be your first task in the end-of-chapter Projects section.

ADVANCING BASIC: Rounding Off Values Printed from Data Tables

The Problem.   Now that you've had your statistics lesson, you've undoubtedly noticed that the computer loves to produce decimal fractions to the umpteenth place. Normally this would not be a problem, but when your goal is to print neat columnar data tables, the computer will zig-zag these numbers all over the line, depending upon how many decimal places it comes up with. The solution is to round off these fractional numbers.

Rounding with the PRINT USING Statement.   There are several options available for the use of this statement on the IBM PC and TRS-80. I will cover only one use: PRINT USING to round off numbers and line up columns on the decimal point. The PRINT USING statement has two parameters: a format string and a print item list. The format string is a series of # characters enclosed within quotes. The placement of a period within the format string determines how rounding will occur. The following variations in the format string produce different printed results for the same print item.

FORMAT STRINGS IN THE PRINT USING STATEMENT

Statements	Printed Output
20 D = 345.239783	
30 PRINT D	345.239783
40 PRINT USING "#####.###";D	345.239
50 PRINT USING "#####.##";D	345.24
60 PRINT USING "########.";D	345
100 PRINT USING "###.#";D;	
105 PRINT ,	
110 PRINT USING "###.#";D	345.2 345.2

(PRINT ZONE 1) (PRINT ZONE 2)

Decimal fractions are rounded automatically in the PRINT USING statement. If the same format string is used repeatedly, the items will be printed in a column, centered on the decimal point. However, moving the items across the line by using commas and print zones requires special attention. The comma that moves the printer over one zone cannot be added to the PRINT USING statement. The only punctuation mark allowed at the end of PRINT USING is a semicolon. The solution is to move to the next print zone using a separate PRINT statement terminated with a comma (as in line 105 above).

PRINT USING would make a definite improvement in the appearance of the mean and standard deviation output from the SEMANTIC DIFFERENTIAL program.

PROGRAMMING EXAMPLE: ROUNDING WITH PRINT USING

IBM PC and TRS-80 program segment	notes
700 PRINT	
720 PRINT "MEAN:"	Row label at left margin.
730 FOR J=1 TO 2	
740 PRINT USING "#####.##";ME(J);	Means printed across row.
741 PRINT ,	Moves to next print zone.
750 NEXT J : PRINT	
800 PRINT "S.D.:"	Row label at left margin.
810 FOR J=1 TO 2	
820 PRINT USING "#####.##";SE(J);	S.D.s printed across row.
821 PRINT ,	Moves to next print zone.
830 NEXT J : PRINT	

Rounding on the Apple IIe. To round off numbers, you'll subject them to a formula based on the INT function (that's to truncate any value to a whole number):

FORMULA FOR ROUNDING NUMBERS

$$RN = INT (NU * 10^{DE} + .5) / 10^{DE}$$

```
where...  RN is the rounded result
          NU is the original number
          DE is the number of decimal places
             for rounding
```

A Rounding Subroutine for the Apple IIe. This is a perfect opportunity to reintroduce subroutines, which I presented in Chapter 5. The rounding subroutine will be a small branch in the program that will subject any number to the above rounding equation, and return the new rounded value in place of the old.

ROUNDING SUBROUTINE FOR THE APPLE IIe

Apple IIe program segment	notes
700 PRINT	
720 PRINT "MEAN:"	Row label at left margin.
730 FOR J=1 TO 2	
735 NU = ME(J) : GOSUB 1000	
740 PRINT RN,	Means printed across row (only two zones used).
750 NEXT J : PRINT	
800 PRINT "S.D.:"	Row label at left margin.
810 FOR J=1 TO 2	
815 NU = SE(J) : GOSUB 1000	
820 PRINT RN,	S.D.s printed across row.
830 PRINT J : PRINT	
840 GOTO 2000	Branch past subroutine.
1000 REM ROUNDING SUBROUTINE	
1005 DE = 2	Use 2 decimal places.
1010 RN = INT (NU * 10DE + .5) / 10^DE	
1020 RETURN	
2000 END	

Closure

With this chapter you have begun polishing your programming skills. You now have all the tools necessary to run a computer-controlled experiment, and at a fairly high level of sophistication! For example, earlier in the learning process your programs printed data on the screen following each trial. That's actually not very useful, since you don't want the subject to see these distracting data printouts. Now you have the capability to store the data on-line as they are obtained. Then, using a separate routine after the testing is over, you can print neatly organized tables. What a difference!

Projects

Stand-alone Projects. Complete the expanded SEMANTIC DIF-FERENTIAL program to the point where both dependent variables are tabled and summarized with means and standard deviations.

Apply the principles of on-line array storage and printing to the latest version of the TIME PERCEPTION programs developed in Chapter 7.

Interface Project. Apply the on-line storage techniques to the ALTERNATING SCHEDULES program developed in Chapter 7.

CHAPTER 9

Off-Line Disk Storage of Subject Data

Computers Have Long-Term Memory

In Chapter 8 you learned about array storage techniques for raw data and summary measures. Array storage is the short-term memory of the computer; to keep your information, you must print out the data before you turn off the computer system. The long-term memory of the system is **disk storage**. Disk storage is nothing new to you, you use it each time you save a program. The statements in the program are stored permanently on the disk itself. In addition, you can also store numbers and text labels.

Disk Files. Just like a manila file folder, the **disk file** is a storage place for text and numeric information. It's the ideal place to put your raw data table, for several reasons.

First, disk storage is convenient, far more so than using the line printer. It's faster, definitely more quiet, and not likely to interfere with the testing of subjects. Of course, you'll still use the printer to get your paper, or hard, copy, but you'll make printouts later, after the test session is over. Second, disk storage makes your personal laboratory a bit more portable. Imagine that you have a TRS-80 system in a general purpose, high-traffic area in the laboratory. Suppose you need to relocate the system temporarily to a private room, so that a special noise- and distraction-free test can take place. Or maybe you would like to transport the system to a cooperating nursery school to test preschoolers in your study. With disk storage you can do these things without lugging the printer around too. The only cost to you is the effort of writing a few more statements within the section of your program that prints a raw data table.

Disk Files in Printout Format. By now you've grown accustomed to the appearance of data printouts. They have clear and concise labels along the top and sides and numbers in the middle. The disk files are going to look exactly the same. In fact, in more than one sense you'll be "printing" onto the disk during the storage process. The printout format file often goes by the name **sequential-access** file, because items are placed in and retrieved from the file in sequence from first to last.

Creating a disk file is remarkably similar to printing a table of data. But before you see just how similar, you first need to learn where the file "folders" are and how to get them out of the file "cabinet."

ADVANCING BASIC: Sequential-Access Disk Files

The OPEN Statement. OPEN is the statement that literally opens the file for you. For a moment, let's talk about parameters. There are three: file channel, mode, and name. If you have any manila folders lying around your desk right now, you can certainly appreciate the need to be able to have more than one file open at the same time. You can do this on some computers as well.

Each disk file is opened on a specific channel, and each channel has a number. So, the computer will know what you mean when you want to put some data into file #1 and take some data out of file #2. That brings us to the real difference between input and output. Each of these actions represents a different file mode, and in sequential-access files you can't do both from the same file at the same time. However, using disk file input is beyond the scope of this book, and you won't have any such assignments.

Finally, you must specify a file name. When you open a file, it's crucial to use the correct name. Disk file names must conform to the same rules as program names, which were covered in Chapter 3. One feature of the file name worth emphasizing is the portion called the *extension*—for instance, the .BAS extension on all IBM PC BASIC programs. All of your disk data files will be given the .OUT extension (/OUT on the TRS-80). This is a handy notation so that you can quickly identify them.

Now that you've read about the OPEN statement and its parameters, here is an example.

OPEN STATEMENT

IBM PC	notes
502 OPEN "TEST1.OUT" FOR OUTPUT AS 3	Specifies file name, output mode, channel number.
	(See also, Appendix E)

TRS-80	notes
502 OPEN "O",3,"TEST1/OUT"	Output mode, channel, file name.

It's a bit different on the Apple IIe. A special control character must be printed before disk statements like OPEN. The Apple IIe regards OPEN as more than a statement. It has all the status of a DOS command, and in order to be recognized the special control character must accompany it. Furthermore, there's no channel number, and in place of a mode designation comes the WRITE command. Here's how it all looks.

STATEMENTS REQUIRED FOR DISK FILE USE ON THE Apple IIe

Apple IIe	notes
502 D$ = CHR$(4)	Special control character.
506 PRINT D$;"OPEN ";"TEST1.OUT"	Channel not used.
508 PRINT D$;"WRITE ";"TEST1.OUT"	WRITE command specifies output mode; a space is required after OPEN and WRITE.

Most of the examples on disk file storage in this chapter will be geared to the same examples used in Chapter 8 (the modified SEMANTIC DIFFERENTIAL program). A quick check back will show you that I am positioning these opening statements just before the nested loops used to print the contents of the raw data array in the SEMANTIC DIFFERENTIAL program.

Sequential-access File PRINT Statements. Now that your printout format file is open, you can print items into it in the same manner that you print items on the screen or line printer. It's a simple process on the Apple IIe. Once a file has been opened, *all* PRINT statements to follow direct the output into the disk file (not the screen or printer). On the IBM PC and TRS-80 there is a special form of the

PRINT statement for use with disk files. It has one parameter: the channel number on which the file was originally opened.

```
PRINT #n, STATEMENT (FOR DISK FILE USE WITH IBM PC AND TRS-80)
```

IBM PC and TRS-80	notes
510 PRINT #3, "RAW DATA: RATINGS" 515 PRINT #3,	File is open on channel 3. Equivalent of "bare" PRINT statement.

You can draw two conclusions from these examples. First, on the IBM PC and TRS-80 the routines to print data tables on the line printer can be easily modified to redirect output to a disk file. After the PRINT just add the #3, (or whatever channel number is matched to that used in the OPEN statement). On the Apple IIe you may not have to change anything. PRINT statements automatically redirect output to the disk once the file has been opened.

How about the PRINT USING statements covered in Chapter 8? To make PRINT USING work with disk file output, simply insert the #3, between the PRINT and the USING (3 is an example of a channel number).

```
PRINT #n, USING STATEMENT (FOR DISK FILE USE WITH IBM PC AND TRS-80)
```

IBM PC and TRS-80	notes
740 PRINT #3, USING "#####.##";ME(J),	When file is open on 3.

The CLOSE Statement. Having opened a file, printed into it, and completed all operations on it, you will need to close it. Once a file is closed, it cannot be accessed again without another OPEN statement. Also, on the Apple IIe closing a file redirects output from PRINT statements back to the screen.

```
CLOSE STATEMENT
```

IBM PC and TRS-80	Apple IIe
900 CLOSE #3	900 PRINT D$;"CLOSE ";"TEST1.OUT"

With all this talk about opening and closing files, you may be wondering whether you can add data to a file after it has been closed.

You can, and it's not difficult. The IBM PC has an append mode, the TRS-80 has an extend mode, and the Apple IIe has an APPEND command. To add data to the end of a disk file, simply open it and specify append mode. If the file is a new one, on the IBM PC and TRS-80 append and extend modes will create new files (just like opening for output). On the Apple IIe, however, the APPEND command may be used only if the file already exists.

```
OPEN STATEMENTS THAT SPECIFY APPEND MODE
```

IBM PC	notes
502 OPEN "TEST1.OUT" FOR APPEND AS 3	Append mode; channel #3.

TRS-80	notes
502 OPEN "E",3,"TEST1.OUT"	Extend mode; channel #3.

Apple IIe	notes
502 D$ = CHR$(4)	Special control character.
506 PRINT D$;"APPEND ";"TEST1.OUT" 508 PRINT D$;"WRITE ";"TEST1.OUT"	APPEND replaces OPEN. WRITE command specifies output mode.

Limitations and Cautions. As you have learned, each system deals with disk file storage differently. While all three systems allow you to access several different files in the same program, the IBM PC and TRS-80 require that a specific channel number be assigned to each file. However, I won't be introducing projects that require more than one file in a single program. There are also system differences in printing statements used to put information into disk files. Certain cautions are also worth mentioning. Be careful to keep file names straight. If you reuse a file name and open it for output, *it will be erased if it is already on disk*. On the other hand, when you are opening a file for appending data, it won't be erased.

A variety of system errors can arise from disk file operations. The most troublesome type would be to attempt to print data into a disk file when the disk is full and cannot store any more information. This is potentially big trouble. You should keep a close watch on disk free space if you are placing many files and/or programs on the same disk. The amount of free space is given at the top of the directory of files on the TRS-80 using the DIR (A) command at TRSDOS level. On the IBM PC you can calculate free space using the CHKDSK utility program. On version 2.0 or higher of PC-DOS/MS-DOS, free space is printed after each directory produced with the DIR command at DOS level. On the Apple IIe you calculate free space using a file management utility program on the DOS 3.3 System Master Disk called by typing RUN FILEM.

An additional caution worth mentioning concerns the file names you give for output files. These file names must be selected with some pattern in mind. For example, they might be a code for the subject whose data they contain. Then you will end up with a separate file for each subject's data. The file names could also contain characters that indicate what experimental condition the data represent. One important implication of these examples is that you will be specifying *a different file name for each run of the program.* So the best approach is to use a string variable in the OPEN statement instead of a string constant. The examples in this chapter show string constants. Let me show you how to use a string variable. First, near the very top of the program, you would request an input to assign a file name to a string variable.

USING STRING VARIABLES TO HOLD DISK FILE NAMES

IBM PC program segment	notes
5 INPUT "ENTER OUTPUT FILE NAME";FF$	Experiment provides this.
502 OPEN FF$ FOR OUTPUT AS 3	Specifies output mode; 3 means channel #3.

TRS-80 program segment	notes
...same as above except...	
502 OPEN "O",3,FF$	Output mode, channel #3.

Apple IIe program segment	notes
502 D$ = CHR$(4)	Special control character.
506 PRINT D$;"OPEN ";FF$	Channel not used.
508 PRINT D$;"WRITE ";FF$	WRITE command specifies output mode; a space is required after OPEN and WRITE.

Let's take some time to discuss practical examples of all the disk file storage options. I have already mentioned why disk file data storage comes in handy. Next, I'll develop a hypothetical application. In Chapter 7 I developed the PAIRED ASSOC STUDY program. Next, I'll develop the PAIRED ASSOC TEST program to exemplify techniques for disk file storage.

The PAIRED ASSOC TEST Program Using Disk File Storage

The Problem. PAIRED ASSOC STUDY was a program that presents a list of paired items for learning. Each pair consisted of a stimulus term on the left and a response term on the right. One way of testing would be to present each stimulus term and require the subject to type in the correct response term. That would be a difficult free-recall test. Maybe if the subject were given 50 repetitions of the study procedure, success would be fairly certain. You could also use a recognition test, where the stimulus term is presented and accompanied by a series of possible response terms. The subject then recognizes the correct response term from among the series. Your first programming decision is to use the PAIRED ASSOCIATE TEST program to carry out the recognition procedure.

The program should be based on a series of trials. Each trial should consist of the presentation of a stimulus term and response options, followed by a request for the subject to select one of the options as the correct response term. Your second programming decision is that the test screen will consist of the stimulus term and possible response term choices, and a prompt to the subject. Each screen will represent a single trial.

After the subject makes a choice, the data should then be stored and analyzed. What dependent variables would be appropriate? There is a frequency count measure in the number of correct trials recorded. There is a duration measure in the process time to make a choice. Your third programming decision is that the raw data stored for each trial will include the actual response, the correct response, and the process time. The data summarized for each subject will include the frequency, percent correct, and average process time for correct choices.

Take a close look at the above paragraphs. They are a prototype of the first step in the process of translating an experimental procedure into a laboratory computer program. You have to make certain general decisions about the form the program will take. You made a decision concerning how the program would display stimuli. Another involved specifying the dependent variable(s). Finally, you decided on the format for the raw and summary data. The next step is to put the program together.

Programming the Test Screen Display. The example is based on the PAIRED ASSOC STUDY program previously developed. Ten words (five pairs) were used as stimuli and were present in DATA statements near the beginning of the program. Since you will be presenting all five response terms as choice options on each trial, you cannot effectively use the READ statement. Before each trial you would have to read one of the five stimulus terms and all the response terms in order to make up the display screen. READ does not give the flexibility required, but arrays do! The solution is to assign all the stimulus and response terms to elements of arrays, then begin the test trials. Now you will learn to work with **string arrays**. Fear not—both string and numeric array storage are based on the same concepts.

ONE-DIMENSION STRING ARRAY HOLDING STIMULUS TERMS

NONCOMPUTER CONCEPT		ONE-DIMENSION ARRAY
verbal item		
Row 1 HOUSE		ST$(1) = HOUSE
2 HORSE		ST$(2) = HORSE
3 HIM		ST$(3) = HIM
4 HOWL		ST$(4) = HOWL
5 HUNT		ST$(5) = HUNT

PROGRAMMING EXAMPLE: ASSIGNING STIMULUS AND RESPONSE TERMS

program segment	notes
...clock reset, etc...	Different by system.
...clock subroutine...	
100 DATA 5	Number of pairs.
110 DATA "HOUSE","HARP"	
111 DATA "HORSE","HOT"	
112 DATA "HIM","HER"	
113 DATA "HOWL","HAPPY"	
114 DATA "HUNT","HAWK"	
300 READ N	5 assigned to N.
305 FOR I=1 TO N	
310 READ ST$(I),RT$(I)	Stimulus and response terms
315 NEXT I	assigned.

Now the ST$ and RT$ arrays contain the stimulus and response terms, respectively. The parameter, number of pairs (also number of trials), is now represented by N.

Each screen display is quite straightforward. As each trial occurs, each stimulus term and all response terms are displayed. I will label each response term with a numeral so that only a single keystroke will be required to make a choice. The program will present one through N trials. As always, a loop will step the program from one trial to the next (the familiar trial loop you've seen before). In addition, a second loop is needed for each screen display. Can you figure out where? Only two categories of stimuli are being displayed: stimulus term (singular) and response terms (all). A loop is needed to display the response terms as choice options. In the example there are five response terms ($N = 5$), so this loop will cycle five times (N times). There is something about this approach that makes this program good only as an example, and actually not usable in the laboratory. While you're working out the steps, see if you can catch the fault.

PROGRAMMING EXAMPLE: DISPLAY OF STIMULUS AND RESPONSE TERMS

IBM PC and TRS-80 program segment	notes
400 FOR I = 1 TO N	Start trial loop.
410 CLS	HOME on Apple IIe
420 PRINT ,ST$(I)	Display stimulus term.
430 PRINT	
440 FOR J = 1 TO N	Start response term loop.
450 PRINT ,J;" ";RT$(J)	Displays item number and response term.
460 NEXT J	

Programming the Response Measures. Next, I want to start a response latency timer and wait for a keystroke that signifies that one of the response terms has been chosen. The subject will press the number key, ⟨1⟩ through ⟨5⟩, that corresponds to the correct match. At this point I want to add a program section based on either the INKEY$ function (IBM PC and TRS-80) or the Apple IIe keystroke entry routine (both introduced in Chapter 6). So, start the latency timer and detect a keystroke on keys ⟨1⟩ through ⟨5⟩. This, by the way, is done within the trial loop because it's all part of a single trial.

PROGRAMMING EXAMPLE: START LATENCY TIMER, DETECT KEYPRESS

IBM PC and TRS-80 program segment	notes
500 GOSUB 50 : START = TIME	Start latency timer.
510 I$ = INKEY$: IF I$ = "" THEN 510	Endless loop until keypress.
520 GOSUB 50 : LAX = TIME-START	Assign value to latency.
530 NI = VAL(I$)	Convert to numeric.

APPLE IIe program segment	notes
...all the above except...	
405 HOME	
407 INPUT "PRESS <RETURN> TO START";R$	Subject clears keyboard as trial starts.
410 HOME	

```
510 KEY = PEEK (-16384)        Keystroke entry routine
512 POKE -16368,0                 (chapter 6).
514 IF KEY > 127 THEN 518      If new key has been pressed.
516 GOTO 510
518 I$ = CHR$(KEY-128)         Convert keystroke to string.
```

Programming the Data Storage. So far, so good. Now think about what has just happened. The trial is over and you now have two pieces of raw data, the response term choice and the process time (response latency). These dependent measures require special attention. What you have in the response choice measure is actually a numeral (1 through 5) representing an array element containing one of the response terms. The variable in question, *I$*, was first a string and had to be converted to a numeric, *NI*. So that makes the actual response term chosen RT$(*NI*). But what's the correct response term? How about RT$(*I*), since items stored in ST$ and RT$ correspond by array position. Now maybe you're starting to see the fault that I mentioned earlier.

The next step is to print the stimulus term, the correct response term, the actual response term, and the process time for that trial. Then print the current values for number correct, percent correct, and average response latency. Current values will be based on number of trials completed. And, of course, when I say *print*, I mean print to a disk file.

The first step then will be to open the disk file. Since the file will be accessed at the end of each trial, on the Apple IIe you'll open it for append mode (to keep adding data to the end of the file). This will allow you to print both on the screen and onto disk by opening and closing the file. On the IBM PC and TRS-80 you can print items into the disk file without affecting the screen display, so you can open the file for straight output mode. This system difference is fairly important, since it determines where in the program the OPEN statements occur. On the IBM PC and TRS-80 they need occur only once at the beginning of the program.

A single CLOSE statement is required at the end of the program. But on the Apple IIe you are opening and closing (using append mode) at the end of each trial. Opening the disk file redirects all printing to the disk. Closing the file redirects all printing back to the screen. Furthermore, on the Apple IIe you must open the file for output mode first, just to establish its existence. Remember, on Apple IIe systems if a file does not already exist, you cannot open it to append data.

You also need to remember that there are five print zones available on the IBM PC and TRS-80 (go back to Chapter 4 if you need a reminder). On the Apple IIe, however, there are no print zones per se when you are using disk output files. You have to make them yourself. I'll cover that right now.

What exactly is a print zone? It's the computer's way of putting items in columns as they are printed. Only the Apple IIe differentiates on-line printing, where print zones are used, from off-line disk file printing, where print zones are not used. The solution is to write statements into the Apple IIe program that produce the print zones. Three important parameters are required to do this. You need to know the zone's width and the length of the item to be printed so you do not attempt to print an item that has more characters than you have space available in a zone (although these "overflows" are bound to occur from time to time). Once you have standardized the width of each print zone, you can use the TAB function to move along the line from zone to zone. It is very important that you *do not use commas anywhere within this routine*. Commas automatically terminate a line that is being written onto disk in Apple IIe systems. Let's look at a routine that will do the job.

A DISK FILE "PRINT ZONE" ROUTINE FOR THE APPLE IIe

Apple IIe program segment	notes
655 P$ = STR$(LAX)	STR$ function converts number to corresponding string.
656 LS = LEN(P$)	LEN function gives length of a string.
660 PRINT P$; TAB(10-L);"PROCESS TIME"	P$ is now LAX in string form (same information); You tabbed 10-LS spaces to expand and fill zone.

A second method for organizing Apple IIe disk file output is to limit yourself to two print zones in all applications. The strategy in this case is to print your text label in the first zone. Then, knowing its exact length, TAB the remainder to a specified column location, such as 20, and print the numeric item. The nice thing about this method is its simplicity and the fact that you need not worry about numeric over-flows. I'll use this technique in the example below.

You'll format your disk file just as you would format your paper printout (hence the term *printout format*). The approach requires that data files be stored on the programming master disk. This means that no extra disks are required. In the examples below I'm throwing in some data summarizing routines, such as summing and averaging, so be on the lookout for them.

PROGRAMMING EXAMPLE: DISK FILE STORAGE

IBM PC and TRS-80 program segment	notes
200 OPEN "TEST.OUT" FOR OUTPUT AS 3	Open the file before procedure begins.
600 PRINT #3, 610 PRINT #3,"TRIAL: ";I 620 PRINT #3,	
630 PRINT #3,"STIMULUS TERM ",ST$(I) 640 PRINT #3,"RESPONSE TERM ",RT$(I)	Note use of I for original items.
650 PRINT #3,"R-TERM CHOICE ",RT$(NI) 660 PRINT #3,"RAW PROCESS TIME ",LAX	Note use of NI. Raw data item.
670 IF NI = I THEN COUNT = COUNT + 1	Checks for a correct choice; if yes, add 1 to COUNT.
680 PRINT #3,"NUMBER CORRECT ",COUNT 690 PRINT #3,"% CORRECT ",(COUNT/I)*100	Summary data item. Summary data item.
700 SLAX = SLAX + LAX	Compute sum of all process times.
710 PRINT #3,"MEAN PROCESS TIME",SLAX/I	Summary data item.
800 NEXT I	End of trial.
810 CLOSE 3 : END	

TRS-80 program segment	notes
200 OPEN "O",3,"TEST/OUT"	

Apple IIe program segment	notes
200 D$ = CHR$(4)	Special character.
206 PRINT D$;"OPEN ";"TEST1.OUT" 208 PRINT D$;"WRITE ";"TEST1.OUT"	OPEN creates the file. WRITE for output mode.
210 PRINT "PAIRED-ASSOCIATE DATA" 212 PRINT D$;"CLOSE ";"TEST1.OUT"	Title printed to file.
580 PRINT D$;"APPEND ";"TEST1.OUT" 582 PRINT D$;"WRITE ";"TEST1.OUT"	APPEND mode used.
600 PRINT 610 PRINT "TRIAL: ";I 620 PRINT	
630 PRINT "STIMULUS TERM";TAB(7);ST$(I) 640 PRINT "RESPONSE TERM";TAB(7);RT$(I)	Note use of I for original items.
650 PRINT "R-TERM CHOICE";TAB(7);RT$(NI) 660 PRINT "RAW PROCESS TIME";TAB(4);LAX	Note use of NI. Raw data item.
670 IF NI = I THEN COUNT = COUNT + 1	Checks for a correct choice; if yes, add 1 to COUNT.
680 PRINT "NUMBER CORRECT";TAB(6);COUNT 690 PRINT "% CORRECT";TAB(12);(COUNT/I)*100	Summary data item. Summary data item.

```
700 SLAX = SLAX + LAX                    Compute sum of all
                                         process times.
710 PRINT "MEAN PROCESS TIME";TAB(3);SLAX/I  Summary data item.

720 PRINT D$;"CLOSE ";"TEST1.OUT"

800 NEXT I

810 HOME : END
```

In the Apple IIe version above I opened the file at line 200, simply to create it on the disk. It was closed shortly thereafter. Without this routine first, the following APPEND statements would not have worked. Notice also that the PRINT statements are plain, since output is redirected to disk. But at the end of the printing routine, the disk file must be closed in order to redirect printing to the screen as the next trial comes along. In the IBM PC and TRS-80 version you don't close the file until the program ends.

Have you figured out the flaw that makes this program inappropriate for use in an actual experiment? It has to do with the way trials are presented. There is no attempt to vary the selection of specific trials so that subjects do not receive a predictable order of presentation. The order of trials is dangerously predictable. It's simply first through last. The *test order* is the same as the *study order*. Response terms are also presented in this same order, further compounding the problem. Under these circumstances *pair* associations cannot be separated from *order* learning. Put simply, the test is so easy it's not valid (as long as subjects know they are on trial 3, they can just push key ⟨3⟩ to select the third response term).

Well then, what is needed? In a word, randomization. (Which is one of the topics to be covered in the next chapter.) For now, just keep in mind that the present version of the PAIRED ASSOC TEST program is merely preliminary.

Additional Format Options for Disk File Storage

In this section I will cover commands and functions that help to make a printout format disk file easier to read and better organized.

Print Zones Reviewed. Once again, I need to talk about print zones. You have five on the IBM PC and TRS-80 and should limit yourself to two on the Apple IIe. Print zones will automatically place your data in columns on the disk (just as they do on paper). As you've seen above in the Apple IIe example, you can design your own column layout using the TAB function. However, note the system differences when using TAB with disk output files. On the IBM PC and TRS-80 the parameter in the TAB statement represents the column that you want to tab to along the line. On the Apple IIe, however, this parameter is the number of spaces that will be skipped along the line. This difference is important, but it's relevant only when you are dealing with TAB and disk file storage.

```
TAB FUNCTION
```

IBM PC and TRS-80 program segment

```
300 PRINT #3, TAB(10);"PART 1";TAB(20);"PART 2";TAB(30);"PART 3";
310 PRINT #3, TAB(40);"PART 4";TAB(50);"PART 5
```

Apple IIe program segment

```
300 PRINT TAB(10);"PART 1";TAB(10);"PART 2";TAB(10);"PART 3"
```

Listing Disk Files on a Screen or Line Printer

Ultimately, you'll want to get a hard copy of your disk data files as well as display them on the screen. This is relatively easy on IBM PC and TRS-80 systems, but on the Apple IIe the operation requires a separate utility program supplied in Appendix G of this text.

```
TYPE COMMAND ON THE IBM PC
```

IBM PC	notes
TYPE TEST1.OUT	This is DOS command for screen output; Use <Ctrl-S> to stop and restart.
TYPE TEST1.OUT<CTRL-P> <CTRL-N>	Directs output to printer. Directs output back to screen; turns off printer; on DOS 2.0 or higher use <Ctrl-P> instead of <Ctrl-N> to turn off printer, or use the PRINT command from DOS level.

LIST COMMAND ON THE TRS-80

TRS-80	notes
LIST TEST1/OUT	TRSDOS command for screen output.
LIST TEST1/OUT(P)	Directs output to printer.

Before you can list disk data files on the Apple IIe, you must first load the LIST OUTPUT program supplied in Appendix G. At this point you should type in this short program (as you would any other BASIC program) and save it on your Apple IIe master disk. Then simply run the program and follow the prompts. For printed output type PR#1 first (to turn on the printer), then run the LIST OUTPUT program.

Closure

Now you know how to handle long-term storage of your research data. You know how to open files for output and append modes, print data into them, format them, and list them on the screen or printer. However, I've only scratched the surface of the file systems available on the computer. For example, I have not talked about input mode since you won't be using it for real-time applications.

One thing that bears repeating is that disk data files are files like any other. Once they exist on the disk, they are handled much the same as programs. They can be deleted, copied, viewed in a directory or catalog, and so on. However, they are not BASIC programs and cannot be used with BASIC commands such as LOAD, SAVE, RUN, and the like. Don't make that mistake. I'll never forget the confused student who kept using SAVE with a disk data file. The data were compressed into a binary machine code and turned into unreadable gibberish. The test sessions were completely wasted. So be careful. Think first, so you don't ruin your data later!

Projects

Convert any two of your previous programs to store data in disk files.

CHAPTER 10

Programming the Experimental Design

The Requirements for Good Experimental Design

Experimental design is the aspect of psychological research that is concerned with the organizational layout and internal validity of an experiment. The **layout** of an experiment shows which variables are being manipulated, measured, and controlled. The **internal validity** of an experimental procedure is maintained if the events and presentations to the subject are controlled, unbiased, and uncontaminated by influence from outside factors. The lessons to be learned about these topics are beyond the scope of this book, however, in this chapter I want to provide a bridge to connect these fundamental concepts with real-time programming strategies.

Layout and Experimental Variables. Out of necessity I have already introduced programming methods that involve certain aspects of experimental design. In particular, I have touched upon the three variables that experimenters work with: independent (IV), dependent (DV), and control (CV) variables. For example, I devoted a chapter to the programming techniques for measuring subject responses. You should recognize measurement as the basis for the DV of the experiment. In another case you developed a program that presented two types of stimuli in a semantic differential task: concrete and abstract words. You should recognize that each type of word represented a level of an IV.

Up to this point I have devoted the most coverage to control variables. CVs are yet another form of parameter in a computer-controlled procedure. For example, each time I (seemingly arbitrarily) decided upon the display duration of a stimulus, or the number of stimuli in a word list, I was designating a CV (and also a program parameter). These are factors that are constant across all levels of all IVs.

In this chapter you will be adding new programming tools to develop research designs. Specifically, you will learn new techniques for the administration of IVs in computer-controlled procedures.

Keeping the Experimental Procedure Unbiased.   This topic has yet to receive much attention. In fact, in Chapter 9 you developed a program that was technically unusable because of its inability to present an unbiased test of memory. In this chapter you will develop the programming techniques needed to remedy that particular problem. In addition, this chapter will provide you with a general set of tools for programming internally valid and unbiased presentations of stimuli and conditions in an experiment.

Between- and Within-Subjects Designs

Independent variables can be easily classified as either between or within subjects. If each level of the independent variable, such as the type of stimulus presented (e.g., concrete vs. abstract words) is presented to a different group of subjects (a concrete group vs. an abstract group), then the variable is **between subjects**. If each level is presented to each subject (each subject receives all levels), then the variable is **within subjects**.

Implications for Programming.   The most obvious implication for you as a real-time programmer is that within-subjects procedures require that a single program provide all the levels (or conditions) of the experiment. One program should do it all. On the other hand, between-subjects procedures require an approach that I'm calling **program templates**, because one "starter" version of the program (a template) will be modified for each level of the IV. Each level of the between-subjects IV will have a separate program.

You've already had some experience using a within-subjects procedure from your work on the SEMANTIC DIFFERENTIAL program (concrete vs. abstract words). In addition, you've already practiced the basics of using program templates as well. Each time you modified an existing program, such as developing PROJECTOR IV from PROJECTOR III, you practiced the program template approach if you first loaded the old version of the program, then modified it, and finally saved it under a new file name.

I'll begin by formalizing some of the principles and procedures behind the use of program templates in general, then work up to specific examples involving between-subjects IVs. Next, you'll tackle the problem of how to program within-subjects experiments and sequence their experimental conditions. Along the way you'll take the current version of the TIME PERCEPTION program and make it suitable for a within-subjects experiment with one IV. Next, you'll cover programming techniques to preserve internal validity and remove a sequence bias from a procedure. That work will culminate in the final development of a working PAIRED ASSOC TEST program.

ADVANCING BASIC: Program Templates

Reviewing What a Template Is. In grade school when you wanted to draw several shapes, for example squares that were exactly the same size, you cut out a template and used it to trace each figure. Once the outline of the square had been drawn, you could add detail to it to make each figure different, though based on the same premise. Program templates are no more complicated. I'll begin with an example you should be very familiar with.

PROGRAMMING EXAMPLE: Clock Templates. It's easy to make a clock template for use with either a DOS clock or the LVB Timer. Simply save a "program" that contains only the clock statements.

DOS CLOCK TEMPLATES

IBM PC and TRS-80 program segment	notes
20 TIME$ = "00:00:00"	SYSTEM "TIME$=00:00:00" on TRS-80; resets clock.
30 GOTO 100	
50 T$=TIME$	Start of clock subroutine
52 H$=MID$(T$,1,2)	
54 M$=MID$(T$,4,2)	
56 S$=MID$(T$,7,2)	
58 HS = VAL(H$) * 3600	
60 MS = VAL(M$) * 60	
62 SS = VAL(S$)	
64 TIME = HS + MS + SS	
66 RETURN	End of clock subroutine
100 REM RESUME PROGRAM	

Now save this template on disk. Use ASCII format, but otherwise proceed just as you would save any other program. Use the file name DOSCLOCK. The DOS clock on the Apple IIe will be based on an internal clock card (Appendix C has the subroutine).

SAVING PROGRAM TEMPLATES IN ASCII FORMAT

IBM PC and TRS-80	notes
SAVE "DOSCLOCK",A	The ,A denotes ASCII format.
(Ok)	

DOSCLOCK is a program template that now contains the clock subroutine. It can be the starting point for the development of any new program. Please note the use of the ASCII format save option (,A). On the IBM PC and TRS-80 it is required for the effective use of templates. The concept of ASCII format saving is not relevant on the Apple IIe, so just save the template in the normal way.

To build a new program around the clock, simply load the clock template as you would any other program, add statements to it (before line 20 or after line 100), and save the program *using a new file name*. If you don't use a new file name, you'll erase the clock template. Now what if you want to add a template to a program that is already under development?

ADVANCING BASIC: The MERGE Command

Getting Set to MERGE Two Programs.   On the IBM PC and TRS-80 you must make sure both component programs (the main program and the template) have been saved in ASCII format. Next, regardless of system, you must make sure that the components do not share any line numbers. What happens if they do? You'll need to renumber one or both according to the steps below. The MERGE command itself is refreshingly simple.

Renumbering Routines.   Suppose that the main program you are developing has DATA statements beginning at line 60. They will obviously cut into the clock subroutine, should you decide to merge the two programs into one. The solution is to renumber the main program, moving the starting line to 200, well above the end of the clock subroutine. I have already covered versions of the renumber command for each system (in Chapter 5); however, below you'll see a special application for renumbering routines. You don't just want to renumber the program; you also want to set a new first line number. This amounts to adding certain parameters to the renumber commands. Follow closely.

RENUMBER, SET NEW FIRST LINE, MERGE SECOND PROGRAM

IBM PC and TRS-80	notes
..."main" program was loaded...	
RENUM 200,,20	Renumbers the program; new first line is 200; increment by 20.
MERGE "DOSCLOCK"	Merges with existing program.
...continue programming...	BE CAREFUL: don't forget to save the new version using correct file name.

Apple IIe	notes
...first save the program on disk...	
RUN RENUMBER	Refers to DOS RENUMBER program.
...the RENUMBER title screen appears...	
press <RETURN>	
LOAD ...main program...	Re-load the program you want to renumber.
& FIRST 200, INC 20	Calls for renumbering; new first line is 200; increments of 20.
& HOLD	Puts current program on "hold."
LOAD DOSCLOCK	Loads the second program; I'll assume DOSCLOCK is a clock card template (Appendix C).
& MERGE	Merges program on hold with second program.
...continue programming...	BE CAREFUL: don't forget to save the new version using correct file name.

If you don't have to renumber, skip everything related to renumbering in the above example. Double-check yourself when using these renumbering and merging commands. Be sure to save the renumbered and merged version of the program. Think of it as what it is: a new program.

Additional Examples of Program Templates.   Imagine that you are programming a between-subjects procedure involving the PAIRED ASSOC STUDY program. There are two groups of subjects. Group 1 will get word list A. Group 2 will get word list B. You'll probably hypothesize that one list will be learned better than the other. At any rate, the program template approach would require that you make two versions of the PAIRED ASSOC STUDY program, each with a different set of DATA statements. The program you run (you're the experimenter) depends upon the group to which the subject has been assigned. You might set up a program template that contains everything but DATA statements. Once you have the template, you can merge any set of DATA statements to complete the process.

Another application might involve changing one or more of the parameters controlling the procedure. For example, imagine you're programming an experiment where the IV is the amount of time the subject has to study a stimulus. This value is a parameter (it could be a constant, or a variable assigned from a DATA statement). Different versions of the test program (for different groups) might be essentially the same except for this value (the value represents a level of IV). This is a very simple version of template usage involving LOAD, change, and SAVE under a new name. LOAD one version of the program, change the parameters or whatever is required to make the new version (for another group), and SAVE under a new name.

Techniques for Sequencing Levels of IV in a Single Program

Back to Within-Subjects Procedures.   In a fully within-subjects procedure each subject is tested with each level of each IV that is present in the design. You had just that case with the last version of the SEMANTIC DIFFERENTIAL program (concrete vs. abstract words). Each set of five trials involved the use of a different category of words. The two categories represented the two levels of the IV.

You had two repetitive cycles operating in that program (it nicely illustrated the use of nested loops): the repetitive cycle of the trials and, outside that, the repetitive cycle of the levels of IV (the two types of words). I didn't call the outer loop the *levels of IV* loop then, but I'm calling it that now.

The most obvious technique, then, for sequencing different levels of a within-subjects IV is with progressively nested loops surrounding the innermost trial loop. Right now you need an example to work with, so turn your attention back to the TIME PERCEPTION program developed in Chapter 7. That was an interface project, so you'll note that the LVB Timer subroutines are used (Apple clock cards are high-speed timers, so an Apple DOS clock can be substituted). To jog your memory, look over the listing again.

```
TIME PERCEPTION program
```

IBM PC and TRS-80 program segment	notes
...LVB parameter statements	Varies by system
...clock reset, etc...	Remember, you'll always have
...clock subroutine...	clock subroutine at 50.
100 DATA 5	
102 DATA 0.6, 0.8, 1.0, 1.2, 1.4	I am not concerned about
	order in this example.
200 CLS	
300 READ FULL	
310 FOR I=1 TO FULL	
320 GOSUB 50 : START = TIME	Begin pretrial timer.
330 GOSUB 50	
340 IF TIME < START + 5 THEN 330	
350 READ OVER	Assign interval value.
400 GOSUB 50 : PRINT CHR$(7);	Sound bell; begin interval
410 START = TIME	timer.
420 GOSUB 50	
430 IF TIME < START + OVER THEN 420	
440 PRINT CHR$(7);	Sound bell
500 PRINT " CHOICES:"	
510 PRINT	
520 PRINT "1 IF LESS THAN A SECOND"	
530 PRINT "2 IF EQUAL TO A SECOND"	
540 PRINT "3 IF MORE THAN A SECOND"	
600 A$=INKEY$: IF A$="" THEN 600	Reading keyboard.
610 PRINT : PRINT "CHOICE=",A$	
620 PRINT : PRINT "ACTUAL=",OVER	Printing results.
700 GOSUB 50 : START = TIME	Posttrial pause timer.
710 GOSUB 50	
720 IF TIME < START + 5 THEN 710	
730 CLS	
800 NEXT I	
1000 END	

APPLE IIe program segment	notes
...same as above except...	
200 HOME	
315 INPUT "PRESS <RETURN> TO START";R$	Needed to "clear" keyboard.

```
600 KEY = PEEK (-16384)          Keystroke entry routine
602 POKE -16368,0                  (chapter 6).
604 IF KEY > 127 THEN 608        If new key has been pressed.
606 GOTO 600
608 A$ = CHR$(KEY-128)           Convert keystroke to string.

730 HOME
```

Note that there are five trials in the program, and in its present form there is no IV! You're going to add the IV right now. But before you do, use the decision list technique that you used in Chapter 9 with the PAIRED ASSOC TEST program to help design a better procedure.

The Problem.   Jazzing up the TIME PERCEPTION program above requires that you add an IV. What are some possible candidates? Varying the sound stimulus used to signal the onset and offset of the time interval might affect judgments. Another idea would be to vary the type of stimulus. Visual and sound stimuli were compared in an earlier version of the program (Chapter 7). Or you could vary the intervals themselves; the length of the stimulus interval might determine the accuracy of the judgment. For example, are short intervals judged more accurately than long intervals? Decision #1: Establish the IV as range of interval.

Now that you have the IV, how many levels are appropriate? As always, start simple. Decision #2: The IV will be presented at two levels, short and long. Short can be defined as a set of values spread around 1.0 seconds in the original example. Long can be defined as a spread around 2.0 seconds (1.6, 1.8, 2.0, 2.2, and 2.4).

Other decisions are required to make this program operational, including how to organize the raw data and whether to produce a printout after the session or write the data to a disk file. I'm leaving all that for later, on the assumption that you are now well-versed in the methods for organizing data (Chapters 8 and 9). I'll take the example just far enough to focus on the sequencing of the two levels of IV chosen.

Making the Modifications Needed.   First you'll have to add the second level of time values in another data statement. Then you'll have to program an outer loop to control the cycle of levels of IV. This loop will repeat two times (two levels of IV). Since you're adding an IV, you'll have to modify the print statements to indicate which level of IV the data refer to. The last modification is the tricky one. Somewhere deep in the interior of the program is a glitch waiting to present itself. Look closely. It's lines 520–540, where the prompt includes A SEC-OND. The A has to go, in favor of either 1 or 2, depending upon which level of IV is in effect. Fortunately, there is a new variable that you can use to represent the number of seconds in that prompt. It is the loop variable (though you don't have a letter for it yet), which will be equal to one on the first cycle (level one, 1 second prompt), and two on the second cycle (level two, 2 second prompt). Now follow closely.

```
PROGRAMMING EXAMPLE: TIME PERCEPTION (IV = Duration of Interval)
```

program segment	notes
...same as above except...	Adhere to system differences.
104 DATA 1.6, 1.8, 2.0, 2.2, 2.4	Level two values.
305 FOR K = 1 TO 2	Start "levels" loop.
520 PRINT "1 IF LESS THAN ";K;" SEC." 530 PRINT "2 IF EQUAL TO ";K;" SEC." 540 PRINT "3 IF MORE THAN ";K;" SEC."	
610 PRINT : PRINT "CHOICE=",A$ 615 PRINT : PRINT "ACTUAL=",OVER 620 PRINT : PRINT "LEVEL=",K	
900 NEXT K	

This isn't the entire program, of course. It's just the new or al-tered statements required to administer the within-subjects IV.

Now I'm ready to move on to the problem of programming se-quences of stimuli, conditions, or whatever. Lack of control in the or-der of presentation of stimuli can be a serious problem, as you saw with the first PAIRED ASSOC TEST program. Toward the end of the next section you'll overhaul that program and finally make it opera-tional for use in the laboratory. And you'll learn a few new tricks along the way.

Scheduling Unbiased Sequences Within a Program

Counterbalancing versus Randomization.   Both counterbalanc-ing and randomization are techniques used to present an unbiased and controlled sequence of conditions or treatments. **Counterbalancing** is by far the easier technique to program. Any counterbalanced sequence (e.g., ABBA) can be established in a multitrial program simply by arranging blocks of DATA statements. In the example below I'll show a counterbalanced (ABBA) arrangement of two levels of time-interval stimuli in the TIME PERCEPTION program.

COUNTERBALANCING CONDITIONS

program segment	notes
100 DATA 5	
102 DATA 0.6, 0.8, 1.0, 1.2, 1.4	Level one values (A).
104 DATA 1.6, 1.8, 2.0, 2.2, 2.4	Level two values (B).
106 DATA 1.6, 1.8, 2.0, 2.2, 2.4	Level two values (B).
108 DATA 0.6, 0.8, 1.0, 1.2, 1.4	Level one values (A).

That's a very simple approach to unbiased scheduling of conditions or parameters in a program. Randomization is a little more involved.

Randomization of conditions or parameters within a sequence ensures that the sequence will be unbiased. Your first step in learning how to apply the randomization technique is to master a general-purpose randomization routine (the TIME PERCEPTION program will continue to serve as the example). Imagine that you needed to randomize the sequence of a group of time-interval stimuli. Pick the five level-one values above, for example. The way they appear in sequence in the DATA statement above could lead you to predict that the subject will catch on quickly and presume that each stimulus is slightly longer than the previous one. The threat of that happening constitutes a source of bias in the procedure. Randomization is a valid corrective measure.

ADVANCING BASIC: The RND Function and Randomization Routines

First, consider the situation. You have five items to randomize. Once you have chosen an item at random, you do not want to duplicate the choice later. Unlike flipping a coin, where two heads in a row is okay, you cannot present the 0.6 value, for instance, more than once in the sequence. You want to randomize *without duplication*. To accomplish this, you need to *keep a record* of each choice as it occurs. How will your program keep a record, or remember each choice? Are you thinking "array"? Let's see how it's done.

The RND Function.   First, you'll need to use the RND function to choose a random number. Since it's a function, it has to be part of a LET statement. There are considerable system differences in the manner in which RND operates. The IBM PC and Apple IIe provide random numbers only in the range 0–1, and the values are all real numbers, not integers. The random numbers will have to be converted to integers before they can be used. The TRS-80 provides random integers between 0 and any specified value. Random number statements, then, are essentially LET statements that incorporate the RND function and the INT function, depending upon the system. On the IBM PC and Apple IIe there is one all-purpose random number statement to produce values within a specified range. There is a separate variation on the TRS-80.

RND FUNCTION AND RANDOM NUMBER STATEMENTS

IBM PC and APPLE IIe program segment	notes
442 H = 5 : L = 1	Parameters for the range; high and low.
443 RAX = INT ((H-L+1)*RND(1))+L	RAX is a random number between H and L (inclusive).
444 C(RAX) = C(RAX) + 1	The C array keeps count of which values of RAX occur.
445 IF C(RAX) > 1 THEN 443	If a value of RAX has already been used, get another.
...program continues...	

TRS-80 program segment	notes
442 H = 5	Parameter for high only.
443 RAX = RND(H)	RAX is a random integer between H and 1 (inclusive).
444 C(RAX) = C(RAX) + 1	The C array keeps count of which values of RAX occur.
445 IF C(RAX) > 1 THEN 443	If a value of RAX has already been used, get another.
...program continues...	

As you can see, the two random number statements (line 443) are similar. The TRS-80 version is more streamlined, however. The key concept for you to master here is the fact that an array was used to keep track of which random numbers were used. Values of RAX are never allowed to be duplicated. As each value of RAX (each random number) was generated, a corresponding element in an array was altered. These array elements are used as counters to differentiate between a random number that has been generated only once (the count will equal 1) and one that has been generated more than once (the count will be greater than 1). Also, values of RAX are simply integers in the inclusive specified range. All this routine does is put the numbers out in a random sequence.

Seeding the Random Number Generator.   When the computer detects the use of RND in a program, it sets up a given series of random number values. That given order of values will remain unchanged unless you "reseed" the random number generator. This operation is akin to shuffling a deck of cards. The rule here, is to reseed the random number generator only once, placing the seeding statement at the start of the program. There are considerable system differences in how this is accomplished.

The Apple IIe requires that a **seed** parameter with a negative sign be used. The value of this seed parameter determines the sequence of random numbers that will be generated. Usually, you don't want to use the same seed parameter more than once throughout the course of an experiment to make sure duplication does not take place. However, on the Apple IIe the seed parameter *must* be a constant, so it must be changed through program editing. On that system you might just want to leave the seed parameter alone.

On the IBM PC you have options. The program will prompt you (the experimenter) for the seed value. To change the seed value, just type in a different number each time. Another option is to use the clock to derive a seed value. You can use the running time reading in seconds as a new seed value.

SEEDING THE RANDOM NUMBER GENERATOR: TRS-80

TRS-80 program statement	notes
12 RANDOM	Reseeds random number generator.

Apple IIe program segment	notes
12 RND(-220)	Reseeds random number generator

IBM PC program segment	notes
...for automatic prompt...	
12 RANDOMIZE	Requests user to enter seed value.
...to use clock to reseed...	
12 GOSUB 50 : RANDOMIZE TIME	The current time value is used as seed value.

The next question concerns how random integers can be used to code the random sequence of conditions or events. To do this, turn your attention once again to the preliminary version of the PAIRED ASSOC TEST program.

PROGRAMMING EXAMPLE: Completing the PAIRED ASSOC TEST Program

Randomizing the Presentation of Response Terms. If you recall, the current status of this program is that it works but is unusable because the stimulus and response terms are presented in the same order in which they are learned. The effect is to leave open the possibility that S-R associations are not required, only matching of the numeric labels on the display screen. The solution is to present both the stimulus terms and the response terms in a random sequence, thereby ensuring that recognition will be based on S-R associations and not on order of presentation. Start by reviewing the program listing in its present form.

THE PAIRED ASSOC TEST PROGRAM: Preliminary Version (chapter 9)

IBM PC and TRS-80 program segment	notes
...clock reset, etc... ...clock subroutine...	Different by system.
100 DATA 5 110 DATA "HOUSE","HARP" 111 DATA "HORSE","HOT" 112 DATA "HIM","HER" 113 DATA "HOWL","HAPPY" 114 DATA "HUNT","HAWK"	Number of pairs.
300 READ N 305 FOR I=1 TO N 310 READ ST$(I),RT$(I) 315 NEXT I	5 assigned to N. Stimulus and response terms assigned.
400 FOR I = 1 TO N 410 CLS 420 PRINT ,ST$(I) 430 PRINT	Start trial loop. Display stimulus term.
440 FOR J = 1 TO N 450 PRINT ,J;" ";RT$(J) 460 NEXT J	Start response term loop. Displays item number and response term.

```
500 GOSUB 50 : START = TIME            Start latency timer.
510 I$ = INKEY$ : IF I$ = "" THEN 510  Endless loop until keypress.
520 GOSUB 50 : LAX = TIME-START        Assign value to latency.
530 NI = VAL(I$)                       Convert to numeric.
```

APPLE IIe program segment	notes

```
...all the above except...

405 HOME
407 INPUT "PRESS <RETURN> TO START";R$  Subject clears keyboard as
410 HOME                                   trial starts.

500 GOSUB 50 : START = TIME
510 KEY = PEEK (-16384)                 Keystroke entry routine
512 POKE -16368,0                          (chapter 6).
514 IF KEY > 127 THEN 518               If new key has been pressed.
516 GOTO 510
518 I$ = CHR$(KEY-128)                  Convert keystroke to string.

...continue program...
```

Here are the major segments of this program. Stimulus and response terms are read and assigned to array elements. A trial loop starts, and each stimulus term is presented (in the order that it was read—thus, the sequence bias). Then, an inner response-term loop starts and presents each response option (also in the order that it was read, compounding the sequence bias). Your goal is to make stimulus term choice random, and sequence of response terms random.

What Original Information Must Be Maintained Following Randomization?   This is a critical section, so study it with care. When you randomize a list of items, you jumble their sequence. But let's say that a subject then selects item number four (whatever that may be) as a response. After randomization, how does your program "know" which of the original items is represented by the response *four*? There is a solution.

Your program must store the original item labels along with the production of a random number. In the PAIRED ASSOC TEST program, this feature is critical to knowing which stimulus term was selected at random and which response term was selected during the recognition test. As you know from running the program in its preliminary form, the subject is required to press a number key between 1 and 5 to indicate the match of a response term to a stimulus term. Since both the stimulus and response terms are displayed in a random order, you have to also keep a record of their *original* list, or array, positions (the subscript values).

You'll be using a simple variable to store the original position of the stimulus term selected at random because only one stimulus variable is displayed on a given trial. But in the case of response terms you'll use another array to store the original list positions. An array is required because all response terms are displayed on a given trial.

When you check out the randomization routines listed below, be very careful to pick out how and where this original information is stored for later use.

PAIRED ASSOC TEST PROGRAM: Adding the Randomization Routines

IBM PC and Apple IIe program segment	notes
...within trial loop above...	

412 H = N : L = 1
413 RAX = INT ((H-L+1)*RND(1))+L
414 CT(RAX) = CT(RAX) + 1
415 IF CT(RAX) > 1 THEN 413
	Begin a randomization
	   routine based on H = N;
	      N = number of trials.
	Note use of CT array.

416 SS$ = ST$(RAX) : SP = RAX	SS$ is the randomly chosen
	   stimulus term; SP is the
	   original array element
	   where SS$ was located.

420 PRINT ,SS$ 430 PRINT	Display randomly chosen stimulus term.

435 FOR G = 1 TO N
436 CR(G) = 0
437 NEXT G
	Start a loop based on N
	Set these array elements to 0.
	   before next set of R terms
	   is randomly chosen.

440 FOR J = 1 TO N	Start response term loop.

442 H = N : L = 1
443 RAX = INT ((H-L+1)*RND(1))+L
444 CR(RAX) = CR(RAX) + 1
445 IF CR(RAX) > 1 THEN 443
	Begin a randomization
	   routine based on H = N;
	      N also = number of pairs.
	Note use of CR array.

446 RR$ = RT$(RAX) : RP(J) = RAX	RR$ is the randomly chosen
	   response term; RP(J) is
	   original array element
	   where RR$ was located.

450 PRINT ,J;" ";RR$ 460 NEXT J	Displays item number and response term.
...continue program...	

TRS-80 program segment	notes
413 RAX = RND(H)	

I have stopped abruptly at the point where the subject is about to indicate a selection response. Now take a close look back over the randomization routines.

Randomizing the Stimulus Terms.   At line 412 I begin the process of selecting a trial at random. The CT array keeps track of those random numbers that have already been used (remember, there will be five trials). Line 416 is critical. In order for the program to know which of the *original* stimulus terms is now assigned to SS$, the corresponding random number (which was used as an array subscript) must be saved. It was assigned to *SP*. When it comes time to reference an element of a raw data array, you'll use *SP* as the subscript for the stimulus term: ST$(*SP*). And of course I display SS$ in line 420.

Randomizing the Response Term List.   Next, beginning at line 442, is the randomization routine for the display of the five stimulus terms. These are the subject's choice options in the memory-matching task. The CR array (different from the CS array) is used to prevent duplicate random numbers. RR$ is a randomly selected response term. The process repeats five times (*N* equals 5). Again, line 446 is critical. The RP array (a new array) is used to store the *original* location in the response term list (the RT$ array) from which the item was chosen. This piece of information is required to decode the subject's response. The subject will simply type one of the number keys representing a value of *J* (one through five), but (and this is a big but), RT$(*J*) is not the response term selected (because of jumbling by randomization).

Next, I'll show the keyboard input routines from the program and add a statement that will automatically determine which response actually was selected.

PAIRED ASSOC TEST PROGRAM: Revised Keyboard Input Routines

IBM PC and TRS-80 program segment	notes
500 GOSUB 50 : START = TIME	Start latency timer.
510 I$ = INKEY$: IF I$ = "" THEN 510	Endless loop until keypress.
520 GOSUB 50 : LAX = TIME-START	Assign value to latency.
530 NI = VAL(I$)	Convert choice to numeric.
560 RI = RP(NI)	Convert choice to original subscript value used in ST$ array.

APPLE IIe program segment	notes
405 HOME	
407 INPUT "PRESS <RETURN> TO START";R$	Subject clears keyboard as
410 HOME	trial starts.

```
500 GOSUB 50 : START = TIME
510 KEY = PEEK (-16384)            Keystroke entry routine
512 POKE -16368,0                    (chapter 6).
514 IF KEY > 127 THEN 518          If new key has been pressed.
516 GOTO 510
518 I$ = CHR$(KEY-128)             Convert keystroke to string.

530 NI = VAL(I$)                   Convert to numeric.

560 RI = RP(NI)                    Convert choice to original
                                     subscript value used in
                                     ST$ array.
```

I added something to the keyboard input routine. Look at line 560. A new variable appears there. *RI* is another version of the subject's response (it will be either 1, 2, 3, 4, or 5). Both *NI* and *RI* are variables representing the subject's response. How can that be? *NI* references the number of the response term displayed after randomization. *RI* references that same response term, but based on its original location in the ST$ array. *RI* will be used as a subscript during the printing of data.

Here is a sample screen produced by this program, with and without the randomization routines. Remember that the original order of items is: 1. HOUSE HARP, 2. HORSE HOT, 3. HIM HER, 4. HOWL HAPPY, and 5. HUNT HAWK.

```
                              screen

                HOUSE

                1. HARP
                2. HOT
                3. HER
                4. HAPPY
                5. HAWK
```

The screen above shows the display without the randomization routines. Now let's see it with the routines.

```
                              screen

                HOWL

                1. HER
                2. HARP
                3. HOT
                4. HAWK
                5. HAPPY
```

The stimulus term chosen is not necessarily the first one, and the response terms are displayed in a random order. The choice labels 1, 2, 3, 4, and 5 are not changed. When the subject responds on the above trial by pressing the ⟨5⟩ key (a correct choice), the program has to know that the subject picked HAPPY and not HAWK (subscript 5 in the original ST$ array). The program knows that 4 in the randomized list was RP(J) in the original list. What is RP(J) equal to? Why 5, of course. I can show the contents of the original ST$ array and the new RP array on the display screen to prove it to you.

```
          screen          |        notes

                          |    original        original position
                          |    ST$ array       values stored in
          HOWL            |                       RP array

          1. HER          |  ST$(1)="HARP"       RP(1)=2
          2. HARP         |  ST$(2)="HOT"        RP(2)=3
          3. HOT          |  ST$(3)="HER"        RP(3)=1
          4. HAWK         |  ST$(4)="HAPPY"      RP(4)=5
          5. HAPPY        |  ST$(5)="HAWK"       RP(5)=4

    (after randomization) |
```

The most critical variables in this revised PAIRED ASSOC TEST program are *SP* and *RI* (*RI* was derived from the RP array), because they allow the program to automatically decode the result of randomized sequences. This is quite logical. You can't jumble a series by randomization and expect to reference the original items afterward unless you retain the information on their original location or value. In the case of an array item subjected to randomization (as with ST$ and RT$ above), those locations are the numeric subscript values (1, 2, 3, 4, and 5).

You're convinced that this step is important, and you think you may understand it. But what is it important for? The answer is data storage or printing. For example, a raw data array cannot be filled with data using random values as the subscripts (or array elements). Raw data arrays require that the original information be retained so that responses are stored in the correct place. In the case of printing raw data, the same requirement holds. You must print raw data based on original array locations, not on the subscript values after randomization. So if you're using an output file method for your raw data table (which is easier, in this case) you'll still need to reference what I'm calling the *original information*. Now let's complete the revision of the PAIRED ASSOC TEST program, and you can see what all this means.

PAIRED ASSOC TEST PROGRAM: Revised Disk File Storage Routines

IBM PC program segment	notes
200 OPEN "TEST.OUT" FOR OUTPUT AS 3	Open the file before procedure begins
600 PRINT #3,	
610 PRINT #3, "TRIAL: ";I	
620 PRINT #3,	
630 PRINT #3, "STIMULUS TERM ",ST$(SP)	Note use of SP for
640 PRINT #3, "RESPONSE TERM ",RT$(SP)	original items.
650 PRINT #3, "R-TERM CHOICE ",RT$(RI)	Note use of RI.
660 PRINT #3, "RAW PROCESS TIME ",LAX	Raw data item.
670 IF RI = SP THEN COUNT = COUNT + 1	Checks for a correct choice based on original values; if yes, add 1 to COUNT.
680 PRINT #3, "NUMBER CORRECT ",COUNT	Summary data item.
690 PRINT #3, "% CORRECT ",(COUNT/I)*100	Summary data item.
700 SLAX = SLAX + LAX	Compute sum of all process times.
710 PRINT #3, "MEAN PROCESS TIME",SLAX/I	Summary data item.
800 NEXT I	End of trial.
810 CLOSE 3 : END	

TRS-80 program segment	notes
200 OPEN "O",3,"TEST/OUT"	

Apple IIe program segment	notes
200 D$ = CHR$(4)	Special character.
206 PRINT D$;"OPEN ";"TEST1.OUT"	OPEN creates the file.
208 PRINT D$;"WRITE ";"TEST1.OUT"	WRITE for output mode.
210 PRINT "PAIRED-ASSOCIATE DATA"	Title printed to file.
212 PRINT D$;"CLOSE ";"TEST1.OUT"	
580 PRINT D$;"APPEND ";"TEST1.OUT"	APPEND mode used.
582 PRINT D$;"WRITE ";"TEST1.OUT"	
600 PRINT	
610 PRINT "TRIAL: ";I	
620 PRINT	
630 PRINT "STIMULUS TERM";TAB(7);ST$(SP)	Note use of SP for
640 PRINT "RESPONSE TERM";TAB(7);RT$(SP)	original items.
650 PRINT "R-TERM CHOICE";TAB(7);RT$(RI)	Note use of RI.
660 PRINT "RAW PROCESS TIME";TAB(4);LAX	Raw data item.

```
670 IF RI = SP THEN COUNT = COUNT + 1          Checks for a correct
                                               choice based on
                                               original values;
                                               if yes, add 1 to
                                               COUNT.

680 PRINT "NUMBER CORRECT";TAB(6);COUNT        Summary data item.
690 PRINT "% CORRECT";TAB(11);(COUNT/I)*100    Summary data item.

700 SLAX = SLAX + LAX                          Compute sum of all
                                               process times.
710 PRINT "MEAN PROCESS TIME";TAB(3);SLAX/I    Summary data item.

720 PRINT D$;"CLOSE ";"TEST1.OUT"

800 NEXT I

810 HOME : END
```

The disk file storage routines for the revised PAIRED ASSOC TEST program must also incorporate the use of *SP* (rather than *I*) as the original stimulus and correct response term subscript. This is done at lines 630 and 640, which print the original stimulus and correct response term. *RI* (rather than *NI*) must be used to print the actual response term chosen on the trial. Furthermore, both *RI* and *SP* must be compared (rather than *NI* and *I*) for the program to determine if the response was correct.

Note the use of the TAB function in the Apple IIe disk output file routine above. TAB in that situation adds spaces to the last item printed. It does not seek a specified column number on the line.

Conclusions on the PAIRED ASSOC TEST Revision. Randomization of a sequence of events or items is a difficult process to manipulate mentally. It is important to develop work habits that use concrete aids to understanding, such as the screen diagrams presented above. When the program is being developed, you can draw these diagrams yourself to plot exactly what you expect your display to look like. In addition, randomization routines depend upon your ability to see the list or sequence in two forms. The first form is, of course, the *original* list or sequence. The second form is produced *after randomization*. You must develop the ability to keep these different forms straight. Pictures, diagrams, and tables that show the translation of one form to the other will be helpful.

Closure

Working with independent variables and unbiased stimulus sequences is tricky business for the real-time computer programmer. But the monster is worth taming because, in doing so, you unlock the true potential of computer control in the behavioral research laboratory. Just keep in mind the basic schematic. Between-subjects IVs are best programmed through the use of program templates. Within-subjects IVs are best programmed through the use of a levels-of-IV outer loop and multiple sets of DATA statements.

Mastery of this new material marks your graduation into the advanced class. From this point forward, I'll talk exclusively about specialized applications for real-time computer techniques. With this chapter you have completed the nuts and bolts objectives for this book.

Projects

On your particular system develop and store on disk the following templates: DOS clock and LVB Timer. Make sure the LVB Timer templates include all the necessary LVB parameter statements specific to each system.

Stand-alone Projects. Run an experiment on paired-associate learning using the two programs developed so far for this procedure: Phase 1 (learning) using the PAIRED ASSOC STUDY program, and Phase 2 (recognition) using the PAIRED ASSOC TEST program. Use the following nonsense syllables as the learning stimulus pairs:

CVC-VCV condition		CVC-CVC condition	
CIC	AVI	CIC	VIV
KUQ	ETO	KUQ	LAL
TIB	IBA	TIB	KIK
UEL	OME	UEL	MAF
FUM	OXU	FUM	HUJ

As you can see, these two conditions are levels of an independent variable. The two columns of stimulus terms are the same, while the two columns of response terms differ: VCV in list one as opposed to CVC in list two. The IV, then, is the composition of the response term syllables. Will VCV versus CVC in the response term position affect the memorability of these lists? You can determine that with your experiment. This project will use program templates because you are to have separate groups of subjects learn each list. In other words, the IV is a between-subjects factor.

Interface Projects. Complete the revised version of the TIME PERCEPTION program presented in the chapter. Program the procedure to store an organized raw data table in a two-dimension array for later printing.

PART FOUR

ADVANCED PROGRAMMING PROJECTS

Chapter 11 deals with special projects in verbal learning and memory. The chapter is designed to round out your real-time programming skills in this field, begun earlier with the PAIRED ASSOC program series. You will develop programs for serial learning and scanning of short-term memory. All the varied techniques presented throughout the book will come together in these advanced projects.

Chapter 12 moves you into the realm of computer graphics by teaching the techniques for low-resolution drawing on the computer screen. These principles are put into use with an advanced project on cognitive processes called the abstraction of visual prototypes procedure.

Chapter 13, the final chapter, caps your exposure to computer graphics by teaching high-resolution line drawing on the screen. You will develop an advanced program to draw lined figures as the stimuli in a preference for visual complexity experiment.

CHAPTER 11

Special Projects in Verbal Learning and Memory

Opening Remarks

As you've seen so far, the experimental procedures for the study of verbal learning, information processing, and cognitive psychology are particularly well suited to control by the computer. This is not a happy accident, but rather a direct byproduct of the way noncomputer procedures are developed in these fields. If there is a common thread among these procedures, it will certainly help your programming skills to know about it. Fortunately, you don't have to look too hard to see it. Just pick any classic verbal learning procedure from the subject matter of your general psychology course. Serial learning is a perfect choice.

The Common Units of Verbal Learning Procedures. As a programmer, your toughest task is to think like a psychologist. Just try it for a moment. In standard serial learning procedures a list of words is presented to a subject. The list is presented a number of times until the words are memorized in their original order. Two phases in the procedure are evident: the **stimulus presentation** phase, and the **memory assessment** phase. Am I suggesting that several different verbal learning procedures can be reduced (more or less) to just two different phases? Yes, I am!

From your knowledge of experimental design, you should recognize that independent variables will usually be manipulated during the stimulus phase, and dependent variables will be measured during the memory assessment phase.

The Common Approach to Programming. All of this apparent standardization is good news for programmers. Your decision sequence for outlining a verbal learning program will always take the same general form. Early decisions will pertain to the choice of independent variables and their levels. As you make these decisions, you will set a variety of parameters controlling stimulus presentation. Further decisions will pertain to the memory assessment phase, and will determine what form the measurement of memory will take.

Goals of This Chapter. In this chapter I will profile two separate but (as you have just learned) related procedures for the study of human memory and information processing—serial learning and the scanning of short-term memory (the Sternberg procedure). You will be developing real-time control programs for each procedure. In addition, you should come away with a logical framework for programming translations of a wide range of verbal learning, memory, and information processing procedures.

PROGRAMMING EXAMPLE: Serial Learning

Essential Features of Serial Learning. First of all, **serial learning,** by definition, involves the memory of a specific sequence of items. The items may be nonsense syllables, letters, words, sentences, or any verbal string. I am, of course, referring to the stimulus presentation phase of the procedure, when I talk about to-be-learned items. There may also be more than one list of items in an experiment. For example, when the independent variable is the imagery value of words, list 1 might contain only words of high imagery, while list 2 might contain only words of low imagery (imagery norms have been published for a wide variety of words). Maybe your hypothesis would be that the high-imagery list will be more completely learned than the low-imagery list. Which brings me to the memory assessment phase. Given that you can program the display of two serial lists, how can you program the measurement of serial memory? That question will be answered shortly.

Stimulus Presentation Phase: DATA Statements. As always, the actual stimuli to be used by the program will be located in DATA statements placed toward the top of the program. A serial word list requires a number of parameters: (a) the number of items in the list, (b) the duration that each item is displayed, (c) the time interval between the display of each item, and (d) the time interval between the end of the stimulus presentation phase and the onset of the memory assessment phase (the retention interval). These are parameters because they must be known in order for the procedure to work. However, each one could easily be the basis for an independent variable. Whatever the case, these values must be present in DATA statements. These data items, along with the actual words to be learned, will comprise a unit of stimulus information.

Let's talk for a minute about trials. It certainly is easy to imagine a learning experiment with more than one trial. Multiple trials pose no special problem for the programmer. In fact, you've already handled that situation. In the examples to follow I'll use a multiple trial procedure, but for the sake of example, I'll include only stimulus units sufficient for two trials.

```
SERIAL LEARNING: Organizing the Stimuli
```

program segment	notes
...clock reset, etc...	Different by system.
...clock subroutine...	
200 DATA 2	Number of trials.
210 DATA 6, 2, 3, 10	Number of items, item duration inter-item interval, and retention interval.
220 DATA "CAT","TOT","DOG"	The item series for trial 1.
230 DATA "BAT","HOG","BOP"	
240 DATA "JOT","GAB","SAD"	The item series for trial 2.
250 DATA "WET","MOP","PUT"	
300 READ NT, NI, DI, DP, DM	Where NT is number of trials, NI is number of items, DI is duration of item, DP is duration of pause between each item, and DM is duration of pause before memory testing.

Stimulus Presentation Phase: Trial Loop. The READ statement at line 300 in the program assigns the parameter values to variables in preparation for starting the trial loop. The trial loop itself is one of the busier segments of the program. It must include (a) an inner item loop to display each item, (b) the centering routine, and (c) two separate interval timers.

SERIAL LEARNING: Programming the Presentation Trial Loop

IBM PC program segment	notes
350 WIDTH 40	IBM PC version only.
400 FOR I = 1 TO NT	Start trial loop.
500 CLS	IBM PC version only.
510 INPUT "HIT <RETURN> TO START";Z$	Allows time to prepare test.
520 CLS	
540 FOR J=1 TO NI	Start item loop.
560 READ W$	Get verbal item.
570 L$(J) = W$	Store original items in original order in a one dimension array.
600 L = LEN(W$)	Begin centering routine
610 HL = INT(L/2)	(see chapter 7).
620 TARG = (40/2)-HL	
630 LOCATE 12,TARG	IBM PC version only.
640 PRINT W$	End of centering routine.
700 GOSUB 50 : START = TIME	Interval timer: duration
710 GOSUB 50	of exposure to item
720 IF TIME < START + DI THEN 710	(see chapter 5).
730 CLS	
800 GOSUB 50 : START = TIME	Interval timer: pause
810 GOSUB 50	between items.
820 IF TIME < START + DP THEN 810	
850 NEXT J	Completes item loop.
900 GOSUB 50 : START = TIME	Interval timer: pause
910 GOSUB 50	before memory assessment.
920 IF TIME < START + DM THEN 910	

...to be continued...

TRS-80 program segment	notes
...same as above except...	
630 PRINT @ (12,TARG*2),;	Moves cursor to line 12, target column.

Equivalencies: IBM PC	TRS-80
CLS	CLS : PRINT CHR$(23);

Apple IIe program segment	notes
...same as above except...	
630 VTAB 12 : HTAB TARG	

Equivalencies: IBM PC	Apple IIe
CLS	HOME

You'll notice that the outer trial loop is still open in the segments shown above. That's because the trial isn't over yet! After the inner item loop completes, and all verbal stimuli have been presented, the program proceeds to the memory assessment phase. This phase will also occur within the trial loop.

Memory Assessment Phase. Think for a moment about how you can measure serial learning and the typical serial position effects. Since the memory for serial position is the critical feature I want to record, I'll choose a recognition test where the subject is prompted with a word from the list and required to assign a number representing its *original* serial position. So you don't want to present the items in the original order, you want to randomize the order. Randomizing the order of verbal items simply means sequencing the numbers 1–6 at random since these are the subscripts of the L$ array (see line 570 above).

First, open a second inner item loop during the memory assessment phase to present each of the original items in a random sequence. After each item is presented, the subject will be asked to type the original ordinal position (1, 2, 3, etc.) for the item. This piece of information will serve as the raw data from the serial memory for the list. Remember, since subjects are prompted with the actual item, this is a recognition test. The raw data, then, will be in the range 1–*NI*, the number of items. What to *do* with the raw data comes next; first, you have to obtain it.

SERIAL LEARNING: Memory Assessment -- Random Selection of Items
and Subject Memory Response

IBM PC program segment	notes
940 FOR G = 1 TO NI 942 CR(G) = 0 : NEXT G	Required as preparation for the random routine.
950 FOR J=1 TO NI 960 CLS	Start item loop again.
1000 H = NI : L = 1 1010 RAX = INT ((H-L+1)*RND(1))+L 1020 CR(RAX) = CR(RAX) + 1 1030 IF CR(RAX) > 1 THEN 1010	Random numbers between 1 and NI (no. of items). Reject RAX if already used.
1100 PRINT ,"POSITION" : PRINT 1110 PRINT L$(RAX);	Semicolon used to prevent return to left margin.
1120 FOR K=1 TO NI 1130 PRINT ,K : NEXT K 1140 PRINT 1150 INPUT "TYPE CORRECT POSITION ";P 1155 CLS	K loop prints numbers 1-NI. P will be the number the subject "assigns" as serial position for L$(RAX); subject must press <return>.

```
1160 IF P = RAX THEN COUNT = COUNT + 1    COUNT will be the number of
                                          times the subject matches
                                          correctly from memory.
...to be continued...
```

TRS-80 program segment	notes

```
...same as above except...

1000 H = NI : L = 1                       Random numbers between 1
1010 RAX = RND(H)                             and NI (no. of items).
```

Equivalencies: IBM PC	TRS-80
CLS	CLS : PRINT CHR$(23);

Apple IIe program segment	notes

```
...same as above except...
```

Equivalencies: IBM PC	Apple IIe
CLS	HOME

I stopped just short of the part of the program where the raw data are stored. You will want to store these data in a disk file. I hope you've noticed how this new program is taking you back and forth through the various procedures we've covered. I want to bring all your knowledge of real-time programming together.

Memory Assessment Phase: Storage of Raw Data.   The first step is, of course, to open a disk file. On the IBM PC and TRS-80 the OPEN statement can occur only once toward the top of the program, and before any statements that are part of the experimental procedure. On the Apple IIe there will also be an OPEN statement near the top of the program. However, there will have to be an APPEND statement at the point just before the actual data are printed into the disk file. These are simply the system differences covered earlier in Chapter 9. Let's first accomplish the initial, and on some systems only, file OPEN statement.

```
SERIAL LEARNING: Raw Data Disk File OPEN Statement
```

IBM PC program segment	notes

```
320 INPUT "ENTER DISK FILE NAME ";F$      Must conform to system rules.
330 OPEN F$ FOR OUTPUT AS 3               Output mode; channel #3.
340 PRINT #3, "SERIAL LEARNING DATA:"     Prints a "heading" in the
342 PRINT #3,                                 disk file.
```

TRS-80 program segment	notes
320 INPUT "ENTER DISK FILE NAME ";F$	Must conform to system rules.
330 OPEN "O",3,F$	Output mode; channel #3.
340 PRINT #3, "SERIAL LEARNING DATA:"	Prints a "heading" in the
342 PRINT #3,	disk file.

Apple IIe program segment	notes
310 D$ = CHR$(4)	Special control character.
320 INPUT "ENTER DISK FILE NAME ";F$	
330 PRINT D$;"OPEN ";F$	
335 PRINT D$;"WRITE ";F$	Output mode.
340 PRINT "SERIAL LEARNING DATA:"	Prints a "heading" in the
342 PRINT	disk file.
345 PRINT D$;"CLOSE ";F$	Closes file.

Line 345 in the Apple IIe segment may look strange, but it's required for what I want to do. Simply put, I'm closing the disk file after only printing a short text heading. That's because I will want to open it again later in APPEND mode. No such worries on the IBM PC or TRS-80.

Next, try to see where you are in the program. I have completed the stimulus presentation phase and the memory assessment phase. Each of these phases is represented within the trial loop. I am now still inside the second inner item loop of the memory assessment phase. After each response by the subject, judging the original serial position of the item, that data must be stored. So you are ready to store that data on disk.

What exactly do you want to store? You want to know the subject's match to the test item, P in line 1150. You also want to know the correct item at that serial position. And after all the items have been tested, you want to know how many correct matches were made.

SERIAL LEARNING: Printing Raw Data Into a Disk File

IBM PC and TRS-80 program segment	notes
1300 PRINT #3, I,L$(RAX),P,L$(P)	Trial no., test item, subject's position response, original item at that position.
1400 NEXT J	Completes the test loop.
1500 PRINT #3, "TRIAL","TEST ITEM",	
1510 PRINT #3, "RESPONSE","ORIGINAL"	
1520 PRINT #3,	

```
1530 PRINT #3, "TRIAL";I;"MATCHES=";COUNT
1540 PRINT #3,
1550 COUNT=0                          Set equal to 0 before next
                                      trial.
1600 NEXT I

2000 CLOSE 3 : CLS : END
```

Apple IIe program segment	notes

```
1200 PRINT D$;"APPEND ";F$        Opens file for append mode.
1210 PRINT D$;"WRITE ";F$

1300 PRINT "TRIAL";TAB(10);I       Trial number.
1302 PRINT "TEST ITEM";TAB(6);L$(RAX)  Prints test item.
1304 PRINT "RESPONSE";TAB(7);P      Prints subject's position
                                    response.
1306 PRINT "POSITION";TAB(7);L$(P)  Prints original item at
                                    that position.
1310 PRINT
1320 PRINT D$;"CLOSE ";F$

1400 NEXT J                         Completes the test loop.

1500 PRINT D$;"APPEND ";F$         Opens file for append mode.
1510 PRINT D$;"WRITE ";F$

1520 PRINT "MATCHES=";TAB(7);COUNT
1530 PRINT "--------------------------"
1540 PRINT D$;"CLOSE ";F$
1550 COUNT=0                        Set equal to 0 before next
                                    trial.
1600 NEXT I

2000 HOME : END
```

No, your eyes do not deceive you. That END statement in line 2000 means it's all over. Don't forget to save this program, and don't forget that your raw data are in a disk file. If you've forgotten how to print the contents of disk files, refer back to Chapter 9.

The section above on printing to a disk output file on the Apple IIe required that print zones be programmed using the STR$, LEN, and TAB functions. These routines were first introduced in Chapter 9. You may also need to reread those sections. You may recall that the TAB function used in a disk output file does not seek a specific column on the line. Instead, TAB adds a specific number of spaces after the previous item.

Closure on the SERIAL LEARNING Program. This program is more flexible than you might think. First of all, you structure the subject's experience by organizing the DATA statements at the beginning of the program. For instance, you could study transfer of training or interference effects by placing different lists in different trial positions in the DATA statements. That would be a within-subjects factor. The list parameters are each the basis for an independent variable. For instance, you have a time delay before the memory assessment phase. This is commonly termed the **retention interval,** since it determines how long the memory must be held before the recognition test. Different values in the DATA statements will determine different retention intervals in the program. If this is a between-subjects variable, use your skills with program templates (Chapter 10) to duplicate the SERIAL LEARNING program and change DATA statements to produce as many versions as you have levels of retention interval. Different groups of subjects will then be tested with different versions of the program.

The point of this lesson and the development of the SERIAL LEARNING program above is to give you some perspective on the entire process of translating an experimental procedure into a real-time control program that will execute it. Another example follows.

PROGRAMMING EXAMPLE: Scanning of Short-Term Memory (Sternberg)

Essential Features of the Scanning Procedure.   When the study of memory goes beyond amount of material recalled, it usually finds itself pondering methods of recall. The question of how information is processed is one of the enduring goals of recent research on human learning and memory. Within short-term memory (STM), a scanning procedure has been hypothesized to show that the amount and type of information to be processed determines the rate of processing. According to this approach, the number of items in a list will determine how fast you can answer a question about the items.

This procedure allows for the study of some interesting independent variables. For example, you can vary the type of question the subject must answer about the items in the list. What difference should that make? Well, suppose that you present a list of concrete nouns for a brief amount of time: CLOCK, MOUNTAIN, RIVER, FOREST, ELEVATOR, BOAT, PALLET. Next, you immediately ask the subject to answer one of two questions about the word VALLEY (this is called the *probe* word): Did the list contain an antonym, or did it contain another word that had a similar sound? One of the questions requires the analysis of meaning, whereas the other requires only analysis of physical-phonetic attributes. Also remember that the subject is given only a brief exposure to the original list (let's say only two seconds for the seven words). Then the probe is presented. Would you say that the physical question will be answered more quickly than the semantic? Most people would, since the subject is given only a quick "snapshot" exposure to the list.

On the other hand, you might contend that the subject's processing speed would depend upon where in the list the key word was located. For example, here are two lists:

List 1: CLOCK, MOUNTAIN, RIVER, FOREST, ELEVATOR, PALLET, BOAT

List 2: CLOCK, PALLET, RIVER, FOREST, ELEVATOR, MOUNTAIN, BOAT

The difference between the two lists is in the location of key words MOUNTAIN and PALLET (referring back to the two types of questions). If the physical question is answered faster for list 2 than for list 1, the subject did not scan the entire list, but instead stopped as soon as the key word (PALLET) was found. So this procedure can be used to study scanning methods in STM. And how about this? Will the physical question for list 2 be answered faster than the semantic question for list 1? Does it take more effort to scan for meaning than for appearance or sound? If these issues are interesting to you, the upcoming programming example will allow you to pursue answers in your personal laboratory.

Stimulus Presentation Phase: DATA Statements. It should be obvious that the lists above will be represented in DATA statements at the top of the program. However, the real challenge is in determining the parameters that will control the MEMORY SCANNING program. Actually, there is good correspondence among different procedures. For example, certain of the parameters in the serial learning procedure are also found here in the memory scanning procedure: (a) number of trials (lists), (b) number of items per list, (c) duration of exposure to the list, and (d) retention interval for the list. There will be additional parameters that are unique to the memory scanning procedure: (e) the type of question—semantic or physical, (f) the probe word, and (g) the correct answer to the question—*yes* or *no*.

In addition, you will have to deal with the problem of experimental design. How many independent variables does this experiment actually have? Well, first I am manipulating the type of question: semantic or physical. I am also manipulating the position of the key word (the target word) in the list: second or sixth. This arrangement can best be shown in a 2 × 2 table of conditions:

Position of Target

	Second	Sixth
Semantic		
Physical		

Type of Question

You should hesitate to make this study completely within-subjects, requiring that all subjects receive all conditions. If the same person had to switch back and forth between semantic and physical questions, a degree of confusion might result that would carry over from trial to trial. This point is debatable, but you have to draw lines somewhere. So, I'll make *type of question* a between-subjects factor, and *position of target* a within-subjects factor. In terms of programming, this decision means that two programs are required. One can be the template for the other, however, with only changes in DATA statements required to make the transformation.

Since the position of target is within-subjects, DATA statements will have to reflect this factor. Two kinds of lists will appear throughout: lists with targets in the second position and lists with targets in the sixth position. The placement of these lists might be counterbalanced. In any case, only two trials will be included in the programming example below. The actual program would have to contain multiple trials. The program example below will pertain to the semantic test condition and the antonym question. The finished program will then be used as a template to develop the second program for the physical-phonetic condition (the similar sound question).

MEMORY SCANNING: Organizing the Stimuli

program segment	notes
...clock reset, etc... ...clock subroutine...	Different by system.
200 DATA 2 202 DATA 7, 2, 5	Number of trials. Number of items, list duration, retention interval.
210 DATA "MEAN THE OPPOSITE OF -- "	Operative part of the "semantic" question.
220 DATA "CLOCK","MOUNTAIN","RIVER" 222 DATA "FOREST","ELEVATOR","PALLET"	List 1.

224 DATA "BOAT"	
226 DATA "VALLEY"	List 1 probe.
228 DATA 2	Probe position; 2 = second.
229 DATA "Y"	Correct answer.
230 DATA "BOLT","ANCHOR","MAPLE"	List 2.
232 DATA "CRAFT","BUZZARD","DARKNESS"	
234 DATA "WOLF"	
236 DATA "LIGHT"	List 2 probe.
238 DATA 6	Probe position; 6 = sixth.
239 DATA "Y"	Correct answer.
300 READ NT, NI, DL, DM	Where NT is number of trials, NI is number of items, DL is duration of list, and DM is duration of pause before memory test (retention interval).
310 READ Q$	Operative part of question.

Stimulus Presentation Phase: Trial Loop. As usual, there will be an outer trial loop, then an inner item loop to complete the stimulus presentation phase. Certainly these are the major organizational components required for this program. The item loop is going to function very much as it did in the SERIAL LEARNING program. A series of items will be read and displayed. However, this time the items will be on the screen all together, not one at a time. Then, after a duration of exposure (DL), the screen will be cleared. After the retention interval (DM) the memory assessment phase will begin. Let's get the MEMORY SCANNING program to that point.

MEMORY SCANNING: Programming the Presentation Trial Loop

IBM PC program segment	notes
350 WIDTH 40	IBM PC version only.
400 FOR I = 1 TO NT	Start trial loop.
500 CLS	IBM PC version only.
510 INPUT "PRESS <RETURN> TO START";Z$	<ENTER> key on TRS-80.
520 CLS	
540 FOR J=1 TO NI	Start item loop.
560 READ W$	Get verbal item.
600 L = LEN(W$)	Begin centering routine.
610 HL = INT(L/2)	
620 TARG = (40/2)-HL	
630 LOCATE J,TARG	IBM PC version only.
640 PRINT W$	End of centering routine.
700 NEXT J	Completes item loop.

```
800 GOSUB 50 : START = TIME          Interval timer: duration
810 GOSUB 50                            of exposure to list.
820 IF TIME < START + DL THEN 810
830 CLS


900 GOSUB 50 : START = TIME          Interval timer: pause
910 GOSUB 50                            before memory assessment.
920 IF TIME < START + DM THEN 910

...to be continued...
```

TRS-80 program segment   notes

...same as above except...

630 PRINT @ (J,TARG*2),;

Equivalencies: IBM PC   TRS-80

               CLS   CLS : PRINT CHR$(23);

Apple IIe program segment   notes

630 VTAB J : HTAB TARG

Equivalencies: IBM PC   Apple IIe

               CLS   HOME

Let's run down the key concepts thus far. First, look at line 630 of the IBM PC version. We are printing each item on line J of the screen. J will, of course, increment from 1 to *NI* as the item loop progresses. The effect will be to print each of the seven items on a separate line. Remember, unlike the SERIAL LEARNING program, you want *all* items in the list exposed at once. Notice also how this is handled for the TRS-80 (line 630). Again, the effect is to print all items, one under the other. Naturally, in order to accomplish this effect, the NEXT J (line 700) must come before the interval timers, and it does. This is another major difference in relation to the SERIAL LEARNING program. Even with these differences, you can't help but appreciate the strong similarity between the two programs. This is all part of the point I'm trying to make about the stimulus presentation phase—that it is fairly standard from procedure to procedure.

Memory Assessment Phase.   Memory assessment in the MEMORY SCANNING program comes in two forms (two dependent variables). The first measure of memory is the *accuracy* of the response to the question about the probe. The second, and the more important of the two, is the *amount of time* it takes to respond. Processing time is the critical measure because it represents how long the subject spent scanning the memory representation of the list. Process timers were discussed first in Chapter 5.

The memory assessment phase begins with the presentation of the question and probe. Then the ball is in the subject's court. The subject must answer *yes* or *no*. In order to reduce the subject's response requirement, you'll use a keystroke entry routine (rather than an INPUT statement, as in the SERIAL LEARNING program). Remember that keystroke entry routines (covered in Chapter 6) allow you to specify just one key—⟨Y⟩ or ⟨N⟩—as the subject's response.

MEMORY SCANNING: Memory Assessment -- Probe Prompt and Keystroke
               Entry

IBM PC and TRS-80 program segment	notes
1000 PRINT "DID A WORD ";Q$;	Print question.
1010 READ P$: PRINT P$;"? (Y/N)";	Get and print probe.
1100 GOSUB 50 : START = TIME	Start process timer.
1110 R$=INKEY$: IF R$="" THEN 1110	Keystroke routine.
1120 IF R$="Y" THEN 1150	
1130 IF R$="N" THEN 1150	
1140 GOTO 1110	Reject all but <Y> or <N>.
1150 GOSUB 50 : PT = TIME - START	Compute process time
	(response latency).
...to be continued...	

Apple IIe program segment	notes
...all the above except...	
1110 KEY = PEEK (-16384)	Keystroke entry routine
1112 POKE -16368,0	(chapter 6).
1114 IF KEY > 127 THEN 1118	If new key has been pressed.
1116 GOTO 1110	
1118 R$ = CHR$(KEY-128)	Convert keystroke to string.

Keystroke entry varies among the three systems. However, the effect is the same. R$ (after line 1120) will be either *Y* or *N*. PT (line 1150) will be the amount of time it took to make a response. At this point you're ready to consider raw data measures and how to manage them.

Memory Assessment Phase: Raw Data Array. I'm going to take a different tack with this program by not immediately printing into a disk file after each trial. Instead, I'll store raw data in arrays for later printing. Why do it this way? First and foremost, to give you the experience of both data storage methods. Secondly, because the research design lends itself easily to array storage.

You have only one independent variable manipulated within this program (because the program is designed for only the semantic question group). That variable is the position of the key item in the list: second or sixth (of course, the subject will not be told where to expect the key item).

Look back at the DATA statements for a moment. Lines 228 and 238 provide a code that indicates which level of the position variable was in effect for a given trial. Now what could this code have to do with storing the raw data in arrays? Well, you can use the code to direct the program to separate array storage routines for each condition (position 2, position 6).

One problem raised by this approach, however, is the need for separate tracking of the two arrays as they are updated during the program. By that, I mean that a single trial loop won't be able to do the job, since *only one condition can be in effect on a given trial.* So, instead of referencing the elements of these data arrays with the trial loop variable, you'll use two additional variables to keep a separate count of trials in each condition. You'll see this clearly in the programming example below. Right now, I'll show you what arrays will be used for data storage.

MEMORY SCANNING: Arrays for Raw Data -- Response to the Probe

---

		One-Dimension Arrays	
		R2$	R6$
		position 2	position 6
Rows (trials)	1	R2$(1)	R6$(1)
	2	R2$(2)	R6$(2)
	..etc..		

MEMORY SCANNING: Arrays for Raw Data -- Processing Time (Latency)

		One-Dimension Arrays	
		T2	T6
		position 2	position 6
Rows (trials)	1	T2(1)	T6(1)
	2	T2(2)	T6(2)
	..etc..		

The R2$ and R6$ string arrays will hold the Y or N responses made after presentation of the probe (line 1110). Two numeric arrays, T2 and T6, will hold the processing time (response latency) required to answer the question posed by the probe (PT from line 1150).

It's true that there are only two trials in this programming example. In an actual experiment there would be multiple trials. In fact, there would be an equal number of second and sixth trials (the two types of lists). Also, you would have to counterbalance the order of lists as you enter them into the DATA statements.

However, 2 trials or 20, the raw data arrays will still work the same way. Just remember to use the proper DIM statement if you intend more than 10 trials.

And while I'm on the subject of arrays, I want you to store the correct answers to the probe question as well. Use the C2$ and C6$ arrays for these (Y or N characters) so that you can make comparisons to the obtained responses (these values are in DATA lists at lines 229 and 239 above).

MEMORY SCANNING: Arrays for Correct Answers

		One-Dimension Arrays	
		C2$	C6$
		position 2	position 6
Rows (trials)	1	C2$(1)	C6$(1)
	2	C2$(2)	C6$(2)
	..etc..		

Next, you need to assign all the necessary values to these arrays. Some will be read as part of the original DATA lists at the top of the program. Others will be obtained from variables defined during the test trial. All these operations occur within the trial loop and are repeated for each trial. As each trial is completed, two separate trial counters (variables) are maintained. These will be N2 for the position 2 condition and N6 for the position 6 condition.

MEMORY SCANNING: Raw Data Arrays

program segment	notes
1300 READ CODE	Get position code (2 or 6); see lines 228, 238.
1310 IF CODE = 6 THEN 1420	Differentiates code values.

```
1320 N2 = N2 + 1          Next section for "2" trial.
1330 R2$(N2) = R$         Increment trial counter.
1340 T2(N2) = PT          Store subject's response.
1350 READ C2$(N2)         Store process time.
1360 GOTO 1500            Read, store correct answer.

1420 N6 = N6 + 1          Next section for "6" trial.
1430 R6$(N6) = R$
1440 T6(N6) = PT
1450 READ C6$(N6)

1500 NEXT I
```

Line 1320 is important. You'll need to know what condition (represented by its CODE value) was in effect for each trial. That's because the data from each condition are stored in different arrays.

Memory Assessment Phase: Printing of Raw Data. For a change of pace, print the raw data on-line after the end of the experimental session. First, suspend the program with an INPUT statement to allow yourself time to debrief the subject. After you have escorted the person out of the lab, you can turn on the system line printer and start the printout by responding to the INPUT statement prompt. This won't be just any ordinary printout. You're going to put some summary statistics into it and make it show average response latency based on N2 or N6 trials for each of the two position conditions.

MEMORY SCANNING: Printing Raw Data From Arrays

IBM PC and TRS-80 program segment	notes

```
2000 CLS
2010 INPUT "SESSION OVER....";Z$     Halts program temporarily.

...when printer is ready, press <return>...

2100 LPRINT "MEMORY SCANNING: RAW DATA -- ACCURACY"
2110 LPRINT
2120 LPRINT "KEY WORD IN POSITION 2"
2130 LPRINT
2140 LPRINT "TRIAL","ANSWER"

2160 COUNT = 0                       To be used to count
                                     number correct.

2200 FOR I = 1 TO N2                 Start trial loop for
                                     condition 2.
2210 IF R2$(I)=C2$(I) THEN A$="RIGHT"
2220 IF R2$(I)<>C2$(I) THEN A$="WRONG"
2230 IF A$="RIGHT" THEN COUNT=COUNT+1
2240 LPRINT I,A$                     Trials within condition
                                     2 are labeled 1 - N2.
2280 NEXT I                          Complete trial loop.
```

```
2290 LPRINT "TOTAL=",COUNT
2310 LPRINT
2320 LPRINT "KEY WORD IN POSITION 6"
2330 LPRINT
2340 LPRINT "TRIAL","ANSWER"

2360 COUNT = 0                                To be used to count
                                              number correct.

2400 FOR I = 1 TO N6                          Start trial loop for
                                              condition 6.
2410 IF R6$(I)=C6$(I) THEN A$="RIGHT"
2420 IF R6$(I)<>C6$(I) THEN A$="WRONG"
2430 IF A$="RIGHT" THEN COUNT=COUNT+1
2440 LPRINT I,A$                              Trials within condition
                                              6 are labeled 1 - N6.
2480 NEXT I                                   Complete trial loop.

2490 LPRINT "TOTAL=",COUNT

2500 LPRINT
2510 LPRINT "----------------------"
2520 LPRINT
2600 LPRINT "MEMORY SCANNING: RAW DATA -- LATENCIES"

2610 LPRINT
2620 LPRINT "KEY WORD IN POSITION 2"
2630 LPRINT
2640 LPRINT "TRIAL","LATENCY"

2660 SUM = 0                                  To be used to compute
                                              mean latency.

2700 FOR I = 1 TO N2                          Start trial loop for
                                              condition 2.
2710 SUM = SUM + T2(I)                        Each latency is summed.
2740 LPRINT I,
2750 LPRINT USING "##.###";T2(I)             Print in column on decimal
                                              point.

2780 NEXT I                                   Complete trial loop.

2790 LPRINT "MEAN=",
2795 LPRINT USING "##.###";SUM/N2

2810 LPRINT
2820 LPRINT "KEY WORD IN POSITION 6"
2830 LPRINT
2840 LPRINT "TRIAL","LATENCY"

2860 SUM = 0                                  To be used to compute
                                              mean latency.

2900 FOR I = 1 TO N6                          Start trial loop for
                                              condition 6.
2910 SUM = SUM + T6(I)                        Each latency is summed.
2940 LPRINT I,
2950 LPRINT USING "##.###";T6(I)

2980 NEXT I                                   Complete trial loop.

2990 LPRINT "MEAN=",
2995 LPRINT USING "##.###";SUM/N6

3000 END
```

Apple IIe program segment	notes
...all the above except...	

```
2000 HOME
2050 PR# 1                                    Sends output to printer.
```

Equivalencies: IBM PC/TRS-80	Apple IIe
LPRINT (etc.)	PRINT (etc.)

```
2120 PRINT "TRIAL";TAB(10);"ANSWER"

2240 PRINT I;TAB(10);A$

2290 PRINT "TOTAL=";TAB(10);COUNT

2340 PRINT "TRIAL";TAB(10);"ANSWER"

2440 PRINT I;TAB(10);A$

2490 PRINT "TOTAL=";TAB(10);COUNT

2640 PRINT "TRIAL";TAB(10);"LATENCY"


2740 DE = 3 : NU = T2(I)
2742 RN = INT(NU * 10^DE + .5)/10^DE      Apple IIe rounding routine;
2750 PRINT I;TAB(10);RN                      see chapter 8.

2790 DE = 3 : NU = SUM/N2
2792 RN = INT(NU * 10^DE + .5)/10^DE
2795 PRINT "MEAN=";TAB(10);RN

2840 PRINT "TRIAL";TAB(10);"LATENCY

2940 DE = 3 : NU = T6(I)
2942 RN = INT(NU * 10^DE + .5)/10^DE
2950 PRINT I;TAB(10);RN

2990 DE = 3 : NU = SUM/N6
2992 RN = INT(NU * 10^DE + .5)/10^DE
2995 PRINT "MEAN=";TAB(10);RN

3000 PR#0 : END                            Restores output to screen.
```

Finally, note the use of the TAB function to format this on-line printout on the Apple IIe. Since it is an on-line printout and not disk file output, TAB seeks the column number specified in its parameter.

Altering the Program Template. Remember, what you have above is one of two programs necessary to do the experiment outlined. You still need to produce the version of MEMORY SCANNING that will ask the physical question about the probe. This is a simple exercise in program templates. First, SAVE the existing MEMORY SCANNING program using a separate name—for example, MS SEMANTIC. Be sure to follow system rules for file names. Next, make one change in the program to prepare it for the physical condition.

MEMORY SCANNING: Changing the Program Template

program segment	notes
215 DATA "HAVE A SOUND SIMILAR TO -- "	Operative part of the physical question.

That's it. Your experiment is ready to roll.

Closure on the MEMORY SCANNING Program. MEMORY SCANNING is your minithesis in real-time computers. It contains nearly all the tools you've worked on throughout the text. You have nested loops, interval timers, process timers, centering routines, 40-column screen, array storage, keystroke entry, computation of a mean, and rounding off of numbers. Once again, you've got yourself a very flexible program in MEMORY SCANNING, since it can work for any verbal stimuli.

Projects

Stand-alone Project. Design an experiment using the SERIAL LEARNING program from this chapter. Use two independent variables in a 2 × 2 between-subjects design. IV #1 is the time interval between items during the stimulus presentation phase. Its two levels are 2 and 10 seconds. IV #2 is the retention interval, with levels of 2 and 120 seconds. Develop a list of 10 concrete nouns as the stimuli. Use only one list (one trial).

Stand-alone Project. Design an experiment using the MEMORY SCANNING program from this chapter. Use two independent variables in a 2 × 2 mixed design. IV #1 is the between-subjects factor—the type of question about the probe (just as in the chapter example). IV #2 is the within-subjects factor—the retention interval at either 5 or 30 seconds. Develop 12 lists (12 trials), each with 7 concrete nouns. Make sure that half the answers to the probe question are correct if ⟨Y⟩ is given, and the other half are correct if ⟨N⟩ is given.

CHAPTER 12

Low-Resolution Graphics and a Special Project in Cognition

Computer Graphics in Real-Time Computer Applications

What Are Computer Graphics Good For?   No one has to remind you that computers can draw pictures. Some of the most sophisticated computer graphics are familiar to almost everyone in the form of computer games and video amusements. This text is not going to teach you those kinds of graphics capabilities for experimental psychology programs. Nevertheless, computer graphics are a part of real-time experimental control, and you will be developing graphics tools for your personal psychology laboratory.

According to your knowledge of experimental design, would you use computer graphics for an independent variable, dependent variable, or something else? In essence, you will use the computer graphics capability on your microcomputer to produce pictorial stimuli that will be varied according to some operational definition of a treatment factor.

Because you are now in the realm of pictures and images, you'll find yourself able to use the computer for more high-level research—namely, cognition and perception. The project you'll be programming for this chapter is a variation on Posner's abstraction of visual prototypes procedure. In Chapter 13, you'll tackle a program for Berlyne's experiment on preference for stimulus complexity.

Let's now look into the simplest kind of graphic stimulus a BASIC program can produce. I'll be talking first about **block graphics.** These are images on the video display that are predetermined by the circuitry within the computer system. Each system has a flexible block graphics capability.

ADVANCING BASIC: Block Graphics on the Apple IIe

The Low-resolution Grid.   In **low-res graphics** mode, where shapes of light rather than points of light are displayed, the Apple IIe screen takes on new dimensions. Up till now, you have programmed in text mode only, and used a 24-line × 40-column grid for the display of text. Now, in low-res graphics mode, you'll have a display divided into two parts: a grid for pictures and a grid for text. The picture space consists of a 40 × 40 grid. In this region, each grid **coordinate** represents a place on the screen where a graphic block image may be displayed. An individual coordinate is referenced by a column grid value and row grid value (e.g. 1,10 or 30,30). Look at the diagram of the low-res grid below.

LOW—RES GRID ON THE Apple IIe

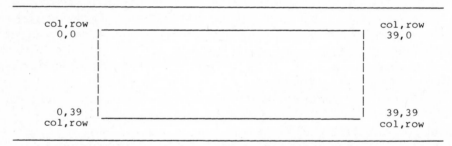

Each of the graphic blocks displayable on the grid is a small rectangular image on the screen. The blocks are about half as tall as text letters, which explains why the graphics grid contains 40 rows. If these block images are displayed in lines, they paint a fairly thick swath of color horizontally or vertically across the grid. I'm using the words *paint* and *color* loosely. I will not delve very deeply into the color-generating potential of any computer system. However, there is a color on the display screen at all times. When the screen is blank, it is black. When it contains text or graphics, it is amber, green, or white depending upon the type of video display in use.

The low-res grid also contains a 4-row × 40-column window for text at the bottom of the screen. You will make good use of this dual capability (graphics and text on the same screen) in Apple IIe low-res graphics. You invoke the low-res graphics mode by using the GR statement. You should immediately set a color using the COLOR statement. The COLOR statement has a numeric parameter that can range from 0 to 15. Just remember that 0 sets screen color to black. Black comes in handy when you want to erase graphics by drawing over a block or line using black color.

GR and COLOR STATEMENT

Apple IIe	notes
300 GR	Invokes low-res graphics, clears the 40 x 40 grid, leaves 4-line text window.
310 COLOR = 10	Sets color (on color monitors up to 16 colors can be used; on monochrome units each color value is a variation of a single hue.
312 HOME	Clears text window.

GR and COLOR must appear in the portion of the program that directly precedes graphics statements. GR must be followed by a COLOR statement whenever you clear the graphics grid. In other words, don't use GR alone.

The PLOT, HLIN, and VLIN Statements. PLOT puts a single block at a specified position within the grid. PLOT requires a column grid and a row grid parameter. HLIN and VLIN each require three parameters. Here are some examples.

LOW-RES GRAPHICS STATEMENTS AND THEIR PARAMETERS

Apple IIe	notes
400 PLOT 2,20	1st value: column grid location. 2nd value: row grid location.
410 HLIN 2,20 AT 10	1st value: beginning column on grid. 2nd value: ending column on grid. 3rd value: row on grid where line is drawn.

```
420 VLIN 2,20 AT 10              1st value: beginning row on grid.
                                 2nd value: ending row on grid.
                                 3rd value: column on grid where
                                 line is drawn.
```

The parameters for any of these graphics statements—COLOR, PLOT, HLIN, and VLIN—may be constants (as in the examples above), variables, expressions. Apple IIe low-res graphics is a very flexible part of Apple's BASIC language (Applesoft).

For a beginning programming example, let's do something with low-res graphics that is a component of the ABSTRACTING PROTOTYPES program to be covered later in the chapter. The problem is simple enough: write a program that will read a series of coordinates from DATA statements, then plot them within the low-res grid.

PROGRAMMING EXAMPLE: Drawing a Design with Graphic Blocks

Apple IIe program segment	notes
500 DATA 8	Signifies number of blocks in the design.
510 DATA 5,5, 10,5, 15,5	3 blocks drawn horizontally at row 5; 5 columns apart.
514 DATA 5,15, 10,15, 15,15	3 blocks drawn horizontally at row 15, 5 columns apart.
518 DATA 5,10	1 block completing left vertical side of design.
520 DATA 15,10	1 block completing right vertical side of design.
800 GR : COLOR = 10	Clear low-res grid.
805 READ NBLOCKS	Number of blocks.
810 FOR I = 1 TO NBLOCKS	Start a loop to draw blocks.
820 READ CG,RG : PLOT CG,RG	CG is column grid value, RG is row grid value.
830 NEXT I	

From this example you learn, first, that DATA statements are a convenient way to set column and row grid coordinate pairs. Next, a loop is a convenient way to draw the figure specified by the list of coordinates. But how did I get the square figure? It's all in which column and row grid coordinates you specify. As you specify these values, you can picture how the figure will take shape as it is being drawn on the 40 × 40 low-res grid. If you understand the grid, and the grid coordinate parameters, you can draw a variety of specific designs.

At this point the Apple IIe is still in graphics mode. This means, among other things, that *you cannot list the program using the entire screen.*

TURNING OFF GRAPHICS MODE WHILE PROGRAMMING

Apple IIe	notes
(]) TEXT : HOME	Invokes text mode and clears screen so that a program may be listed.

Typing these statements after the] prompt will allow you to return the computer to text mode and edit the program statements. Without these, you would only be able to work within the four lines of the small text window at the bottom of the low-res graphics grid.

ADVANCING BASIC: Block Graphics on the IBM PC and TRS-80

Blocks as Graphics Characters.   Low-res graphics on the IBM PC and TRS-80 does not involve a graphics mode per se, but instead deals with certain graphics characters that are displayed just like any letter or numeric character. This capability can be functionally similar to Apple IIe low-res graphics. I will focus on one particular graphics character: a solid block image given the ASCII code 219 on the IBM PC and 191 on the TRS-80. The other graphics characters and their ASCII codes may be obtained from the technical manuals.

The Block Graphics Grids.   On the IBM PC and TRS-80 you have two separate grid sizes available for low-res block graphics. (A graphics adapter card must be installed in your IBM PC for this to work.) That's because these systems support either a 40- or 80-column width in text mode, and block graphics is essentially done in text mode. You have 24 rows and either 40 or 80 columns, depending upon how your program sets width. I covered these width statements in Chapter 7, but I'll refresh your memory here.

CHANGING SCREEN TO 40-COLUMN WIDTH

IBM PC	TRS-80
110 WIDTH 40	110 CLS : PRINT CHR$(23);

CHANGING SCREEN TO 80-COLUMN WIDTH

IBM PC	TRS-80
110 WIDTH 80	110 CLS

Printing ASCII 219 and 191. You may remember ASCII codes from my coverage of them in Chapter 6 to detect presses on special keys. In Chapter 7 you learned how to sound the bell signal by using PRINT CHR$(7). The situation here is exactly the same in order to display the graphics block represented by ASCII 219 or 191.

PRINTING A BLOCK CHARACTER (ASCII 219 or 191)

IBM PC program segment	notes
100 BLOCK$ = CHR$(219)	Assigns code 219 to the string variable BLOCK$
110 WIDTH 40	Sets 40 columns.
120 KEY OFF	Turns off function key line.
510 PRINT BLOCK$;	Prints the graphics character at current cursor position.

TRS-80 program segment	notes
100 BLOCK$ = CHR$(191)	Assigns code 191 to the string variable BLOCK$
110 CLS : PRINT CHR$(23);	Sets 40 columns.
510 PRINT BLOCK$;	Prints the graphics character.

In line 100 above, you see a shortcut method for printing a given ASCII code. Since you'll find CHR$(219) to be bulky, simply assign the character (it's a string constant, after all) to a variable. Once that has been done, the variable can be printed whenever and wherever you want.

There are no specific statements to draw with these blocks. You have to print the block characters just as you would print a standard text character (a letter or numeral). The special programming problem you face here is how to position the cursor where you want it before printing the graphics character.

Positioning the Cursor on the IBM PC. On the IBM PC the LO-CATE statement (introduced in Chapter 4) will move the cursor to a specified row and column location. LOCATE also will work with variables such as the row and column parameters.

POSITIONING THE CURSOR BEFORE PRINTING AN IBM PC GRAPHICS CHARACTER

IBM PC program segment	notes
100 BLOCK$ = CHR$(219)	Specific block character.
110 WIDTH 40	Sets 40 columns.

```
120 KEY OFF                          Turns off function key line.

300 DATA 30,10                       Print at column 30, row 10.

400 READ CG,RG                       column and row grid values.

500 LOCATE RG,CG                     Row value first, then column.

540 PRINT BLOCK$;                    Graphic block displayed.
```

It's much the same on the TRS-80. However, you have to alter the PRINT @ statement to multiply the target column by 2 since you will be in 40-column mode (I introduced this catch in Chapter 7).

Positioning the Cursor on the TRS-80.   Imagine how the subject will feel as the cursor jumps around the screen during graphics printing. You can fix this potential problem by turning off the cursor. That's done by printing a special character function, CHR$(15); on the TRS-80. You can turn it back on again with CHR$(14);.

Let's say you wanted to display a horizontal line of blocks. Once you had printed the first block on the target row, you could continue to print on that row to draw the graphics line. Drawing a horizontal line would require that you use PRINT @ to place the cursor where you wanted to begin to draw. Then, using a loop, you could repeatedly draw blocks on the line. I am not going to incorporate line drawing in the programming example; you can pick up the fundamentals by experimenting. For the chapter programming assignments all you need to know is that PRINT @ will be used in roughly the same way as LOCATE on the IBM PC. To make this example more realistic, I'll read one pair of grid coordinates first.

POSITIONING THE CURSOR BEFORE PRINTING A TRS-80 GRAPHICS CHARACTER

TRS-80 program segment	notes
100 BLOCK$ = CHR$(191)	Specific block character.
110 CLS : PRINT CHR$(23);	Sets 40 columns.
120 PRINT CHR$(15);	Turns off cursor.
300 DATA 30,10	Print at column 30, row 10.
400 READ CG,RG	Column and row grid values.
500 PRINT @ (RG,CG*2),;	Times 2 required in 40-column mode.
540 PRINT BLOCK$;	Graphic block displayed.

By now it should be clear why you must multiply the column grid value CG by 2. It's required to use PRINT @ in 40-column mode. One more thing: If you want the cursor back on again for programming, simply type PRINT CHR$(14) with no line number.

Low-res Graphics and Text on the Same Screen.   The IBM PC (with graphics adaptor) and TRS-80 also allow both block graphics and standard text printing on the same screen. There is no text window per se. Simply move the cursor to the location desired and print the text desired. However, don't forget that your graphics grid is the same 24 × 40 or 24 × 80 arrangement used for displaying text. Don't send your cursor below row 24!

Programming a Concept Learning Procedure

Abstraction of Visual Prototypes.   One of the approaches taken in research on concept learning has been to test the ability to classify stimuli and assign them to categories. Presumably, once the fundamental categories have been identified, people can be given any new stimulus variation, and they will successfully assign it to an established grouping. The process of identifying a single category for a series of different stimuli has been referred to as the *abstraction of a prototype*. The entire process has been regarded as a model of how concepts are learned. The prototype itself is not part of the set of stimuli to be classified, yet it is represented in the cognitive process of the subject as the hypothetical average of all the various stimuli that were judged. Research on this phenomenon has been done by Posner and his associates. Your programming project will be to implement a real-time control program, using low-res graphics, that is derived, in part, from one of Posner's classic visual prototype procedures.

Broad Outline of the Procedure.   You'll begin by presenting two sets of designs on the graphics grid. Within each set, a specific stimulus design will be a distortion of a standard figure, either a square or a cross. To produce these distortions, you'll randomly select certain blocks to be moved off their original location in the standard figures. Obviously, if you distort only one block in a figure, the change will be minimal, making it easier to abstract a prototype (or classify individual stimuli within the same set). Under that condition the process of averaging many distortions should occur fairly quickly. On the other hand, if you distort many blocks, the abstraction process should take longer.

What is this abstraction process? Simply put, subjects must assign each stimulus to one of the two sets. In so doing, they indicate that as they become more familiar with the stimuli (the distorted designs), they are better able to determine which are in common with each other. It is specifically the prototype, or standard design, that is the common element. No subject will be shown this design, however.

The number of blocks that are distorted would make an appropriate independent variable in this procedure. Furthermore, the number of classification trials required to reach complete success in categorizing distortions would make a good dependent variable. For example, to the untrained eye these designs will look like scattered patterns of blocks. However, with experience, each subject will get better at the classification process, and eventually see every distortion as a stimulus from one of the two possible categories. At the point where this performance occurs, a prototype has been abstracted and a concept has been formed.

Specific Steps for the Programmer.   This is a challenging program to organize, but I'll try to keep it simple. First of all, what specific stimuli does the program require in order to work? There will be two sets of distorted designs based on two separate standards. Although the standards will never be drawn, their coordinate pairs are required in order to make the distortions. As a result, each standard design must be represented in the program by its corresponding grid coordinate pairs (column, row) provided in DATA statements.

Next, how do you determine the specific distortion? You will manipulate the *number* of distorted blocks, not which blocks are distorted. You'll determine the latter by random selection (using routines similar to those covered in Chapter 10). I've designed this IV to be a between-subjects factor. That means you'll have *separate* versions of the program, one for each level of the IV. Let's have two levels of distortion: two blocks out of eight (25%), and four blocks out of eight (50%). Remember, the level of distortion depends upon how many blocks are moved from their original location in the standard figure. So now you know what the independent variable will be, and what the two experimental conditions are.

How will the program know which distortion (set #1 or #2) to display on which trial? Again, it will be determined at random. You'll pick, at random, whether to display a distortion of the square (set #1) or the cross (set #2). It'll be like flipping a coin.

What kind of distortion will actually be programmed? You'll distort by either adding or subtracting two units from the grid value. The direction (addition or subtraction) will be determined at random.

Finally, what will you measure? You will keep a running count on how many distorted figures are classified correctly—that is, correctly assigned to set #1 or #2. When performance reaches eight correct in a row (regardless of set chosen), the experiment will stop. The value of eight correct will serve as a specific criterion for performance. The final raw data will be the number of trials (presentations) of each type of design required to reach that criterion.

DATA Statements and Program Parameters. You need to specify the exact grid locations for the standard designs: set #1 will be a square; set #2 will be a cross. Your program will be referring to these two sets and their grid coordinates repeatedly throughout the program. In fact, each time you draw a figure, you'll run through a given set from top to bottom.

What if you assign these column and row values to elements of an array? In fact, two two-dimension arrays will do the trick. You can have a single array for the column grid values in each set. That would be an 8 × 2 matrix. You should do the same with the row grid values. That way, when the program draws a distortion from set #1, it simply references the array elements in column 1 of each two-dimension matrix. Let's begin to see how all this takes shape.

ABSTRACTING PROTOTYPES: DATA Statements -- Set #1 and #2

program segment	notes
...clock reset, etc...	
...clock subroutine...	
150 DATA 2, 2	2 sets, level of distortion (2 blocks or 4 blocks).
160 DATA 8	Accuracy criterion (8 right).
200 DATA 8	8 blocks in set #1 (square).
210 DATA 5,5, 10,5, 15,5	3 blocks drawn horizontally.
214 DATA 5,15, 10,15, 15,15	3 blocks drawn horizontally.
218 DATA 5,10, 15,10	2 blocks along the verticals.
230 DATA 8	8 blocks in set #2 (cross).
240 DATA 5,10, 10,10, 15,10	6 blocks drawn horizontally.
242 DATA 20,10, 25,10, 30,10	
244 DATA 15,5, 15,15	2 blocks drawn vertically.
300 READ NSETS, LEVEL	Number of sets, number of blocks to distort.
310 READ CRIT	Accuracy criterion (8 right).
350 READ N : FOR I = 1 TO N	
360 READ CCL(I,1), RRW(I,1)	Grid values in set #1.
370 NEXT I	
380 READ N : FOR I = 1 TO N	
390 READ CCL(I,2), RRW(I,2)	Grid values in set #2.
400 NEXT I	

Let's look at a table of what is now stored in the two arrays CCL and RRW. The essential feature to keep in mind as you look over the array tables below is this: a column subscript of 1 in each array automatically references the list of grid coordinates for stimulus set #1, and a subscript of 2 references similar values for set #2. Something that might also be mentioned is the potential for adding sets to this design. It would be no problem for the program.

	CCL Array		RRW Array	
	Set		Set	
	#1	#2	#1	#2
Block 1	5	5	5	15
Block 2	10	10	5	15
Block 3	15	15	5	15
etc.	5	15	10	5
	etc.		etc.	

Drawing a Distorted Stimulus.   This segment of the ABSTRACTING PROTOTYPES program is the guts of the entire procedure. The objective here will be to draw a figure based on three separate random selections: (a) set number—1 or 2, (b) either a column grid value or row grid value change, and (c) direction of distortion—add or subtract. Take yet another look at the two standard arrays above. You know how to plot their coordinates. What you'll need to do is change a given number of those coordinates before you plot them.

Let's take the example of a distortion based on set #1, at LEVEL = 2 (25%). Your goal, then, would be to choose two of the eight pairs in set #1, then add or subtract the two units of grid space to one of the grid coordinates in each pair to offset the original block. Step 1 is to copy the complete set of column and row grid coordinates from the standard into another array. I'll call this third 8 × 2 array FINAL. Step 2 requires that you generate a series of random integers (determined by the value of LEVEL). Each time you get a random integer, go to that row in the FINAL array. Then, decide (at random) whether to distort the column grid value or the row grid value. Finally, decide (at random) whether to add or subtract from the number you are distorting. Ultimately, the FINAL array will contain the column and row grid coordinate values that will compose an individual distorted design. Now let's translate this scenario into program statements.

ABSTRACTING PROTOTYPES: Creating a FINAL Array of Grid Values

Apple IIe and IBM PC program segment	notes
...continued from above...	
600 H = NSETS : L = 1	Parameters for RND range.
602 SET = INT((H-L+1)*RND(1))+L	Choose set # at random.
610 FOR I = 1 TO 8 612 FINAL (I,1) = CCL (I,SET) 614 FINAL (I,2) = RRW (I,SET) 616 NEXT I	Copy values row by row. Copy column grid value. Copy row grid value.
630 FOR I = 1 TO 8 : C(I) = 0 632 NEXT I	C array keeps count of random numbers selected.
640 HH = 8 : L = 1 642 FOR I = 1 TO LEVEL 644 RAX = INT((HH-L+1)*RND(1))+L 646 C(RAX) = C(RAX) + 1 648 IF C(RAX) > 1 THEN 644	Parameters for RND range. Loop determines distortions. If RAX has already been selected, get another.
650 H = 2 : L = 1 652 RV = INT((H-L+1)*RND(1))+L	RX is either the column grid value (if = 1) or row grid value (if = 2).
660 H = 1 : L = 1 662 RD = INT((H-L+1)*RND(1))+L	RD signifies either add (if = 1) or subtract (if = 2).
670 IF RD=1 THEN FINAL(RAX,RV)=FINAL(RAX,RV)+2 672 IF RD=2 THEN FINAL(RAX,RV)=FINAL(RAX,RV)-2	
674 NEXT I	

TRS-80 program segment	notes
...continued from above...	
...same as above except...	
602 SET = RND(H)	Choose set # at random.
644 RAX = RND(HH)	
652 RV = RND(H)	

These randomization routines are the same as those covered in Chapter 10; there are just many more of them. Let's recap what's happening in this latest segment of the ABSTRACTING PROTOTYPES program.

First, at 600–602, a random generator produces an integer between 1 and the number of sets involved (NSETS = 2 in the example). This, in effect, determines which set will be distorted on this specific trial. Next, lines 610–616 copy the column grid and row grid values from the standard designs (stored in the CCL and RRW arrays). The new 8 × 2 array is FINAL. Only elements of the FINAL array will actually be distorted. I don't want you to distort the original arrays holding the standard values. Then comes the tricky part, beginning at line 642. A loop repeats until the proper number of blocks have been picked at random and distorted in a random direction (by adding or subtracting). The C array (line 630) was needed to prevent repetitions in random numbers. All in all, this segment is quite complex, so study it until you know it.

Drawing the Distortion and Requesting a Classification.   This next segment has two parts. First, you want to draw the distorted design. The program still knows which set number this distortion was derived from because the variable SET holds that value (1 = square or 2 = cross in this example). The drawing statements are the same as those used previously, only this time the column grid and row grid values will be drawn from the FINAL array. Once the design is on the screen, you want to prompt the subject with a text question asking for a categorization (set 1 or set 2?).

ABSTRACTING PROTOTYPES: Drawing Distorted Figure, Recording
                        Categorization

Apple IIe program segment	notes
...continued from above...	
680 GR : COLOR = 10	Invoke graphics, clear grid.
682 HOME	Clear text window.
690 FOR I = 1 TO 8	
700 PLOT FINAL(I,1),FINAL(I,2)	Place each block on the grid.
710 NEXT I	
720 PRINT "WHAT SET IS FIGURE FROM: ";	
730 FOR I = 1 TO NSETS	
740 PRINT I;	
750 NEXT I	
760 INPUT R	R is the set number typed by the subject as a response.

IBM PC program segment	notes
140 BLOCK$ = CHR$(219)	Specific block character.
142 WIDTH 40 : KEY OFF	

```
680 CLS                                    Clear screen.

690 FOR I = 1 TO 8

692 CG = FINAL(I,1)                        CG is column grid value.
694 RG = FINAL(I,2)                        RG is row grid value.
700 LOCATE RG,CG

708 PRINT BLOCK$;                          Graphic block displayed.

710 NEXT I

715 LOCATE 22,1
720 PRINT "WHAT SET IS THE FIGURE FROM ";
730 FOR I = 1 TO NSETS
740 PRINT I;" ";
750 NEXT I
760 INPUT R                                R is the set number typed by
                                           the subject as a response.
```

TRS-80 program segment	notes

```
140 BLOCK$ = CHR$(191)                     Specific block character.



142 PRINT CHR$(15);                        Turn off cursor.

680 CLS : PRINT CHR$(23);                  Clear screen.

690 FOR I = 1 TO 8

692 CG = FINAL(I,1)                        CG is column grid value.
694 RG = FINAL(I,2)                        RG is row grid value.
700 PRINT @ (RG,CG*2),;

708 PRINT BLOCK$;                          Graphic block displayed.

710 NEXT I

720 PRINT @ (22,1), "WHAT SET IS THE FIGURE FROM ";
730 FOR I = 1 TO NSETS
740 PRINT I;" ";
750 NEXT I
760 INPUT R                                R is the set number typed by
                                           the subject as a response.
```

Now focus your attention on the variable R. This variable is the subject's classification response. It represents the set number assigned to the distorted figure. Of course, during the first few trials the subject will have little confidence in these responses. However, as exposure to the distortions continues, these classification responses should become more and more accurate. In other words, the subject should eventually have a string of successful match-ups.

Determining When the Response Criterion is Reached. Your objective is to keep track of any unbroken string of successful judgments. The criterion for completion of the procedure is eight consecutive correct classifications. If, at any time, the subject should respond in error, you must start counting the eight all over again. Clearly, you need a simple counting statement to keep track of progress toward the criterion.

ABSTRACTING PROTOTYPES: Reaching the Response Criterion

program segment	notes
800 IF R = SET THEN RCOUNT=RCOUNT+1	If R is correct, count upward.
810 IF R <> SET THEN RCOUNT=0	If R is wrong, reset counter.
815 T = T + 1	Keep count of no. of trials.
820 IF RCOUNT = CRIT THEN 900	Session over, print results.
830 GOTO 600	Session continues with next trial.
900 PRINT "NO. TRIALS TO CRITERION=";T	No. of trials is the DV.
1000 END	

That's all there is to this example. As you look back over the AB-STRACTING PROTOTYPES program, you should see several familiar programming techniques including randomization, control of cursor movement, and input of subject responses. You should also come away with the knowledge that the program was designed to be flexible, with built-in potential for new levels of the amount of distortion independent variable. Furthermore, any figure may be used as long as it fits within the confines of the available graphics grid.

Altering the Program Template. You will recall that this example is for only one level of the IV. To produce a second version, one that can be used with the second level of IV, simply change the DATA statement at line 150.

ABSTRACTING PROTOTYPES: Changing the Level of IV

Apple IIe or TRS-80 program segment	notes
150 DATA 2, 4	2 sets, level of distortion is 4 blocks.

Closure

Low-res graphics have great potential as a means for generating experimental stimuli. With this chapter you've only scratched the surface. You may now be curious about the full range of graphics characters available on the TRS-80 and IBM PC (with graphics adaptor installed). If so, simply consult the ASCII tables in the relevant technical manual. Refer to the manual also for specific instructions on how to manipulate color on the Apple IIe in low-res graphics mode.

CHAPTER 13

High-Resolution Graphics and a Special Project in Perception

High Versus Low Resolution in Computer Graphics

In this chapter I'm going to focus on the use of **high-resolution (high-res)** point and line graphics. The example will be a version of Berlyne's classic procedure to measure preference for stimulus complexity. You'll learn how to program with high-res graphics on the Apple IIe and IBM PC systems (IBM PC must have the color graphics adaptor).

ADVANCING BASIC: Point and Line Graphics on the Apple IIe

The High-Resolution Grid.   As you have learned from your earlier work with low-res graphics, the screen dimensions are different when you're dealing with the graphics grid. The high-res grid is 280 columns × 160 rows, as diagramed below.

HIGH-RES GRID ON THE Apple IIe

Each *point* on this grid—each grid coordinate—is a spot of color on the display screen. High-res graphics will allow you to display individual image points and thin *lines* on the screen. High-res graphics applications will also involve a small window for 4 lines × 40 columns of text at the bottom of the screen.

You invoke high-res graphics by using the HGR statement. You must set the color immediately following HGR. This is done with the HCOLOR statement. The numeric parameter for HCOLOR may range from 0 (black) to 5. Remember that on a monochrome monitor each of these color values is a different tint of the monochrome color.

HGR and HCOLOR STATEMENT

Apple IIe	notes
300 HGR	Invokes high-res graphics, clears the 280 x 160 grid, leaves 4-line text window.
310 HCOLOR = 3	Sets color.
312 HOME	Clears text window.

Of course, HGR and HCOLOR must precede the portion of your program that uses high-res graphics capabilities.

The HPLOT Statement.   HPLOT can put a single point or a line of color within the high-res grid. Like other graphics drawing statements, HPLOT requires parameters to do its job. These parameters are values that represent column and row grid coordinates. The parameters may be numeric constants, variables, or expressions (the results of the calculation of an equation). Let's now review the two versions of the HPLOT statement: one for points, the other for lines.

HPLOT STATEMENT AND ITS PARAMETERS

Apple IIe	notes
400 HPLOT 2,20	1st value: column grid location, 2nd value: row grid location.
410 HPLOT 2,30 to 100,30	Draws a line between two grid coordinate pairs.
420 HPLOT TO 120,150	Continues a line to specified coordinate pair.

Your programming example is a routine that will serve you later in the PREFERENCE FOR COMPLEXITY program. Your objective here will be to read a series of grid coordinates from DATA statements and draw a figure on the grid.

PROGRAMMING EXAMPLE: Drawing Lined Figures

Apple IIe program segment	notes
500 DATA 4	Number of lines in figure
510 DATA 10,30	Starting coordinate pair (col,row).
520 DATA 100,10, 90,90, 20,120, 10,30	Remaining pairs.
800 HGR : HCOLOR = 3	Clear high-res grid.
802 HOME	
805 READ NLINES	Number of lines.
810 READ C,R : HPLOT C,R	First point drawn.
820 FOR I = 1 TO NLINES	
830 READ C,R : HPLOT TO C,R	Connects a series of coordinates.
840 NEXT I	

Take a close look at the approach used in this example. The first step was to plot the starting point, the single coordinate pair from which the remainder of the figure would be drawn. The second step involved using a loop to read four additional coordinate pairs. These four pairs completed the corners of a figure with four sides. In other words, a figure with four sides was drawn with five operations. It was done that way to take advantage of the HPLOT statement that continued drawing from a previous coordinate. Of course, before I could continue drawing, I had to have a point on the screen in the first place. That's why five coordinate pairs appear in the example, even though the figure has only four lines. One more thing. Notice that the final coordinate pair is the same as the starting pair. This ensures that the figure will be closed.

As with low-res graphics on the Apple IIe, you must cancel the graphics mode before you can continue to program using the entire screen.

TURNING OFF GRAPHICS MODE WHILE PROGRAMMING

Apple IIe	notes
(]) TEXT : HOME	Invokes text mode and clears screen so that a program may be listed.

Typing these statements after the] prompt will allow you to return the computer to text mode and edit the program statements. Without these you would only be able to work within the small text window at the bottom of the high-res graphics grid.

ADVANCING BASIC: Point and Line Graphics on the IBM PC

The IBM PC can produce exciting and vivid graphics. You must, however, have the optional color graphics adaptor.

The Medium-resolution Grid.   Did I say medium? That's right. The IBM PC has a medium-res grid and a high-res grid, both for point and line graphics. The difference relates to the ability to draw in color. Medium-res works on both color and monochrome video displays. All my examples here will be monochrome, even on color-capable video displays. But so that they can work on most color or monochrome equipment, I'll limit my examples to medium-res applications. The medium-res grid is 320 columns × 200 rows. For high-res applications consult your technical manuals.

MEDIUM-RES GRID ON THE IBM PC

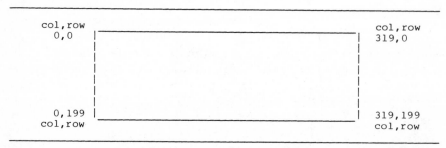

Medium-resolution graphics will allow you to display a wide range of images and designs. I'm using medium-res here because I want the examples on the IBM PC to use approximately the same scale as those on the Apple IIe, although line graphics on the Apple are called hires. Don't let these differences in labeling disturb you. The IBM PC does have a separate hi-res mode with an ultrafine line-drawing capability. Medium-res will do quite nicely for our programming examples, however. Its basic capabilities include single image points and individual lines, and its complex functions include shapes, and figures filled with color. The IBM PC gives you considerable drawing power within its BASIC language.

Unlike the Apple IIe, the IBM PC does not provide a separate text window. Any text may be printed anywhere on the screen using all the standard methods.

You invoke the medium-res grid by using the SCREEN statement. This statement requires a numeric parameter: 0 to invoke pure text mode, 1 to get medium-res graphics, and 2 to get high-res graphics.

SCREEN STATEMENT

IBM PC	notes
300 SCREEN 1	Invokes medium-res graphics grid.
310 CLS	Clear screen.

The PSET, PRESET, and LINE Statements.   These three statements are the bread and butter of IBM PC graphics. They each require grid coordinate pairs as their parameters. PSET and PRESET require a single grid coordinate pair and place a single image point at that spot. PSET illuminates the specified point with color, while PRESET erases the point (colors it the same as the background). LINE draws a straight line image between two points, or from the last point drawn to a new point.

POINT and LINE STATEMENTS AND THEIR PARAMETERS

IBM PC	notes
400 PSET (2,20)	1st value: column grid location, 2nd value: row grid location.
405 PRESET (2,20)	Erases point drawn in 400.
410 LINE (2,30)-(100,30)	Draws a line between two grid coordinate pairs.
420 LINE -(120,150)	Continues a line to specified coordinate pair.
430 LINE (2,30)-(100,30),0	Erases line drawn in 410.

So you see that the IBM PC gives you all the typical high-res capabilities. The above point and line statements are all that you require to program the PREFERENCE FOR COMPLEXITY procedure. However, you really should get exposed to the other IBM PC graphics statements. Maybe you'll develop a unique laboratory application for them.

Boxes, Circles, and Painting. Need to draw a square or rectangular figure? Or a circular figure? It's no problem. You can even "paint" the interior of any figure or graphic space.

DRAWING BOXES AND CIRCLES, "PAINTING"

IBM PC program segment	notes
460 LINE (10,10)-(50,50),,B	Draws a box: 1st coordinate pair is upper-left corner; 2nd pair is lower-right corner.
470 LINE (10,60)-(50,110),,BF	Draws and "fills in" a box with specified corner coordinates.
480 LINE (10,60)-(50,110),0,BF	Erases the box drawn and filled in 470.
490 CIRCLE (100,100),25	Draws a circular outline centered at column,row coordinate; 3rd parameter is the radius.
495 PAINT (90,90)	If the specified grid point is "inside" an outline figure (box or circle), the figure "fills in" with color.

The IBM PC version of the brief programming example is shown below. Remember, your objective here is to read a series of grid coordinates from DATA statements and draw a figure on the grid.

PROGRAMMING EXAMPLE: Drawing Lined Figures

IBM PC program segment	notes
500 DATA 4	Number of lines in figure
510 DATA 10,30	Starting coordinate pair (col,row).
520 DATA 100,10, 90,90, 20,120, 10,30	Remaining pairs.
800 SCREEN 1 : CLS	Clear high-res grid.
805 READ NLINES	Number of lines.
810 READ C,R : PSET (C,R)	First point drawn.
820 FOR I = 1 TO NLINES	
830 READ C,R : LINE -(C,R)	Connects a series of coordinates.
840 NEXT I	

This example does precisely the same thing as the high-res routine on the Apple IIe. In that sense, there is very close correspondence between the two systems when it comes to point and line drawing. The differences are clear, nevertheless. The IBM PC relies on PSET and LINE statements to do the job that HPLOT statements did on the Apple IIe. Now let's plunge ahead to the PREFERENCE FOR COMPLEXITY program.

Programming a Visual Perception Procedure

Preference for Visual Complexity.   This will be your line graphics programming example. Since line graphics are not available on the standard TRS-80 system, I will deal here only with the Apple IIe and IBM PC.

The simple premise of this programming example is that people prefer complex stimuli over simple ones. A good question to ask at this point is what form this preference takes. You could consider the preference to be an aesthetic judgment, such as a response on the dimension of *pleasing . . . displeasing*. This should conjure up memory traces of the SEMANTIC DIFFERENTIAL programs used as earlier programming examples. You'll pay special attention to the dimension that relates to reference.

One of the convenient aspects of this example is that, as you read the phrase *preference for visual complexity,* you are exposing yourself to the broad boundaries for research design on this topic. For example, the primary, or obvious, independent variable jumps out at you from that phrase: *visual complexity* is a primary IV. Levels of visual complexity may be developed through the systematic variation of the visual stimulus, whatever form that is.

Simply put, that's where computer graphics comes in. The graphics statements in BASIC that I've covered in this chapter will allow for systematic manipulation of the complexity of the visual stimulus to be presented to subjects.

And what about the dependent variable? At the very least, it should be obvious by a process of elimination. *Preference* is the DV. You may want to define preference specifically in terms of an aesthetic judgment or a pleasantness dimension. Whatever specific definition you use, the measurement of a response to the visual stimulus will be a *rating,* or the assignment of a number. That's where an individual preference score in this procedure will come from. But to make this example really challenging, let's record a second DV in the form of the *processing time* required to make a preference judgment. The last time you programmed a process (or reaction) timer was in the MEMORY SCANNING procedure in Chapter 10, so it should be fairly fresh.

To make it seem as simple as possible, you might think of the procedure this way. Subjects will give a numbered response after they study a drawing. Low values will signify that they did not like the drawing; high values will signify that they did.

Specific Steps for the Programmer. The PREFERENCE FOR COMPLEXITY program has a fairly simple outline. An individual trial in the procedure should occur as follows: (a) A certain drawing is put on the screen using graphics capabilities. (b) A prompt for the scaled rating response is displayed to ask whether the subject likes or dislikes the figure. (c) The raw rating response is stored according to the experimental condition represented in the specific stimulus figure.

How do you want to vary the visual complexity of the figures to be judged? Consider the graphics manipulations you have available to you for the program. One sure way to manipulate complexity is to draw figures varying in the number of lines they possess. Another way might be to manipulate the form of the figure, such as making it either open or closed. (A closed figure will have its final line reconnected to its point of origin.) As always, two IVs are enough to keep most experimenters happy. You'll have two variables in your program: the number of lines, and the form (open vs. closed).

Next, should the experiment be a within- or between-subjects design? Since you haven't programmed a completely within-subjects procedure lately, do it that way. It will be a good chance for you to see how one program can do an entire two-factor experiment.

DATA Statements and Program Parameters. DATA statements for this program will be clustered into sets. This step will help to organize the parameters and stimuli required for each trial in the procedure. Let's consider what each set of DATA statements must contain: (a) the number of lines to be drawn—IV #1, (b) whether the figure was open or closed—IV #2, (c) the first grid coordinate pair, and (d) the remaining grid coordinate pairs. Of course, the actual closing of a figure is determined by whether the final grid coordinate pair is the same as the first coordinate.

The general program parameter that also must be specified is the number of trials. In addition, use disk file storage (just to keep from getting rusty). The program will request a specific disk file name from the experimenter.

You could have multiple trials in each of the four possible combinations of the two IVs, but I'm not going to that extreme in this sample program. I'll show only one trial for each combination in the 2 × 2 research design. You'll use two levels of number of lines—3 versus 9—and the two levels of open versus closed.

In a program that presented multiple trials within each of these categories, the raw data would need to be summed and averaged by category or level of IV. To accomplish this, I'm coding each level as follows: three lines gets a code of 1, nine lines gets a code of 2, open figure gets a code of 1, and closed figure gets a code of 2. You'll be using these codes as subscript references in raw data arrays. This coding of levels of IV is not new. You did the procedure in Chapter 11 in connection with your MEMORY SCANNING program to label each level of the probe position variable.

PREFERENCE FOR COMPLEXITY: DATA Statements, Program Parameters

program segment	notes
...clock reset, etc... ...clock subroutine...	
200 DATA 4	4 figures to be drawn.
210 DATA 3, 1, 2 211 DATA 50,50 212 DATA 100,90, 20,120, 50,50	3 lines; Closed figure.
220 DATA 9, 2, 2 221 DATA 20,100 222 DATA 40,20, 60,90, 110,10 223 DATA 220,110, 225,80, 180,75 224 DATA 50,120, 37,155, 20,100	9 lines; Closed figure.
230 DATA 9, 2, 1 231 DATA 10,10 232 DATA 20,33, 200,42, 51,34 233 DATA 78,50, 85,120, 110,12 234 DATA 135,24, 139,99, 145,140	9 lines; Open figure.
240 DATA 3, 1, 1 241 DATA 200,34 242 DATA 15,79, 145,99, 39,145	3 lines; Open figure.

The DATA statements at 210, 220, 230, and 240 all show the levels of IV coded numerically. The first value in each statement is the actual number of lines in the figure. The second value is the code for the number of lines IV (1 = 3, 2 = 9). The third value is the code for the open–closed IV (1 = open, 2 = closed). Remember, these codes are going to be used as subscript variables for raw data arrays so that data can be stored according to the level of IV that it relates to.

Trial Loop and Figure Drawing Statements.   The next step is to start a trial loop. Within that loop will be nested the figure loop. This inner loop will do the work of actually drawing the picture.

PREFERENCE FOR COMPLEXITY: Trial Loop and Drawing Statements

IBM PC program segment	notes
...continued from above...	
400 READ NTRIALS	Number of trials.
420 FOR T = 1 TO NTRIALS	Start trial loop.
430 SCREEN 1 : CLS	Clear med-res grid.
435 INPUT "HIT <RETURN> TO START ";Z$	Allows subject to start trial.
440 READ NLINES	Number of lines.
450 READ V1,V2	Codes for IV #1, IV #2
460 READ C,R : PSET (C,R)	Plot first point.
470 FOR L = 1 TO NLINES	Start line loop.
480 READ C,R : LINE -(C,R)	Draw each line.
490 NEXT L	

Apple IIe program segment	notes
...same as above except...	
430 HGR : HCOLOR = 3 : HOME	Clear hi-res grid.
431 VTAB 21	Position cursor within 4-line text window.
435 INPUT "HIT <RETURN> TO START ";Z$	Allows subject to start trial; facilitates Apple keystroke entry routine.
460 READ C,R : HPLOT C,R	Plot first point.
480 READ C,R : HPLOT TO C,R	Draw each line.

At this point the figure is drawn. The next step requires that the program prompt the subject for a preference rating.

Displaying the Rating Scale Prompt—Recording the Dependent Measures.   The text prompt that will serve as the basis for the subject's rating response need be only a simple sentence conveying that the scale may range from one number to another. Let's use 1 through 9 to give the subjects a wide range for assigning preference. On Apple IIe systems this message will be printed within the four-line text window at the bottom of the display area. On the IBM PC the program needs to position the cursor at the appropriate line, then print the message.

When it comes to dependent variables, you have two. First, you want to record the actual rating given by the subject for each figure. Second, you want to record the amount of time it took to make that decision (the processing time). Processing time measures (or reaction times) require a keystroke entry routine to remove the need to press the ⟨return⟩ key. The last time you used keystroke entry was in the MEMORY SCANNING program (Chapter 11).

PREFERENCE FOR COMPLEXITY: Measuring Ratings and Processing Times

IBM PC program segment	notes
500 LOCATE 22,1	Position cursor near bottom of screen.
510 PRINT "LOW- 1 2 3 4 5 6 7 8 9 -HIGH"	
520 PRINT "ENTER YOUR PREFERENCE RATING";	
530 GOSUB 50 : START = TIME	Start process timer.
540 R$ = INKEY$: IF R$ = "" THEN 540	Keystroke entry routine.
550 R = VAL(R$)	String entry is converted to a number.
560 GOSUB 50 : PT = TIME - START	Processing time is obtained.

Apple IIe program segment	notes
500 VTAB 21	Position cursor within text window.
510 PRINT "LOW- 1 2 3 4 5 6 7 8 9 -HIGH"	
520 PRINT "ENTER YOUR PREFERENCE RATING";	
530 GOSUB 50 : START = TIME	Start process timer.
540 KEY = PEEK (-16384)	Keystroke entry routine
541 POKE -16368,0	(chapter 6).
542 IF KEY > 127 THEN 544	If new key has been pressed.
543 GOTO 540	
544 R$ = CHR$(KEY-128)	Convert keystroke to string.
550 R = VAL(R$)	String entry is converted to a number.
560 GOSUB 50 : PT = TIME - START	Processing time is obtained.

Now you have two pieces of raw data: the numeric rating, R, and numeric processing time, PT. These will need to be stored in an array. I planned ahead for this eventuality by assigning codes to each level of each IV in the parameter segment above.

Array Storage of Raw Data. There are two variables involved in the process of array storage of these measures, V1 (for IV #1) and

V2 (for IV #2). I planned for V1 to code the level of number of lines and V2 to code the level of open–closed. These little details allow for the luxury of simply using V1 and V2 as subscript values in two-dimension arrays that will store the raw data for each of the two dependent variables. You'll be able to keep a running sum of ratings and processing times as a function of each of the four combinations of the two-factor design. In table form the arrays look like this.

TWO–DIMENSION ARRAYS TO STORE SUMS OF RATINGS AND PROCESSING TIMES

```
                    R Array                      PT Array

                    Ratings                  Processing Times

                  values of V2                 values of V2
                  (open-closed)                (open-closed)

                  1        2                    1        2
                 .___.___.                     .___.___.
  values      1  |   |   |          1          |   |   |
  of V1          |___|___|                     |___|___|
  (3 vs. 9)    2 |   |   |          2          |   |   |
                 |___|___|                     |___|___|
```

The rows of each array will be referenced by a subscript of 1 for three-line figures, and 2 for nine-line figures. The columns will be referenced by a subscript of 1 for open figures and 2 for closed figures. All four possible combinations are neatly covered by these V1 and V2 values, originally read from DATA statements before each figure was drawn.

You'll be updating each array element by summing or adding on each new raw data value. You can analyze the sums directly or compute an average by dividing each sum by one-fourth the number of trials (NTRIALS/4).

PREFERENCE FOR COMPLEXITY: Array Storage of Raw Data

program segment	notes
...continued from above...	
570 R(V1,V2) = R(V1,V2) + R	Add raw rating to a sum.
580 PT(V1,V2) = PT(V1,V2) + PT	Add raw processing time to a sum.
590 NEXT T	Complete trial loop.

The last segment for this program will be the phase where the subject's performance is printed into a disk output file as a permanent record.

Disk Output File.   Once all the trials have been completed, the program can then print to a disk file the sums and means for each dependent variable at each level of each IV. Since the data were originally stored in two-dimension arrays, it should seem logical that the disk file printing will be done using nested loops. Two-dimension arrays are usually manipulated using nested loops.

PREFERENCE FOR COMPLEXITY: Disk Output File

IBM PC program segment	notes
150 CLS : KEY OFF	Clear; remove key labels.
155 INPUT "ENTER DISK FILE NAME";FF$	Requests file name from experimenter before test session begins.
600 OPEN FF$ FOR OUTPUT AS 3	See also Appendix E.
605 CLS	Clear screen after session.
610 PRINT #3, "RATINGS:" : PRINT #3,	Table heading.
620 PRINT #3, ,"OPEN",,"CLOSED"	1st row heading.
630 PRINT #3, ,"3-LINE","9-LINE",	2nd row heading.
640 PRINT #3, "3-LINE","9-LINE"	
650 PRINT #3, : PRINT #3, "SUMS",	
660 FOR I = 1 TO 2 : FOR J = 1 TO 2	Prints R array.
670 PRINT #3, R(I,J),	
680 NEXT J : NEXT I	
690 PRINT #3, : PRINT #3, "MEANS",	
700 FOR I = 1 TO 2 : FOR J = 1 TO 2	Prints Means computed from
705 PRINT #3, R(I,J)/(NTRIALS/4),	R array.
706 NEXT J : NEXT I	
707 PRINT #3, : PRINT #3,	
710 PRINT #3, "PROCESS TIMES:" : PRINT #3,	
720 PRINT #3, ,"OPEN",,"CLOSED"	1st row heading.
730 PRINT #3, ,"3-LINE","9-LINE",	2nd row heading.
740 PRINT #3, "3-LINE","9-LINE"	
750 PRINT #3, : PRINT #3, "SUMS",	
760 FOR I = 1 TO 2 : FOR J = 1 TO 2	Prints PT array.
770 PRINT #3, PT(I,J),	
780 NEXT J : NEXT I	
790 PRINT #3, : PRINT #3, "MEANS",	

```
800 FOR I = 1 TO 2 : FOR J = 1 TO 2        Prints Means computed from
805 PRINT #3, PT(I,J)/(NTRIALS/4),            PT array.
806 NEXT J : NEXT I

807 PRINT #3, : PRINT #3,

810 CLOSE 3

1000 END
```

Doing the same disk output file routine for the Apple IIe requires programming specific print zones in Apple disk files. You may recall that a similar solution was first developed in Chapter 9. In the example there, however, I needed only two zones; here you need five separate zones across the line. This next segment is fairly complex, so you might want to reread the pertinent sections of Chapter 9 before wading in.

Apple IIe program segment	notes
`150 HOME`	
`155 INPUT "ENTER DISK FILE NAME";FF$`	Requests file name from experimenter before test session begins.
`595 D$ = CHR$(4)`	Special character for disk file statements.
`602 PRINT D$;"OPEN ";FF$` `604 PRINT D$;"WRITE ";FF$`	
`605 HGR : HCOLOR = 3 : TEXT : HOME`	Clear screen after session.
`610 PRINT "RATINGS:" : PRINT`	Table heading.
`620 PRINT TAB(15);"OPEN";` `622 PRINT TAB(26);"CLOSED"`	1st row heading.

`630 PRINT TAB(15);"3-LINE";`
`632 PRINT TAB(9);"9-LINE";`
`634 PRINT TAB(9);"3-LINE";`
`640 PRINT TAB(9);"9-LINE"`
	2nd row heading.

`650 PRINT : PRINT "SUMS";TAB(11);`	
`660 FOR I = 1 TO 2 : FOR J = 1 TO 2`	Prints R array.
`662 P$ = STR$(R(I,J))`	STR$ function converts number to string.
`664 LS = LEN(P$)`	LEN function gives length of the string.
`666 PRINT P$;TAB(15-LS);`	Tab 15-LS spaces to P$ to fill print zone.
`680 NEXT J : NEXT I`	
`685 PRINT`	

```
690 PRINT : PRINT "MEANS";TAB(10);

700 FOR I = 1 TO 2 : FOR J = 1 TO 2        Prints means from R array.

701 M = R(I,J)/(NTRIALS/4)                 M is the mean.

702 P$ = STR$(M)                           STR$ function converts
                                             number to string.
704 LS = LEN(P$)                           LEN function gives length
                                             of the string.
705 PRINT P$;TAB(15-LS);                    Tab 15-LS spaces to P$ to
                                             fill print zone.
706 NEXT J : NEXT I

707 PRINT : PRINT

710 PRINT "PROCESS TIMES" : PRINT           Table heading.

720 PRINT TAB(15);"OPEN";                    1st row heading.
722 PRINT TAB(26);"CLOSED"

730 PRINT TAB(15);"3-LINE";                  2nd row heading.
732 PRINT TAB(9);"9-LINE";
734 PRINT TAB(9);"3-LINE";
740 PRINT TAB(9);"9-LINE"

750 PRINT : PRINT "SUMS";TAB(11);

760 FOR I = 1 TO 2 : FOR J = 1 TO 2         Prints PT array.

762 P$ = STR$(PT(I,J))                      STR$ function converts
                                             number to string.
764 LS = LEN(P$)                            LEN function gives length
                                             of the string.
766 PRINT P$;TAB(15-LS);                    Tab 15-LS spaces to P$ to
                                             fill print zone.
780 NEXT J : NEXT I

785 PRINT

790 PRINT : PRINT "MEANS";TAB(10);

800 FOR I = 1 TO 2 : FOR J = 1 TO 2         Prints means from PT array.

801 M = PT(I,J)/(NTRIALS/4)                 M is the mean.

802 P$ = STR$(M)                           STR$ function converts
                                             number to string.
804 LS = LEN(P$)                           LEN function gives length
                                             of the string.
805 PRINT P$;TAB(15-LS);                    Tab 15-LS spaces to P$ to
                                             fill print zone.
806 NEXT J : NEXT I

807 PRINT : PRINT

810 PRINT D$;"CLOSE ";FF$

1000 END
```

Please be reminded of the special rules for using the TAB function for disk output format on the Apple IIe. This rule was introduced in Chapter 9. TAB in this situation *does not seek a specific column on the line.* Rather, it adds a specified number of spaces following the last item printed. This effect applies to disk file output only. If it were on-line printing, TAB would seek the column specified by its parameter.

Well, there you have it. The PREFERENCE FOR COMPLEXITY program is another complete learning experience, since it contained so many of the tools and routines that you've learned throughout the book.

Closure

The IBM PC and Apple IIe give a high degree of control over graphics in BASIC. I recommend that you begin integrating graphics on a small scale and build gradually. The more you read and study the literature in the fields of human experimental psychology (information processing, cognition, memory, and perception) the more opportunities you will find for your newly developed computer graphics skills.

APPENDIX A

The LVB Interface

Introduction

Each of the four I/O circuits described in the text—Switch Input, Relay (output), DC Driver (output), and Precision Timer—is located on an I/O card. These cards are designed to be plugged into slots inside the main housing cabinet of the interface. Carefully unpack all components and lay them out in a clean area. You will need wire, a wire cutter and stripper, a soldering iron, solder, and a small screwdriver. The component parts are listed below.

```
LVB INTERFACE COMPONENTS from Med Associates, Inc.
                          East Fairfield, VT 05448
                          (802) 827-3825
```

```
    Main Cabinet (Bus Extension 1080-01) containing motherboard
      and 5 volt power supply

        5-pin power bus edge connector

        Ribbon Cable

I/O Cards

        Switch Input card (1080-38) and 10 pin top edge connector

        Relay card (1080-40) and 24 pin top edge connector

        DC Driver card (1080-18) and 10 pin top edge connector

        Precision Timer card (1080-54A or 1080-54)*
```

Internal Computer Adapter card (IBM PC, TRS-80, or Apple IIe)

28-volt DC power supply (provided by you or as an LVB
   component 1080-02)

---

* The 1080-54 card has been superseded by the 1080-54A.
The 1080-54A is the card covered in this text;
see Appendix B for software notes on the 1080-54.

Assembly and Wiring Instructions for the LVB Interface

Technical Manuals Provided With the LVB Interface.   These manuals are reference materials for the procedures outlined here. You should read them carefully; they are much more complete than the instructions given below. The instructions given here are intended as the minimum required to get the system operational for the purposes of projects outlined in this text.

Before Starting.   NEVER CONNECT OR DISCONNECT ANY COMPONENT OF THE INTERFACE SYSTEM UNTIL YOU ARE CERTAIN THAT ALL POWER SOURCES (COMPUTER, LVB CABINET, AND 28 V DC SUPPLY) ARE TURNED OFF.

Step 1.   Remove the black metal cover from the LVB cabinet by unscrewing the eight small screws that retain it. If you inspect the inside of the cabinet, you will see the interface **motherboard,** as it is called in computer lingo.

Next, turn the cabinet so that the power-on switch is near you and to the right side. The small 5-volt power supply should be near you, mounted vertically on the left inside wall of the cabinet. (This has nothing to do with what I will refer to as the 28-volt power supply.) Figure 1 shows how the cabinet should look at this point.

There are two sets of buses. A **bus** is a circuit that transports signals to and from the computer and a series of peripheral devices. The large bus that travels along the right side of the motherboard is extended from the computer. The small bus that travels along the left side of the board carries the 28-volt power supply connections. The motherboard has six positions to accept I/O cards. Each I/O card slides down from above so that its two edge connectors plug into the matching paired receptacles on the motherboard. Early models have a small two-position toggle switch on the motherboard. This should be set to the Apple side for all systems covered here (IBM PC, Apple IIe, and TRS-80 Model III/4). Newer units do not have this switch.

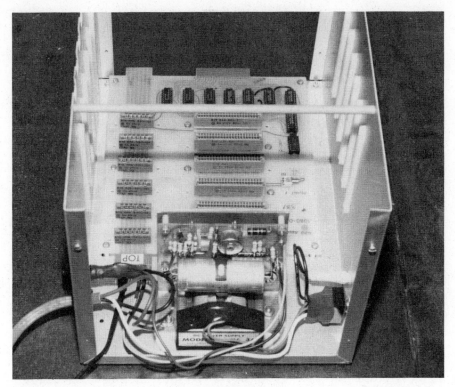

Figure 1.   LVB Cabinet with cover removed.

Step 2.   Let's focus on the 28-volt power bus for a moment. Your LVB cabinet may already have a 28-volt supply. If not, you'll need to connect an external 28-volt DC power source to this bus. The positive and negative (ground) wires from the power source should be soldered to the matching pins on the small power bus edge connector supplied with the LVB Interface. This edge connector is usually packed in a plugged-in position on one end of the bus. Note that +28 and −28 are clearly marked on the motherboard to help you make those power supply connections correctly. You have to get this right in order not to damage your equipment.

Step 3.   Next, you need to connect the computer extension bus, on the motherboard, to the computer itself, using the flat ribbon cable supplied with the interface unit. This cable has an edge connector at each end. It doesn't matter which end you connect to what, but any connection made must show the cable to be aligned in the down position (the cable is "flowing" downward out of the connector). Figure

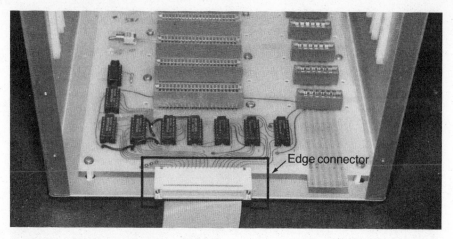

Figure 2. Shows connection of ribbon cable to motherboard.

2 shows the aligned-down connection of the ribbon cable to the exposed edge on the motherboard. These edge connectors are awkward to attach. The best method is to rock the connector onto the exposed edge, first getting the left side onto the edge, then pushing the right side of the connector forward to make a firm attachment.

Next, connect the other end to the computer—easier said than done. With the IBM PC and Apple IIe you must first install an adapter card inside the IBM or Apple system unit. For the IBM PC this card may be plugged into any available expansion slot. On the Apple IIe use slot #2. The technical manuals for the computer and the LVB Interface will be your guide on removal of the system unit cover and installation of the card into one of the expansion slots. Figure 3 shows the connection card and ribbon cable in place inside an IBM PC expansion slot. Figure 4 shows the connection card and ribbon cable in place inside an Apple IIe expansion slot.

If you don't feel confident about messing around inside your computer, call your local computer dealer and get the service technician to do it. On the TRS-80 the adapter card is a small device that simply plugs onto an exposed edge on the bottom of the computer (see Figure 5).

Step 4. Now you should have the LVB Interface connected to the computer, and a 28-volt power supply. Next you are ready to go back inside the LVB cabinet and install the I/O cards.

I'll start with the Switch Input card. On the "business" side of this card you should see lots of integrated circuit chips and a small rectangular device with eight tiny switches on it. This is a **dip switch**

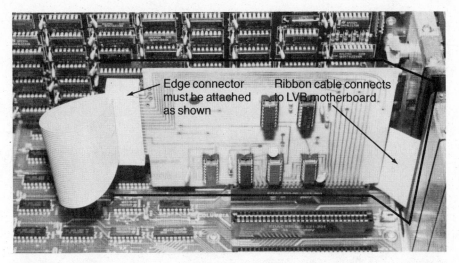

Figure 3.   Adapter card in an IBM PC expansion slot. (Note that any available slot may be used.)

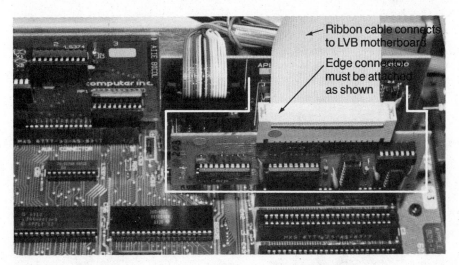

Figure 4.   An adapter card in an APPLE IIe expansion slot #2.

(see Figure 6) used to set the port number for the card. The eight dip switches themselves are labeled using the binary number system (128, 64, 32, 16, 8, 4, 2, 1), allowing up to 256 different port codes. Why use the binary system? This way the dip switch unit needs only eight switches to cover those 256 possibilities, as opposed to 256 separate switches. Without the binary coding the I/O card would have to be

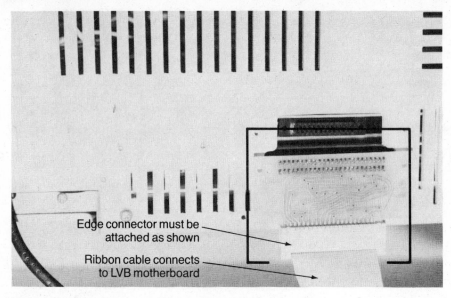

Edge connector must be
attached as shown

Ribbon cable connects
to LVB motherboard

Figure 5. An adapter card in a TRS-80 expansion slot.

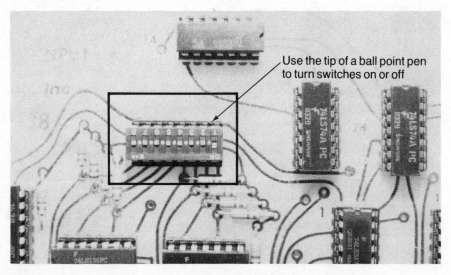

Use the tip of a ball point pen
to turn switches on or off

Figure 6. Location of a dip switch on an LVB input card.

the size of a billboard in order to house all those dip switches! Each
computer system (IBM PC, TRS-80, and Apple IIe) will require different switch settings. Consult the Dip Switch Settings chart on page 219.

For example, on the TRS-80 the port number for the Switch Input card is number 1, so the number 1 dip switch should be on, all others off. The Relay card has port number 30. This translates into dip switches 16, 8, 4, and 2 on, all others off. Remember, it's binary, so 16 + 8 + 4 + 2 = 30; hence the dip switch is set for port number 30. The port setting for the Precision Timer card is 10. Switches 8 and 2 must be on, all others off.

LVB I/O CARD DIP SWITCH SETTINGS AND PORT NUMBERS (IBM PC)

```
            dip switches                    port number      I/O card

  8   7   6   5   4   3   2   1
 (128 64  32  16  8   4   2   1)
         off      off off off off             208          Switch Input
  on  on      on


  8   7   6   5   4   3   2   1
 (128 64  32  16  8   4   2   1)
                 off off     off              242          Relay
  on  on  on  on          on                               (output)


  8   7   6   5   4   3   2   1
 (128 64  32  16  8   4   2   1)
     off          off off off off             176          DC Driver
  on      on  on                                           (output)


  8   7   6   5   4   3   2   1
 (128 64  32  16  8   4   2   1)
                 off off off off              240          Timer
  on  on  on  on
```

LVB I/O CARD DIP SWITCH SETTINGS AND PORT NUMBERS (TRS-80)

```
            dip switches                    port number      I/O card

  8   7   6   5   4   3   2   1
 (128 64  32  16  8   4   2   1)
 off off off off off off off                   1           Switch Input
                             on


  8   7   6   5   4   3   2   1
 (128 64  32  16  8   4   2   1)
 off off off                 off               30          Relay
         on  on  on  on                                    (output)


  8   7   6   5   4   3   2   1
 (128 64  32  16  8   4   2   1)
 off          off off off off off              96          DC Driver
     on  on                                                (output)
```

8	7	6	5	4	3	2	1		
(128	64	32	16	8	4	2	1)		
off	off	off	off		off		off	10	Timer
				on		on			

LVB I/O CARD DIP SWITCH SETTINGS AND MEMORY MAP VALUES (Apple IIe)

(Note: Internal Computer Adapter Card in Slot #2)

dip switches								binary	memory map	I/O card
8	7	6	5	4	3	2	1			
(128	64	32	16	8	4	2	1)			
	off		off	off	off	off	off	160	-16224	Switch Input
on		on								
8	7	6	5	4	3	2	1			
(128	64	32	16	8	4	2	1)			
	off		off	off		off	off	164	-16220	Relay
on		on			on					(output)
8	7	6	5	4	3	2	1			
(128	64	32	16	8	4	2	1)			
	off		off	off	off	off		161	-16223	DC Driver
on		on					on			(output)
8	7	6	5	4	3	2	1			
(128	64	32	16	8	4	2	1)			
	off		off	off	off		off	162	-16222	Timer
on		on				on				

Once the dip switches are set, the four I/O cards can be inserted in any of the six available slots in the LVB cabinet. Again, this process is awkward, so apply very firm rocking pressure downward as you seat the two exposed edges of each card firmly into the edge connectors on the motherboard. The sides of each card should fit within the grooves attached to the walls inside the cabinet (see Figure 7). The DC Driver card should be installed in the last slot away from the on/off switch. This is to allow access to the special switches and dial controls on this card.

Step 5.   Now you're ready for a big step: connecting test apparatus to the Switch Input, Relay, and DC Driver cards. Cables for this purpose are available from Med Associates. If you don't have these, you can make custom connections. Both kinds of connections require that you understand how to wire a switch.

Mechanical switches (like those present in response levers and output relays) exist in one of two states: open or closed. The response lever on your operant chamber will be labeled at each of three wiring

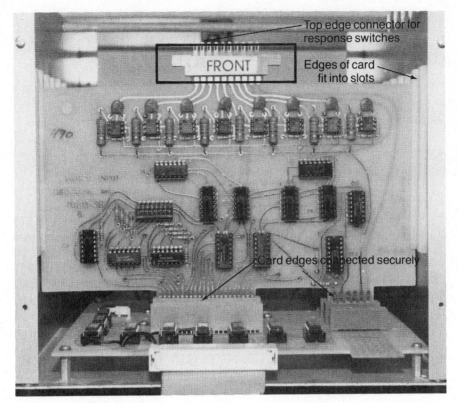

Figure 7. LVB input card plugged into a motherboard.

posts on the plastic switch housing: Common (Com or C), Normally Open (NO), or Normally Closed (NC). For this application the wiring is quite simple.

First, get out the unwired edge connector for the Switch Input card. It's the one with 10 tabs coming out from the top. The side with the FRONT sticker on it should face the side of the cabinet where the ribbon cable plugs in. You must connect the −28-volt pole of the external power supply to the Common post of the response lever. This is the negative (ground) side of the circuit. The pin third from the right on the edge connector (embossed with #8) must be connected to the Normally Open post of the lever (thereby completing the input circuit for Channel 1). You have to make these solder connections to get the Switch Input card operational.

The other seven input lines are available, should you want to expand your system; the interface projects in this text use only one input channel (one response lever), however. The table below summarizes all these wiring options. Methods for controlling the card from BASIC are covered in Chapter 6.

SWITCH INPUT CARD: CONNECTING RESPONSE SWITCHES EDGE CONNECTOR

embossed number on green edge connector	Channel number	Channel label used in programming
1	8	128
2	7	64
3	6	32
4	5	16
5	4	8
6	3	4
7	2	2
8	1	1
9	+ 28 volts (but not wired)	
10	- 28 volts (but not wired)	

Two circuits to control outputs are available in the LVB Interface. The Relay card contains eight separate relays (remotely controlled switches). These can be used to turn a variety of devices on and off. An application that quickly comes to mind is the slide-advance on a carousel projector. Only one lesson in this text makes special use of the Relay card; for more on it, consult the LVB technical manuals. I am considering the Relay card as optional equipment for the purposes of the text. Nevertheless, the table below shows the wiring pattern for the edge connector atop the Relay card. It has two rows of twelve small metal pins sticking up on the top. Each wiring pin is embossed with a tiny letter or number next to it. The pins are functionally clustered in groups of three.

RELAY CARD: CONNECTING OUTPUT DEVICES TO EDGE CONNECTOR

on green edge connector		Channel number	Channel label used in programming
embossed label	relay function		
A	NO	1	1
B	NC		
1	Common		
2	NO	2	2
3	NC		
C	Common		

(The remaining connections are shown in the LVB technical manual)

Operation of the Relay card is covered in Chapter 7.

I will focus most of your attention on the DC Driver card as the output controller because it was specially designed to operate the 28-volt devices used in operant learning apparatus. In the lessons in this text you will operate a feeder/dipper (whichever you have) and a white cue light (this cue light may be located above the lever or as a chamber house light). Unlike the response lever, which just moves voltage along, these outputs draw a voltage load to do some work. The feeder/dipper draws a substantial load to operate its internal motor. The cue light draws light loads to illuminate its filament. All output devices will require +28 volts DC to their positive wiring post, supplied from the + pole of the 28-volt external power supply. The other post on each device will return the voltage directly to the DC Driver card in the interface. The DC Driver card completes the circuit by grounding the output signal.

To recap, each output device—feeder/dipper or cue light—has two wiring posts, one for +28 volts from the power supply + pole, and the other for voltage coming out of the device on a wire to the DC Driver card. Now let's look at the edge connector for the DC Driver card.

DC DRIVER CARD: CONNECTING OUTPUT DEVICES TO THE EDGE CONNECTOR

embossed number on green edge connector	Channel number	Channel label used in programming
1	1	1
2	2	2
3	3	4
4	4	8
5	5	16
6	6	32
7	7	64
8	8	128

9	+ 28 volts (but not wired)
10	− 28 volts (but not wired)

First, you must connect the feeder/dipper to channel #1 (the extreme leftmost pin on the edge connector). Next, connect the cue light to channel #2. If you trace the flow of voltage through these devices, you'll find that you supply + 28 volts from the external supply to the positive pole on the device. From the other pole a wire comes back to the DC Driver card.

The DC Driver card contains eight channels. On the card are

mounted a mode switch, and a pulse dial control for each channel. The mode switches are located on an eight-switch dip panel. Switching a dip switch to *on* sets the pulse mode for that channel. Pulse mode, as the name implies, causes the device to pulse—that is, to go on and then off rapidly. The corresponding pulse dial control allows you to set the actual duration of that pulse (use a small screwdriver to adjust this dial). Pulse mode is required for the feeder/dipper.

The other choice is level mode. When a dip switch is *off*, the level mode is in effect. Level mode turns the device on and leaves it on until it is explicitly turned off. Level mode is required for the cue light in the operant chamber. All the relevant instructions for operating the DC Driver card from BASIC are covered in Chapter 7.

There is one all-important caution that cannot be repeated too many times. The DC Driver card is turned on when the LVB main power switch is turned on. This is an unavoidable characteristic of the hardware that can lead to permanent damage in the output devices. You must counter this situation by ALWAYS following the power-up sequence below.

```
POWER-UP SEQUENCE
```

```
     1.   Turn on LVB main power switch (metal toggle switch)
     2.   Turn on computer system peripherals (display, printer)
     3.   Turn on computer
     4.   Start system with master disk
     5.   Run application program that uses LVB interface:
              An early program statement MUST turn off the
              DC Driver card (see chapter 7)
     6.   Turn on the 28-volt external power supply
```

APPENDIX B

The LVB Precision Timer (1080–54)

For those who are using the LVB Interface with the early model 1080–54 Precision Timer card, the following shows the correct clock subroutine. For a discussion of the derivation of these statements, see the LVB technical manuals.

LVB PRECISION TIMER: CLOCK SUBROUTINE (1080-54 ONLY)

IBM PC program segment	notes
10 TCLVB = 240 12 TDLVB = 241	LVB parameter statements.
20 OUT TCLVB, 64+2 30 GOTO 100	Reset Timer; use .1 sec count.
50 OUT TCLVB, 128+2 52 T1 = INP(TDLVB) 54 OUT TCLVB, 4+2 56 T2 = INP(TDLVB) 58 T3 = (INT(T1/16))*1000 60 T4 = (T1-(INT(T1/16))*16)*100 62 T5 = (INT(T2/16))*10 64 T6 = (T2-(INT(T2/16))*16) 66 TIME = (T3 + T4 + T5 + T6)/10 68 RETURN	First statement of subroutine. Last statement of subroutine.

TRS-80 program segment	notes
...same as above except...	
10 TCLVB = 10 12 TDLVB = 11 18 OUT 236, 16	LVB parameter statements. Turn on ports (TRS-80 only).

```
Apple IIe program segment                notes

Assumes adapter card in slot #2 (see Appendix A)

10 TCLVB = -16222                        LVB parameter statements.
12 TDLVB = -16221

20 POKE TCLVB, 64+2                       Reset Timer; use .1 sec count.
30 GOTO 100

50 POKE TCLVB, 128+2                      First statement of subroutine.
52 T1 = PEEK(TDLVB)
54 POKE TCLVB, 4+2
56 T2 = PEEK(TDLVB)
58 T3 = (INT(T1/16))*1000
60 T4 = (T1-(INT(T1/16))*16)*100
62 T5 = (INT(T2/16))*10
64 T6 = (T2-(INT(T2/16))*16)
66 TIME = (T3 + T4 + T5 + T6)/10
68 RETURN                                 Last statement of subroutine.
```

APPENDIX C

Clock Cards for the Apple IIe

The Apple IIe is capable of accepting a real-time clock as an added expansion board installed inside the system cabinet. A number of manufacturers offer products of this type. This clock card gives you the functional equivalent of the DOS clock on the IBM PC and TRS-80. Apple IIe clock cards are operated by software similar to that used with DOS clocks.

This Appendix lists a clock subroutine for selected real-time clock cards for the Apple IIe. If your system has one of these cards installed, simply substitute the subroutine listed to achieve true stand-alone capabilities (no interface required) on the Apple IIe. All clock subroutines must begin at line 50 to fit into programming examples in the text.

```
"THE CLOCK" BY MOUNTAIN COMPUTER, INC.
"TIMEMASTER II H.O." BY APPLIED ENGINEERING (Mountain Computer mode)
"THUNDERCLOCK PLUS" BY THUNDERWARE, INC. (Mountain Computer format)
"PROCLOCK" BY PRACTICAL PERIPHERALS, INC. (Mountain Computer format)
```

Apple IIe program segment	notes
IMPORTANT: Card shown is installed in slot #5.	
20 D$ = CHR$(4)	Allows program control of DOS commands
30 GOTO 100	
50 PRINT D$	Clock subroutine begins.
51 PRINT D$; "PR#5"	Sets output to clock card.
52 PRINT D$; "IN#5"	Sets input from clock card.
54 INPUT " ";T$	

```
56 HS = VAL(MID$(T$,7,2))              Time string conversions:
58 MS = VAL(MID$(T$,10,2))               Hours,
60 SS = VAL(MID$(T$,13,2))               Minutes,
62 FS = VAL(RIGHT$(T$,4))                Seconds,
64 HS = HS * 3600                        Fraction of second,
66 MS = MS * 60                          Hours to seconds,
68 TIME = FS + SS + MS + HS              Minutes to seconds.
70 PRINT D$; "IN#0"                    Sums to produce running time.
72 PRINT D$; "PR#0"                    Returns input to keyboard.
74 RETURN                              Returns output to screen.
                                       Last line of subroutine.
```

APPENDIX D

The TIMER Function for PC-DOS 2.1 and Apple Macintosh

Microsoft, Inc., the company that provides the operating system (PC-DOS) and BASIC language for the IBM PC, also supplies many other manufacturers. Most notable are the many IBM PC work-alike computers (Compaq, Columbia, Corona, and many others). Other systems relying on Microsoft are the so-called MS-DOS machines (Tandy 2000, Texas Instruments, Hewlett Packard, and many others). When IBM PC commands and BASIC statements are presented in the text, they refer to *version 1* of the PC-DOS/MS-DOS operating system and BASIC. Newer versions are available from time to time. Of particular importance is version 2.1 (or higher) of PC-DOS BASICA, which has a unique system timing function. This function is also available on the Microsoft BASIC available for the Apple Macintosh (Macintosh BASIC is very similar to the BASICA on the IBM PC).

The new timing function, called TIMER, returns the digital running time, including fractions of a second, since the system was first turned on. To use it, you need only a one-line clock subroutine.

TIMER FUNCTION (PC–DOS 2.1 or higher, Apple Macintosh)

program segment	notes
50 REM CLOCK SUBROUTINE	
60 TIME = TIMER	
70 RETURN	

Technically, a separate clock subroutine is not needed to access the TIMER function. I have demonstrated it this way so as to be consistent with the lessons in this book.

APPENDIX E

Early Version of the OPEN Statement on the IBM PC

If you have no success with the OPEN statement as described in Chapter 9, it may be that your IBM PC or MS-DOS system is not equipped with GW BASIC. Instead, you have an earlier version of BASIC with a different type of OPEN statement. Older BASICs will also not allow APPEND mode in disk file operations. On early BASICs use the following OPEN statement.

```
OPEN STATEMENT (for systems without GW-BASIC)
```

IBM PC	notes
502 OPEN "O",3,"TEST1.OUT"	"O" Specifies output mode; 3 means channel #3.

APPENDIX F

Using Versions of PC/MS-DOS 2.0 or Higher

There is always development in the software industry, and the growth of the PC/MS-DOS operating system (Microsoft, Inc.) is no exception. If you are using an IBM PC or work-alike system (AT&T, Columbia, Compaq, Corona, Eagle, Tandy, Tava, and a slew of others), you have an implementation of this operating system. But which *version* do you have? The version number should be clearly printed on the master disk supplied with the system and in your technical manual.

All the IBM PC lessons in this textbook were written with the 1.– versions of DOS in mind. If you have a higher version, you'll be able to do more and do some of the same things more easily. Let's review some of the pertinent advantages of the 2.–versions of DOS.

Implications for Programming

There is only one relevant improvement that will affect how you write real-time control programs using the 2.–versions. BASICA (GW BASIC) on the PC-DOS 2.1 (and higher) has a new TIMER function. This is covered separately in Appendix D.

Implications for System Operations

It is in system operation that 2.–versions of PC/MS-DOS make a difference and allow smoother operations.

More Storage Space on Each Disk. Disks formatted with 2.–versions can store 360K of data (360,000 bytes), as opposed to 320K in 1.–versions.

The PRINT Command in DOS. The PRINT command in DOS is a substitute for the disk output file listing routines covered for the IBM PC in Chapter 9. In 2.–versions, when you want to print a disk file on the line printer, simply type PRINT followed by the file name after the DOS prompt (A⟩). Press ⟨return⟩ if the [prn:] prompt appears. It's that simple. Another nice feature of PRINT is that it uses the available memory in the computer to accomplish background printing (like a print buffer), thereby freeing up the computer more quickly after each file is sent to the printer.

The VERIFY Command in DOS. With 2.–versions, get in the habit of setting VERIFY ON before invoking BASICA. This will ensure that all disk output file operations will get checked for verification, thereby lowering the risk of an error that could prevent data from being retrieved later.

The GRAPHICS Command in DOS. In 2.–versions, if you type GRAPHICS before invoking BASICA, you will have the capability to print any graphics screen on a graphics-compatible dot matrix printer. This can be a big help in documenting the graphics stimuli you use in a real-time control program, as you can get a printed copy of your pictures. To activate the screen print operation, hold the ⟨shift⟩ key and press ⟨PrtSc*⟩. Graphics printing can be canceled by pressing the ⟨Esc⟩ key. It may take a few minutes to print a single screen.

APPENDIX G

The LIST OUTPUT Utility Program for the Apple IIe

Working with disk output files on the Apple IIe requires a separate program to display or print the contents of those files. It's a relatively simple program, but you may find the statements used in reading data from a disk file somewhat confusing. This text covers only printing data into a disk file; the technical manuals cover all aspects of file access. For now, type in this utility program and save it on your master disk. Below the listing is an example of how to run the program.

LIST OUTPUT Program for the Apple IIe

program segment	notes
10 REM LIST OUTPUT	
20 ONERR GOTO 250	Causes the program to close the input file in a normal way after attempting to read past the last item.
30 DIM LN$(1000)	
40 RE$ = CHR$(13) : D$ = CHR$(4)	Special characters.
50 TEXT : HOME : PRINT	Turn off graphics and clear.
60 INPUT "ENTER DISK FILE NAME: ";FF$	
70 PRINT : POKE 34,4	Sets top of scroll at line 4.
80 PRINT D$;"OPEN ";FF$	
90 PRINT D$;"READ ";FF$	Read mode.
120 FOR K = 1 TO 1000	Reads up to 1000 lines.
122 GET CH$: PRINT CH$;	Read one character from file.
124 IF CH$ = RE$ THEN 200	
125 LN$(K) = LN$(K) + CH$	Concatenate characters on line.
126 GOTO 122	Endless loop until RETURN is found.

```
200 PRINT LN$(K)
210 NEXT K
250 PRINT D$;"CLOSE ";FF$
300 TEXT : END
```

Running LIST OUTPUT

---

for screen display only

(]) RUN LIST OUTPUT

...then type the name of the file to be listed

---

for listing on the line printer

(]) PR#1

(]) RUN LIST OUTPUT

...then type the file name

APPENDIX H

Experimental Procedures with DEC Mainframes

Digital Equipment Corporation (DEC) mainframe computers are quite common on campus. The three systems that I'll deal with here are the DECSystem 20 series, the PDP-11 series, and the VAX series. Each of these mainframes supports a BASIC language that is quite similar to the Microsoft BASICA on the IBM PC. There are important differences among them, however.

There's No Such Thing As DOS

That's a major difference! Each DEC mainframe supports its own operating system. However, many of the commands are surprisingly similar to the PC/MS-DOS operating system found on the IBM PC. Of course, on the mainframe users have no access to flexible disks and disk drives, as on micros. There is disk storage, but it's inside the computer center and not apparent to the individual user sitting at a terminal.

Here are some IBM PC commands (taught in the text) that are unchanged on the DEC mainframes when you are at the system level (sometimes called **monitor mode** on the mainframe).

235

DEC OPERATING SYSTEM COMMANDS THAT MATCH IBM PC DOS COMMANDS

	notes
DIR	Lists a directory of your files.
TYPE filename.ext	Types a disk file on your terminal; filename signifies the root of the file, .ext signifies the file extension (the concept of the two-part file name was covered in chapter 3).
PRINT filename.ext	Prints a disk file on the line printer inside the computer center.
DEL filename.ext	Deletes a file from disk.

BASIC Commands on DEC Mainframes

DEC mainframes support several different forms of BASIC. Machines in the 20 series and the PDP-11 series usually have some version of BASIC-PLUS. The VAX series has VAX-11 BASIC. This text can be adapted for use with DEC mainframes, but thorough documentation on the particular DEC BASIC will be required. The most fundamental BASIC commands are listed here, but keep the DEC technical manuals close by.

BASIC COMMANDS THAT APPROACH IBM PC BASIC COMMANDS

	notes
NEW filename	Clears current memory, initializes a new BASIC program.
OLD filename	Clears current memory, calls an existing BASIC program from disk.
RUN	Executes the program in memory.
SAVE	Writes the BASIC program in memory to disk.
REPLACE	Equivalent of SAVE used with existing programs on certain DEC systems.

Of course, you can LIST and DEL a specified range of line numbers, much the same as it is done on the IBM PC (see Chapter 3).

BASIC Statements

The important consideration with respect to BASIC statements on the DEC mainframes is what you *cannot* do. For example, you have no statements or functions to operate an interface (OUT, POKE, INP, PEEK). That should be obvious, since there is no interfacing capability; only stand-alone projects are possible. At this point, I'll cover special routines in BASIC that will substitute for IBM PC BASICA capabilities.

Clearing the Screen.   To control the cursor and the screen, you first must make sure that you have set up your video terminal for VT52 mode. If you don't know what this means, or how to do it, you'll need technical assistance from the computer center. Once that's done, you may control the cursor and screen by printing certain escape sequences. They're called that because they begin with the escape character, ASCII 27.

ESCAPE SEQUENCES FOR VT52 MODE

	notes
`100 ES$ = CHR$(27)`	Assigns ASCII 27 to a string variable.
`500 PRINT ES$;"H";`	Homes the cursor (puts it in the upper left corner).
`510 PRINT ES$;"J";`	Erase screen to right and below cursor.
`520 PRINT ES$;"H";ES$;"J";`	Home and clear screen; same as CLS on IBM PC.
`530 PRINT ES$;"K";`	Erase current line to right of cursor.
`540 PRINT ES$;"A";`	Moves cursor up one row.
`550 PRINT ES$;"B";`	Moves cursor down one row.
`560 PRINT ES$;"C";`	Moves cursor right one column.
`570 PRINT ES$;"D";`	Moves cursor left one column.
	Important: Both the : and \ characters are used to separate statements on the same line in DEC BASIC; find out which character to use on your system.

Next, you want to have the equivalent of the LOCATE statement on the IBM PC (covered in Chapter 4). On DEC mainframes this is done using a special user-defined function called FNCURSOR. Below are the defining statements for the function. They should appear only once, before the part of the program that uses cursor movement applications.

FNCURSOR FUNCTION SUBSTITUTES FOR THE IBM PC LOCATE STATEMENT

program segment	notes
100 ES$ = CHR$(27)	
110 DEF FNCURSOR(L,C)	User-defined function.
120 PRINT ES$;"Y";CHR$(L+31);CHR$(C+31);	
130 FNEND	Used in BASIC-PLUS; (END DEF is equivalent in VAX-11 BASIC).
500 FX = FNCURSOR(22,1)	Moves cursor to row 22, column 1; equivalent to LOCATE 22,1 on IBM PC.

The screen dimensions on the VT52 terminal are 24 rows × 80 columns. The parameters of the FNCURSOR function (as it is used on line 500) can also be variables or equations.

Real-time Clock Operations. Here is the big difference between the IBM PC and the DEC mainframes. DEC mainframes are **time-shared** machines that divide their time among many separate users all working simultaneously. For this reason timer readings are almost always distorted (slowed) by the fact that the mainframe is not spending all its time on one user's job. In practical terms, then, the mainframe is not usable for research per se, because the timer values will be inaccurate—usually all longer than actual running time. Nevertheless, the mainframe can be used for demonstrations and for learning the principles of real-time control. In Chapter 5 you learned all about clock subroutines for the micros. Here is the substitute clock subroutine for DEC mainframes.

CLOCK SUBROUTINE FOR DEC MAINFRAMES

program segment	notes
50 TT = TIME(0)	Assigns time-of-day in measured in seconds; IMPORTANT: the variable TT must be used because TIME is reserved in DEC BASIC; all interval and process timers must be modified accordingly.
60 RETURN	equivalent to the IBM PC DOS Clock routine.

Low-res Block Graphics.   You can get block graphics on the VT52 terminal. On DEC mainframes BASIC requires that you specifically enter a graphics mode in order to draw blocks. While in graphics mode, you can print only uppercase alphabetic text. However, you can exit graphics mode, print any text, and then reenter graphics mode, to continue drawing blocks.

LOW-RES BLOCK GRAPHICS ON THE DEC MAINFRAMES

program segment	notes
100 ES$ = CHR$(27)	
800 PRINT ES$;"F";	Enter graphics mode.
810 BLOCK$ = CHR$(97)	Assigns the block shape to a string variable; equivalent to statement used in chapter 12.
830 PRINT BLOCK$;	Prints block at cursor location.
840 PRINT ES$;"G";	Exits graphics mode; you must exit graphics mode before you can display text on the screen; reenter graphics mode to continue displaying block graphics.

You move the cursor in graphics applications using the same FNCURSOR function shown above.

Generating Random Numbers.   BASIC on DEC systems also has a random number routine for generating random integers within a specified range.

RANDOM NUMBER STATEMENTS

program segment	notes
120 RAX = INT ((H-L)*RND+L)	Random integer within the the range specified by H (high value) and L (low value)

I could never cover all the possible comparisons between DEC mainframes and the IBM PC in this appendix. However, the coverage above will get your stand-alone projects running on the DEC equipment.

APPENDIX I

Reading Simultaneous Inputs from the LVB Interface

Using Logical Operators to Decode LVB Switch Inputs

You were referred to this appendix from chapter 6 where I introduced lessons on how to detect responses on switches using the LVB Switch Input card. Although it is not required for exercises in this text, you may find yourself having to process simultaneous switch inputs from the LVB Interface. This appendix will provide you with the routines to accomplish this, but first you'll have to learn about the logical operators OR and AND.

Logical operators complement relational operators and like relational operators, are often used in IF-THEN statements. You will recall that relational operators involve the symbols $<$, $>$, and $=$, alone or in combination. Logical operators involve words that connect two values *logically*. I'll consider two of these words, OR and AND, as they apply to controlling the LVB Interface.

Switch Input and the Logical OR. The logical OR within an IF-THEN statement means *either or*, and allows you to compare one value against several others within a single statement. You need this capability to interpret simultaneous switch closures because the LVB Interface returns the *sum* of the binary equivalents of each switch channel closed. Let me refresh your memory for these concepts. The terminology I am using here requires close reading. Consider this table from chapter 6.

NUMERIC CHANNEL LABELS AND CORRESPONDING BINARY BIT NUMBERS

BIT NUMBER	7	6	5	4	3	2	1	0
CHANNEL LABEL	128	64	32	16	8	4	2	1
CHANNEL NUMBER	8	7	6	5	4	3	2	1

Focus attention on the channel labels for a moment. These are the binary equivalents of the corresponding channel numbers. The Switch Input card returns data in the form of a channel label or sum of labels (in the case of simultaneous inputs). For example, imagine that you have three possible inputs wired to the channels labeled 1, 2, and 4 (the first three channels on the Switch Input card)—three separate response levers in an operant chamber. Also for the sake of example, assume that it is possible for the subject to press any combination of the three simultaneously. Here's what the LVB Interface could report:

SIMULTANEOUS SWITCH INPUTS: Channels 1, 2, and 4

possible switch closures	binary equivalent
involving channel 1	
1	1
1 and 2	3
1 and 4	5
1 and 2 and 4	7
involving channel 2	
2	2
1 and 2	3
2 and 4	6
1 and 2 and 4	7
involving channel 4	
4	4
1 and 4	5
2 and 4	6
1 and 2 and 4	7

As you look over this table, think in plain English about what can happen when simultaneous switch closures are received by your program. The switch wired to channel label 1 was closed if the interface returns a value of 1, 3 (1 + 2), 5 (1 + 4), or 7 (1 + 2 + 4). You should see that 1 is a part of each of the three possible binary sums.

I'll put this example into an IF-THEN statement using OR to compare an input of 1 against itself and the three possible summed values from the interface. I'll be modifying the program from chapter 6 that simply counted operant lever presses.

SIMULTANEOUS SWITCH INPUTS: Using OR in the IF-THEN Statement

IBM PC and TRS-80 program segment	notes
...LVB parameter statements...	Varies by system.
300 LEVER = INP(SLVB)	Assigns active channels.
310 IF LEVER = 0 THEN 300	Determines if a channel is active (not zero).

320 IF LEVER=1 OR LEVER=3 OR LEVER=5 OR LEVER=7 THEN C1=C1+1

	notes
330 GOTO 300	

Apple IIe program segment	notes
...same as above except...	
300 LEVER = PEEK(SLVB)	

Line 320 is what it's all about. Here the logical OR is used to compare the input (the variable *LEVER*) with each of the possible binary values that could contain it. If any comparison in the statement is true, then you increment the counter for the lever on that channel—lever one (C1 = C1 + 1). Getting this routine to work for all three possible levers is easy. Simply extend the rule already demonstrated.

SIMULTANEOUS SWITCH INPUTS: Using OR in the IF-THEN Statement

IBM PC and TRS-80 program segment	notes
...LVB parameter statements...	Varies by system.
300 LEVER = INP(SLVB)	Assigns active channels.
310 IF LEVER = 0 THEN 300	Determines if a channel is active (not zero).

```
320 IF LEVER=1 OR LEVER=3 OR LEVER=5 OR LEVER=7 THEN C1=C1+1
322 IF LEVER=2 OR LEVER=3 OR LEVER=6 OR LEVER=7 THEN C2=C2+1
324 IF LEVER=4 OR LEVER=5 OR LEVER=6 OR LEVER=7 THEN C3=C3+1
```

	notes

```
330 GOTO 300
```

Apple IIe program segment	notes
...same as above except...	
300 LEVER = PEEK(SLVB)	

A Different Approach Using the IBM PC and TRS-80.   Logical operators on the IBM PC and TRS-80 also allow for the direct comparison of binary equivalents of numbers. The capability to compare numbers directly means that you don't have to list each binary sum separately in the IF-THEN statement. Another change is that here you use the logical AND to ask the question whether the Switch Input value *contains* the channel label you're interested in. Here is the above program segment in a different form for use on the IBM PC and TRS-80.

SIMULTANEOUS SWITCH INPUTS: Using AND in the IF-THEN Statement

IBM PC and TRS-80 program segment	notes
...LVB parameter statements...	Varies by system.
300 LEVER = INP(SLVB)	Assigns active channels.
310 IF LEVER = 0 THEN 300	Determines if a channel is active (not zero).
320 IF LEVER AND 1 THEN C1=C1+1 322 IF LEVER AND 2 THEN C2=C2+1 324 IF LEVER AND 4 THEN C3=C3+1	
	notes
330 GOTO 300	

This capability is quite different and streamlines the IF-THEN statements. Line 320, for example, compares the binary equivalent of the variable *LEVER* with the binary equivalent of 1 to determine if 1 is *within LEVER*. The result is true if *LEVER* is equal to 1, 3, 5, or 7.

APPENDIX J

Controlling Simultaneous Outputs with the LVB Interface

Adding and Subtracting Multiple Outputs

You were referred to this appendix from chapter 7 where I introduced lessons on how to turn on equipment in the laboratory using the LVB DC Driver and Relay cards. Although it is not required for exercises in this text, you may find yourself having to produce simultaneous outputs using the LVB Interface. This appendix will provide you with the routines to accomplish this. The required programming is based on the simple notion that you must reference the *sum* of the channel labels making up the simultaneous output. The channel labels for DC Driver or Relay output are shown below.

NUMERIC CHANNEL LABELS AND CORRESPONDING BINARY BIT NUMBERS

BIT NUMBER	7	6	5	4	3	2	1	0
CHANNEL LABEL	128	64	32	16	8	4	2	1
CHANNEL NUMBER	8	7	6	5	4	3	2	1

Focus attention on the channel labels for a moment. These are the binary equivalents of the corresponding channel numbers. Next, consider this example. Imagine that you have three possible output devices wired to the channels labeled 1, 2, and 4 on the Relay card (the first three channels on the card)—channel 1 is a white light, channel 2 is a red light, and channel 4 is a blue light. Also, for the sake of example, assume that it is possible for the presentation of the lights to overlap in any combination. Here's what the LVB Interface could produce:

SIMULTANEOUS RELAY OUTPUTS: Channels 1, 2, and 4

possible relays on	binary equivalent
involving channel 1	
1	1
1 and 2	3
involving channel 2	
2	2
1 and 2	3
involving channel 4	
4	4
1 and 4	5
2 and 4	6
1 and 2 and 4	7

As you look over this table, think in plain English about what can happen when simultaneous outputs are produced by your program. Following the example of the three stimulus lights, the interface can process output values of 1, 2, 3 (1 + 2), 4, 5 (1 + 4), 6 (2 + 4), and 7 (1 + 2 + 4). These include the possible binary sums of the channel labels 1, 2, and 4. If your program produces an output using one of these sums, the corresponding channels will be turned on simultaneously. To turn *off* individual channels, subtract the appropriate channel label from the original sum. To turn off all channels specify a parameter of zero. In the example below, I'll turn each light on in progression, then reverse the sequence. I'll put a 5-second interval between each change in the output.

SIMULTANEOUS OUTPUTS: Adding and Subtracting Channel Labels

IBM PC and TRS-80 program segment	notes
...LVB parameter statements...	Varies by system.
...clock subroutine...	
400 WL = 1	White light on channel 1.
410 RL = 2	Red light on channel 2.
420 BL = 4	Blue light on channel 4.
500 XX = 0	Initialize parameter value.

```
510 GOSUB 1000                          Turn off all relays.
530 XX = XX + WL : GOSUB 1000           White alone.
540 XX = XX + RL : GOSUB 1000           White and Red.
550 XX = XX + BL : GOSUB 1000           White, Red, and Blue.
560 XX = XX - WL : GOSUB 1000           Red and Blue.
570 XX = XX - RL : GOSUB 1000           Blue alone.
580 XX = XX   BL : GOSUB 1000           All lights off.

900 GOTO 2000

1000 REM- SUBROUTINE CONTROLS LIGHTS
1002 OUT RLVB,XX
1005 GOSUB 50 : START=TIME              Start interval timer.
1010 GOSUB 50
1020 IF TIME < START+5 THEN 1010
1030 RETURN

2000 END
```

Apple IIe program segment   notes

...same as above except...

```
1002 POKE RLVB,XX
```

Glossary

Applesoft   The name of the BASIC language on the Apple II series of computers.

Arrays   Special variables that can store lists of values organized by row and column coordinates. Arrays can be one or two dimensional.

ASCII code   The standard number given each alphabetic, numeric, and graphics character in the computer system's character set.

ATTRIB   The command that assigns a protection against deleting files on the TRS-80.

BACKUP   The disk duplication program on the TRS-80. Can be used to make a working system master or backup. The target disk must be formatted first.

backup disk   The second copy of your working master disk. You should periodically make a backup of your disk in order to maintain a secure copy for use if your working disk should fail, get lost, or be damaged.

BASIC   (Beginner's All-Purpose Symbolic Instruction Code)—The computer language used for programming in this book.

BASICA   (1) The name of BASIC on the IBM PC and compatibles. (2) The command at DOS level that invokes the BASIC language interpreter.

bell code   ASCII 7. Produces a beep or tone with the statement PRINT CHR$(7).

between-subjects design   An experiment in which each experimental condition contains different subjects. Treatment differences are tested using different groups of subjects.

block graphics   A system for drawing designs on the screen with a special "block" image.

BREAK   A key on the TRS-80 used to interrupt a program.

CATALOG   The DOS command on the Apple IIe used to obtain a directory of the disk contents.

channel   A specific I/O circuit on an LVB Interface card.

channel label   A binary number signifying a specific channel. Assigned in the LVB parameter statements.

CHR$ A BASIC string function to convert the ASCII code to its corresponding character.

CHR$ (4)   ASCII 4 is the special control character used before Apple IIe disk file commands.

CHR$ (191)   ASCII 191 is the solid rectangular block image used in block graphics on the TRS-80.

CHR$ (219)   ASCII 219 is the solid rectangular block image used in block graphics on the IBM PC.

CIRCLE   A BASIC statement on the IBM PC used to draw a circular figure in graphics.

clock subroutine   A routine, always beginning at line 50, that contains the DOS clock or LVB Timer statements.

CLOSE   A BASIC statement that terminates disk file access for a given file.

CLS   A BASIC statement on the IBM PC and TRS-80 that clears the screen and puts the cursor in the upper left corner. On the TRS-80 it also sets the width to 80 columns.

COLOR   A BASIC statement on the Apple IIe to set screen color in low-res graphics. Fifteen colors (or shades of a monochrome) are possible; 0 indicates black.

concatenation   The adding together of two or more strings with a plus sign in a LET or PRINT statement.

constant   A numeric constant is an integer or real number. A string constant is one or more characters to be considered as text.

CONTROL   A special key on the left side of the IBM PC and Apple IIe keyboards used in certain keystroke sequences.

CONTROL/ALT/DELETE   The keystroke sequence to restart the IBM PC. Press and hold both ⟨CONTROL⟩ and ⟨ALT⟩ while you press and release the ⟨DEL⟩ key.

CONTROL/BREAK   The keystroke sequence to interrupt a program on the IBM PC.

CONTROL/C   The keystroke sequence to cancel a DOS command on the IBM PC, and to interrupt a program on the Apple IIe.

CONTROL/NUM-LOCK   The keystroke sequence to stop the screen on the IBM PC from scrolling during video listings. Press any key to resume scroll.

CONTROL/OPEN-APPLE/RESET   The keystroke sequence to re-start the Apple IIe. Press and hold both ⟨CONTROL⟩ and ⟨OPEN-APPLE⟩ while you press and release the Reset button.

CONTROL/RESET   The keystroke sequence to stop program execution on the Apple IIe.

CONTROL/S   The keystroke sequence to stop the screen on the Apple IIe from scrolling during video listings. Press any key to resume scroll.

CONTROL/U   The keystroke sequence to cancel the program line you are in the process of typing on the IBM PC.

CONTROL/X   The keystroke sequence to cancel the program line you are in the process of typing on the Apple IIe.

COPYA   The Apple II series DOS 3.3 disk duplication program. Can be used to make a working master disk or backup. Automatically formats the target disk before copying to it.

counting statement   A form of the LET statement used to increment a variable by one each time the statement is executed.

DATA   A BASIC statement that holds a list of numeric or string constants to be read and used in sequence.

DC driver   An output circuit in the LVB Interface for −28-volt DC apparatus.

debug   To correct flaws or typographical errors in a program.

DEC   (Digital Equipment Corporation)—A manufacturer of computer equipment and software, known primarily for mainframe computer systems.

default drive   The disk drive that is used to start up the computer system.

DEL   (1) A DOS command on the IBM PC to remove a file from disk. (2) A BASIC command on the Apple IIe used to remove a line or a range of lines from a program.

DELETE   (1) A DOS command on the Apple IIe to remove a file from disk. (2) A BASIC command on the IBM PC and TRS-80 to remove a line or range of lines from a program.

dependent variable (DV)   A factor in the subject's behavior that is measured as part of an experiment. The DV quantifies the subject's reaction to the manipulation of the independent variable.

DIM   A BASIC statement that sets the maximum number of elements (rows, or rows and columns) in an array.

DIR   The DOS command on the IBM PC and TRS-80 used to obtain a directory of the disk contents.

disk   The magnetic device used for permanent storage of information.

DISKCOPY   The disk duplication program on the IBM PC and compatibles. Can be used to make a working master disk or backup. Automatically formats the target disk before copying to it.

disk drive   The internal or external component into which flexible disks are inserted. The part of the system that reads and writes information onto the disk.

DOS   (disk operating system) The set of programs and commands that allows the computer system to store, read, and manage information on disk.

DOS 1.25   An early version of PC/MS-DOS.

DOS 2.0   The current version of MS-DOS supplied with IBM PC–compatible computers.

DOS 2.1   The current version of PC-DOS supplied with the IBM PC and PCjr.

DOS 3.3   The current version of DOS supplied with the Apple IIe or IIc computers. The Apple II and Apple II+ may be upgraded to run DOS 3.3.

DOS clock   A system feature controlled by a subroutine that returns timer values to a program for use in controlling or measuring processes.

DOS clock reset   Specific statements for the IBM PC and TRS-80 that can set the time of day equal to 00:00:00.

END   The final statement in a BASIC program.

extension   The last three characters of a file name. On the IBM PC the extension is separated from the main part of the file name by a period. On the TRS-80 it is separated from the main part of the file name by a slash.

file   A unit of information stored on disk. A specific name is associated with each file.

file channel   The channel number on which the file will be open.

file mode   The condition of a disk file open for input, output, or appending.

file name   The name you give to each file and program on disk.

flexible disk   An inexpensive magnetic storage device. Also called floppy disk.

FOR   A BASIC statement, the first part of a FOR-NEXT loop.

FORMAT The DOS command on the IBM PC and TRS-80 used to prepare an old or new disk to hold information. Formatting old disks effectively erases their existing information.

GOSUB A BASIC statement that executes a subroutine from within the main program.

GOTO A BASIC statement that causes the execution of a program to branch to a specified line.

GR A BASIC statement on the Apple IIe that invokes low-res graphics. It must be followed by the COLOR statement.

GW BASIC The name of the enhanced BASIC on the IBM PC and compatibles. Its advanced features include color graphics and music.

HCOLOR A BASIC statement on the Apple IIe used to set screen color in high-res graphics. Five colors (or shades of a monochrome) are possible; 0 indicates black.

HGR A BASIC statement on the Apple IIe used to invoke high-res graphics. HGR must be followed by the HCOLOR statement.

high-res (high-resolution) graphics A form of computer graphics that uses points and lines of color as the basis of designs on the screen.

HLIN A BASIC statement on the Apple IIe that draws a horizontal line in low-res graphics.

HOLD A command used within the RENUMBER program on the Apple IIe to store a program before merging it with a second program.

HOME A BASIC statement on the Apple IIe that clears the screen and places the cursor in the upper left corner.

HPLOT A BASIC statement on the Apple IIe that plots a point on the high-res screen or draws a line between two points.

HTAB A BASIC statement on the Apple IIe that places the cursor at a specific column along its current line.

I/O INPUT/OUTPUT, the exchange of information or signals to and from the computer.

IF-THEN A two-part BASIC statement to test a logical relational question and branch to a program line based on the outcome of that test.

independent variable A factor representing the conditions that were manipulated by the experimenter. Each independent variable (IV) must have at least two conditions, or levels, associated with it.

INKEY$ A BASIC string function on the IBM PC and TRS-80 to allow reading single keystrokes from the keyboard.

INP A BASIC function on the IBM PC and TRS-80 to examine the status of a port used with LVB Interface input.

INPUT A BASIC statement that stops the program and requests that the user type a number or string assigned to a variable.

INT A BASIC function that truncates a real number into an integer by dropping, not rounding, the decimal fraction.

integer A whole number that may not have a decimal fraction.

interval timer A real-time clock used to control the passage of a precise amount of time.

keyboard locked A condition in which the computer does not respond to keystrokes. To unlock, interrupt or break the program and, if necessary, restart DOS.

KEY OFF A BASIC statement or command that turns off the function key labels on the IBM PC display.

keystroke entry routine A series of statements on the Apple IIe designed to read single keystrokes.

KILL A BASIC command or statement that removes a file from disk.

latency A time measure representing how long it took the subject to make a response.

LEN A BASIC function that returns the number of characters in a specified string.

LET A BASIC statement that assigns a constant, a variable, or the results of a computation to a variable.

line One or more BASIC statements, beginning with a unique number.

LINE A BASIC statement on the IBM PC used to draw a line in graphics mode. LINE can also be used to draw boxes.

line printer The printing unit that creates paper copies of material from the computer.

LIST (1) A BASIC command to display a line or range of lines in a BASIC program. (2) A DOS command on the TRS-80 used to display or print a disk file.

LOCATE A BASIC statement on the IBM PC that places the cursor at a specific row and column screen coordinate.

LOCK A BASIC command that prevents deletion of a disk file on the Apple IIe.

LOAD A BASIC command used to transfer a program from disk to main memory.

loop   A series of statements in a program that are repeated a specified number of times.

loop variable   The variable in a FOR statement that determines which specific cycle of the loop is currently being executed.

low-res (low-resolution) graphics   A form of computer graphics that uses block images as the basis for designs.

LPRINT   A BASIC statement on the IBM PC and TRS-80 that prints a constant, a variable, or the results of a computation on the line printer.

LVB Interface   An optional peripheral device that allows a microcomputer to send and receive signals from an external apparatus.

LVB parameter statements   A series of LET statements that specify port numbers and memory map values for the LVB Interface.

LVB Precision Timer   The real-time clock circuit within the LVB interface.

LVB Switch input   The input circuit in the LVB Interface.

mainframe   A large, high-speed centralized computer system, with mass storage capacity, serving many users on a time-shared basis.

main memory   The random access memory within the computer's circuitry used for programs and data storage when the computer is on.

memory map   The computer's internal structure, with each circuit and function designated by a specific value. The Apple IIe uses a memory map system for I/O with the LVB Interface.

memory map values   Values assigned in the LVB parameter statements on the Apple IIe.

MERGE   (1) On the Apple IIe, a command used within the RENUMBER program to combine two programs into one. (2) On the IBM PC and TRS-80, a BASIC command to combine the specified program with one already in main memory.

microcomputer   A small desktop or portable computer system, usually serving one user at a time.

MID$ A BASIC string function to extract a substring from within a string.

nested loops   The condition when one loop starts and stops within another loop—that is, when one repetitious process is included within another repetitious process.

NEW   A BASIC command used to clear any program from main memory and start fresh.

NEXT   A BASIC statement that is the closing statement of a FOR-NEXT loop.

OPEN   A BASIC statement used to prepare a disk file to receive information from a program.

OUT   A BASIC statement on the IBM PC and TRS-80 to change the status of a port used with LVB Interface output.

output file   A unit of information created by a program and stored on disk.

PAINT   A BASIC statement on the IBM PC used to fill an enclosed graphics figure with color.

parameter   A value that controls or determines a process within a program.

PEEK   A BASIC function used on the Apple IIe to examine the status of individual memory locations used for LVB Interface input.

PEEK (−16336)   Used in a LET statement on the Apple IIe to produce sounds: LET S = PEEK (−16336).

PLOT   A BASIC statement on the Apple IIe used to display a single low-res graphics block.

POKE   A BASIC statement used on the Apple IIe to change the status of individual memory locations used for LVB Interface output.

port   A given I/O line in the computer used with the LVB Interface. A data line takes signals from the LVB Interface into the computer. A control line puts signals from the computer into the LVB Interface. The IBM PC and TRS-80 use a port system.

PR# 0   A statement or command that directs output display to video screen on the Apple IIe.

PR# 1   A statement or command that directs output display to the line printer on the Apple IIe.

PRESET   A BASIC statement on the IBM PC used to erase a single point in graphics mode drawn with PSET.

PRINT   A BASIC statement that displays a constant, a variable, or the results of a computation.

PRINT @   A BASIC statement on the TRS-80 that causes printing to occur at a specific row and column coordinate.

PRINT CHR$(23);   A BASIC statement on the TRS-80 used to change the screen width to 40 columns and use enlarged print mode.

PRINT USING   A BASIC statement on the IBM PC and TRS-80 that allows printouts to be formatted in precise columns. Values with decimal fractions can be rounded with PRINT USING.

PRINT USING #n   The equivalent of PRINT USING for use with disk output files on the IBM PC and TRS-80.

print zones   A series of preset columns along the width of the video display or line printer.

processing time   The amount of time it takes for a subject to perform a task. A latency measure of behavior.

program   A series of instructions that enable the computer to function automatically.

prompt   A symbol, word, or phrase that, when displayed, calls for some action by the user.

PSET   A BASIC statement on the IBM PC used to plot a single point in graphics mode.

RANDOM   A BASIC statement on the TRS-80 that reseeds the random number generator.

random access memory   Used for temporary storage of program statements, arrays, and variables.

RANDOMIZE   A BASIC statement on the IBM-PC that reseeds the random number generator.

reaction time   A latency measure representing how long it took a subject to respond following a specific stimulus.

READ   A BASIC statement that assigns individual elements of a DATA list to variables.

real number   A number that has or may have a decimal fraction.

real-time clock   A DOS clock or interface timer circuit used by programs for precise control and measurement of time.

real-time programming   Use of a computer to control a process that depends upon precision timing in either measurement or control.

Relay   An output circuit in the LVB Interface for general switching of apparatus.

REM   A BASIC statement that begins the text of a comment or note inserted within a program listing, but not executed.

REMOVE   A DOS command on the TRS-80 to remove a file from disk.

RENUM   A BASIC command on the IBM PC and TRS-80 used to renumber the lines of a program.

RENUMBER   A DOS utility program on the Apple IIe used to renumber the lines of a program and/or merge one program with another.

reserved words   On the IBM PC and TRS-80, character sequences that cannot be used as BASIC variable names. On the Apple IIe they also cannot be part of variable names.

RESTORE   A BASIC statement that makes the next READ statement start at the top of the DATA list.

RETURN   A BASIC statement that completes a subroutine.

RND   A BASIC function that returns a random number.

RUN   A BASIC command to start execution of a BASIC program.

SAVE   A BASIC command to transfer a program from main memory to disk.

SCREEN   A BASIC statement on the IBM PC used to switch between text mode, medium-res graphics, and high-res graphics.

sequential-access file   A type of file that must be read or written from the beginning. The user does not have direct immediate access to individual records within the file. The file type used for disk output files.

SHIFT/@   A keystroke sequence to stop the screen on the TRS-80 from scrolling during video listings. Press any key to resume scroll.

SOUND   A BASIC statement on the IBM PC and TRS-80 used to produce auditory tones.

SQR   A BASIC function to compute the square root of a constant, variable, or equation.

statement   A specific instruction within a BASIC program line. When a single program line contains more than one statement, they are separated by a colon.

STR$ A BASIC string function that converts a numeric value to its corresponding string of characters.

subroutine   A segment within a BASIC program that can be executed repeatedly during a single run of the main program.

subscript   A number that references a particular element of an array. Used along with the array's name to reference a specific value within the array. Two-dimension arrays have both row and column subscripts.

summing statement   A form of the LET statement used to keep a running total of a series of values.

SYSTEM   A BASIC command on the TRS-80 to allow execution of DOS commands from within BASIC level.

system master disk   The disk that you use to start up the computer system. Always use a working copy of the system master disk supplied by the manufacturer.

TAB   A BASIC function used to move along a line during printing. TAB refers to specific columns on the video display, line printer, or disk file. However, in Apple IIe disk output files the TAB function adds a given number of spaces wherever it is used.

template   A program or program segment that can serve as the starting point for additional program development.

TEXT   A BASIC statement or command on the Apple IIe that switches the display from graphics mode to text mode. TEXT should be followed by HOME.

TIME$ A BASIC string function returning the time of day on the IBM PC and TRS-80.

toggle (between drives)   To switch from one disk drive to another.

trial loop   A specific FOR-NEXT loop within a program to control the presentation of a series of trials in an experiment.

TRSDOS   The version of DOS supplied with Tandy TRS-80 Model III, 4, and 4P computers.

truncate   To drop off characters.

TYPE   A DOS command on the IBM PC used to display or print a disk file.

UNLOCK   A BASIC command that allows deletion or modification of a locked disk file or the Apple IIe.

utilities   Special programs that perform useful computer management functions.

VAL   A BASIC function to convert a string of numbers to their numeric equivalent.

value   A numeric quantity.

variable   A numeric variable is a word or acronym that holds the value of a number. A string variable holds a unit of text.

variable name   A word or acronym used to represent a variable.

VERIFY   (1) A BASIC command on the Apple IIe to compare the program in main memory to its version on disk. (2) A DOS command on the TRS-80 to control whether all disk access is accompanied by verification checks.

VLIN   A BASIC statement on the Apple IIe that draws a vertical line in low-res graphics.

VTAB   A BASIC statement on the Apple IIe that places the cursor at a specific row up or down its current column.

WIDTH   A BASIC statement on the IBM PC used to change the column dimensions of the video display between 40 and 80. The screen is automatically cleared.

within-subjects design   An experiment where all conditions are experienced by each subject. Differences are tested within each subject. Subjects provide their own control or comparison.

working disk   The copy of the system master disk that you use for day-to-day operations.

Index